Routledge Revivals

L. T. Hobhouse

First published in 1931, *L. T. Hobhouse* is an amalgamation of the late social philosopher, L. T. Hobhouse's personal life and academic work. The first part of this volume is a brief biography by Mr. J. A. Hobson, with added impressions by personal friends and colleagues. It is followed by an account of his philosophy and sociology written by Professor Morris Ginsberg, his pupil and successor at the London School of Economics. Third section consists of some collected essays illustrative of his various capacities and interests. This book will be of interest to students of philosophy and sociology.

L. T. Hobhouse

His Life and Work

J. A. Hobson and Morris Ginsberg

Routledge
Taylor & Francis Group

First published in 1931
by George Allen & Unwin Ltd

This edition first published in 2022 by Routledge
4 Park Square, Milton Park, Abingdon, Oxon, OX14 4RN

and by Routledge
605 Third Avenue, New York, NY 10017

Routledge is an imprint of the Taylor & Francis Group, an informa business

© 1931 George Allen & Unwin

Publisher's Note
The publisher has gone to great lengths to ensure the quality of this reprint but points
out that some imperfections in the original copies may be apparent.

Disclaimer
The publisher has made every effort to trace copyright holders and welcomes
correspondence from those they have been unable to contact.

A Library of Congress record exists under LCCN: 95234144

ISBN: 978-1-032-35094-3 (hbk)
ISBN: 978-1-003-32526-0 (ebk)
ISBN: 978-1-032-35095-0 (pbk)

Book DOI 10.4324/9781003325260

L. T. HOBHOUSE

L. T. HOBHOUSE

HIS LIFE AND WORK

by

J. A. HOBSON

and

MORRIS GINSBERG

WITH SELECTED
ESSAYS & ARTICLES

LONDON
GEORGE ALLEN & UNWIN LTD
MUSEUM STREET

FIRST PUBLISHED IN 1931

PREFACE

THE death of Leonard Trelawny Hobhouse in the summer of 1928 not only brought sorrow to a wide circle of personal friends, but inflicted a heavy loss on learning and on many causes of practical reform. At the request of his relations I undertook to prepare this volume, whose title indicates its contents. Mr. C. P. Scott, the veteran editor of the *Manchester Guardian* during the thirty years of Hobhouse's association with that paper, writes an Introductory Note. In preparing the Memoir which follows, I am deeply indebted both to Mr. Scott and to various other named or unnamed friends who were associated with Hobhouse as colleagues and friends in various periods of his career as thinker, teacher, writer, and practical reformer.

The most substantial part of the book consists of the account and interpretation of his philosophical and sociological teaching by his pupil, friend, and successor, Professor Morris Ginsberg. The last part comprises a selection from his otherwise inaccessible writings, mostly essays in journalism, illustrative of the wide range of his interests and literary attainments.

J. A. HOBSON

January 1931

PREFACE

INTRODUCTION

It was during a delightful companionship of five years, from the autumn of 1897 to the autumn of 1902, that I saw most of Hobhouse and came to know him best. During the whole of that period I was in constant communication with him and discussed with him, as a leader-writer, the events of the day and the policy of the paper.

He wrote very rapidly, and I have a picture of him in my mind, sitting with his eyes about three inches from the table—for he never wore spectacles—and pen coursing rapidly and continuously over the paper. Then, in less than half the time that most men would take, his tall figure would stalk into my room and deliver the goods.

His work, involving as it did nightly attendance at the office, was never allowed to interrupt his own studies, and he would himself say that this was their not least fruitful period. He thought and wrote in the mornings on his own themes, equally he worked in the evenings on the innumerable topics with which a daily newspaper is concerned. The combination was arduous, but he did not find it inconvenient. He even held that the one task helped the other, and at least it is certain that his habit of looking at the problems of the day against the larger background of knowledge and principle which was natural to him gave to his writing a force and consistency which it must otherwise have lacked.

He was a powerful thinker, but his dominant characteristic was ever his humanity. Where questions of right were concerned he never blinded himself. His work for the paper in Manchester covered the whole difficult period of the Boer War. On the merits of this enterprise the paper took the unpopular side and he was heart and soul with it. It was the same with his approach to domestic questions. The older libertarian Liberalism had done its work and the task of Liberals was no longer to gain power for the unenfranchised, but to teach the new electors how to use it.

Labour questions, so called, had not yet assumed the importance now justly assigned to them, but he was one of the first and most ardent of the thinkers on social subjects to recognise their vital importance. It was with the same largeness of view that he approached foreign policy. He saw in the other nations of Europe not so much competitors to be outwitted or latent enemies to be prepared against as neighbours from whom much could be learnt and with whom benefits might be exchanged.

His deepest instinctive belief and hope was in human progress. It was in that belief that in the flush of youth he set out, as those who knew him best can testify, and it was to that, against all the discouragement of circumstance, that he ever clung. His temperament was not sanguine, and it was inevitable that his faith should at times be tried. He recognised that it rested in part on assumption. Yet for him the conception of progress was indispensable to any tolerable framework of society. The whole modern outlook of suspicion and hate in the relations of nations was to him wholly alien. He could no more carry an unreasoning antagonism into his attitude towards other nations than he could towards other men.

With such a feeling and such a faith it was inevitable that he should suffer, and hard were some of the blows that he received. He struggled, as did every Liberal worth his salt, against the impending catastrophe of the Great War, and it was only the violation, against every principle of international right, of Belgian territory by the German forces that rallied him once for all to the side of the Allies. But he was no friend of a dictated peace, and would have spared Europe a year of war and some millions of lives so soon as he judged that the capital object of the war had been achieved by the vindication of international right and the defeat of a lawless aggression. For me his figure stands as an imposing expression of intellectual power allied to an almost childlike friendliness. No one surely ever better earned the title of the friend of man.

C. P. SCOTT

CONTENTS

L. T. HOBHOUSE
A MEMOIR

BY J. A. HOBSON

CHAPTER I

SCHOOL AND COLLEGE DAYS

LEONARD TRELAWNY HOBHOUSE was born on the 8th of September, 1864, at St. Ive, a village near Liskeard, Cornwall, where his father, Reginald Hobhouse, was rector for fifty-one years, holding the office of Archdeacon of Bodmin during the period 1877–92. The Hobhouse family were prosperous merchants of Bristol during the eighteenth century, the first known ancestor having lived at Minehead towards the end of the seventeenth century. The father of the Archdeacon was a man of great distinction in the public service, occupying successively the posts of Solicitor to the Customs and the Treasury, Permanent Under-Secretary to the Home Office, Keeper of the State Papers. Reginald Hobhouse received his education at Eton and Balliol, of sound, though not brilliant, mental attainments, and best known to his Oxford contemporaries as having rowed in the 'Varsity boat in 1839 and having been President of the O.U.B.C. Ordained in 1848, he was presented with the Crown living of St. Ive, which he held until his death in 1895. In 1851 he married Caroline Salusbury Trelawny, of Harewood House, Calstock, a member of an old and famous Cornish family. Leonard was the youngest of seven children, the two eldest of whom died in infancy. The youngest daughter, Emily, who became well known in later years as *the*, or even *that*, Miss Hobhouse, though four years his elder, was his closest companion in childhood, and their deep attachment lasted until her death, which preceded his by two years.

Of his parents Leonard writes:[1]

"My mother was a first-rate companion. Not young (she was thirty-nine when Emily was born and nearly forty-four when I followed), she lived with us on the footing

[1] In an Appendix 4, ch. i, of Miss F. Ruth Fry's *Life of Emily Hobhouse*.

which is supposed to be the discovery of the modern generation, and took us about with her as companions, exercising no discoverable discipline. She was extremely vivacious, and could be very witty, so that some of her sharp retorts became a tradition in the family. She read French, German, and Italian with ease and pleasure, and taught me Latin before I went to school. What was more, she used to read aloud to us. It was she who introduced us to Mr. Micawber and Mrs. Gamp, and the first ambition in passing from infancy to childhood was to be allowed to sit up for the reading.

"My father was certainly much more apart, but he was never untender or unkind. I do not recollect his ever punishing any one of us. That sort of fear was not within our horizon. But he was remorseless in exacting duty and the repair of neglect, and a few mild words of disapproval fell from him with tons weight, and not on us alone. He was for us all an incarnation of justice and iron rectitude, which we took as of course as a part of the natural framework of things, so much so that it was only with surprise and lingering incredulity that we came to discover that such a standard is not universal. His sole guide was duty, for us as for himself, and of the psychological effect of the regime he seems to have had no glimpse."

"Our childhood", writes Leonard, "was extremely happy", though his sister gives a different impression. The death of the mother in 1880 was a great blow to the family, for "incarnate justice and iron rectitude" do not of themselves go far towards a happy home. Emily gives an exceedingly depressing picture of the later years, with a narrow life of parish work, supervised by a pious narrow-minded taciturn valetudinarian who seldom forgot that he was a clergyman. For Leonard, who only spent portions of his vacations from school and university at St. Ive, and whose bright intelligence and high spirits lit up the home and evoked an emotional response from father as from sister, the scene showed very different. There was a deep affection between him and his father, and when the Archdeacon lay a-dying his most urgent desire was that he might see Leonard. It must, however, have been a source of great pain to his father, who retained throughout his life a rigid orthodoxy in religion and a narrow conservatism in politics, to discover how even in his schooldays Leonard's mind was moving towards unorthodoxy and liberalism.

He began his school life at the age of eight or nine—"His departure", writes his sister Emily in her reminiscences, "was a dreadful blow. First his curls had to be cut off, which spoilt his beauty"—at a preparatory school in Exmouth, where he remained until 1877, when at the age of twelve he entered Marlborough College, where he remained until he entered his university life in 1883 with a scholarship to 'Corpus'. Mr. L. E. Upcott, a Marlborough master, gives the following interesting impressions of his school life.

"Leonard Hobhouse came to Marlborough College in 1877. My first acquaintance with him revealed him as no ordinary boy. He got into the Upper Fifth Form after winning a Senior Scholarship, refused to do more than the minimum of work, and sat complacently at the bottom of the form, the despair of his form-master. It was not unusual for clever small boys to take things easily after a spell of exertion, but this was carrying matters too far. I sent for him and expostulated roundly, pointing out that he would lose his promotion to the Sixth that year, and so be parted from his contemporaries and friends. The remonstrance seemed to have no effect. Perhaps there was some trouble behind that I did not know of. The end of term found him at the bottom. I had to examine the form: Hobhouse was first, went up eight places (on combined form and examination work) and got his promotion. He stood out from the rest in the concise point and originality of his answers, his style. I could not help myself; the form-master most

B

generously justified me. Afterwards one of his friends said to me, 'Sir, it wasn't you; it was we who coached him.' Many years later, a relative of mine, attending his lectures at Kingsway, was introduced to him. He sent me a message: 'Ask Mr. Upcott if he remembers saying to me, "Hobhouse, I always knew you were a knave, and now I know that you are a fool too".' That message was a fine stroke of genuine and generous humour: it touched me deeply.

"In the Sixth Form, where I taught as Assistant to the Master, we were excellent friends; he did admirable work for me. I kept for my own use afterwards some 'Versions Chiefly by L.T.H.'—one in particular, I remember, of part of Wordsworth's *Laodamia*. But all this was in the regular course of study, and we had then a set of brilliant boys in the Sixth, boys who seemed to respond to stimulus, but are themselves the stimulant. It was his own line of private reading that marked the future man. The Sixth Form had an admirable library of its own; it was an incentive to special study. From it Hobhouse culled and read books on social and political science; among others those of J. S. Mill and Herbert Spencer, and Mazzini's Essays. The last was his great find; I remember my surprise when he told me of his discovery. These studies of his made him a remarkable figure at the School Debating Society, in which he would staunchly uphold his belief in Democracy.

"It was a pleasure to me that my old College chose him as scholar. I met him again later in the rooms of a Balliol man—he had a group of friends there—and recollect hearing the remark, 'Hobhouse is working, of course, in his usual steam-engine style'."

A lifelong friend, his contemporary at Marlborough and Oxford, Mr. Maurice Llewelyn Davies, gives a fuller account of his school life.

"Leonard Hobhouse came to Marlborough in January 1877 when he was twelve years old. I had then been already two terms at the school. We both left for Oxford in the summer of 1883.

"He had previously been at a preparatory school on the Devon coast, of which in some respects his recollections were unfavourable. In later years he spoke with strong disapproval of the frequency and severity with which caning was resorted to. The teaching must, however, have been fairly efficient, and well suited to prepare boys for Marlborough (the headmaster had formerly been on the staff there), since Leonard took a very good place for his age and advanced rapidly through the school.

"This was due much more to sheer cleverness, ease of acquisition, and strong memory, than to steady application. His character was late in developing, and in his early years at Marlborough he showed few signs of the strength of purpose, and persistent energy, which marked his life and work later on. As a young boy, he was already very lovable for his warmth of feeling and transparent sincerity; but it was not until he reached the Sixth Form that his underlying qualities began to be discernible.

"He was in the Sixth, I believe, for four years, and was head of the school for the last of these years. This was unquestionably an important period in the formation of his mind and character. We were fortunate in two of the Sixth Form masters: W. M. Furneaux, afterwards Headmaster of Repton and Dean of Winchester, who was a stimulating teacher all round, and in his Divinity lessons took what was for the date an advanced Broad Church line; and L. E. Upcott, to whose wide cultivation many generations of Marlburians owed their first real appreciation of the classics, and in particular of classical (and other) poetry and art. First-rate lectures on English literature were also given to the Sixth by A. H. Beesly.

"As Senior Prefect, Hobhouse came into close contact with the kindly, humorous, and sensible headmaster, G. C. Bell, between whom and the school the head boy had to act as a sort of liaison officer, or buffer state. This experience of practical administration was no doubt of value to him. Many years afterwards Bell was asked whether he had read Hobhouse's philosophical books. He threw up his hands and exclaimed, 'I have hatched a duck!'

"It was at Marlborough, I believe, and chiefly as a result of Upcott's teaching, that Hobhouse became interested in philosophy, and began to show the feeling so characteristic of him, that its conclusions were of real and serious importance for the conduct of life.

"Politics, too, now became an absorbing interest. Brought up in a Conservative home, he naturally at first took the same line as most other boys in the school. I remember his remarking once naïvely how unpleasant it must be to have a surname like Chandler or Butcher, which showed the low origin of one's family: a reflection remote indeed from his later line of thought. Some time before he left Marlborough he became a keen Radical. This change may have been partly due to the influence of the masters (the Common Room at this time was very preponderantly Liberal), though I do not think this was ever unfairly exercised. Among the boys there was a great deal of very free discussion of political (and I may add of religious) subjects: in the School Debating Society the debates on current politics were always the longest and hottest. It is probable, though I do not know to what extent it was the case, that Leonard was also coming under Liberal influences in his family. His uncle, Sir Arthur (afterwards Lord) Hobhouse, was about this time actively interesting himself in politics; at the general election of 1880 he fought, along with John Morley, one of the crucial contests, in the old borough of Westminster. His generous and sympathetic outlook would certainly then have been attractive and congenial to Leonard, as it was later.

"He was one of the editors of the school paper, the *Marlburian*, and among his contributions which I recall were an article upon George Eliot, and another upon Mill and Mazzini. He was not, however, one of those whose literary work in boyhood is mature and remarkable.

"The end of Leonard's term of office as Senior Prefect was marked by a big function, Prince Leopold attending the prize-giving. It fell to Leonard to compose and read to him an address of welcome from the school. He was subjected to much chaff beforehand by his Radical friends, but got through very well, with the minimum of obsequiousness. He relieved his conscience by moving some weeks before a Republican motion in the Debating Society!"

It is not without significance that Leonard Hobhouse was in some respects 'a difficult boy'. His masters did not easily understand his Cornish temperament and the strong emotional strains set up in adolescence by his intellectual break away from the stern religious orthodoxy of his home. A letter from the Headmaster of Marlborough in January 1882 to his father, pressing him to let Leonard spend another year at school before entering for an Oxford scholarship, urges the following considerations:

"Your boy is not, like some lads, old for his age—he is, on the contrary, rather childish and immature for his years, and his scholarship and classical knowledge are ragged and imperfect, partly from his periodical fits of slackness. For these reasons he is by no means a boy whom I should select to send to the University exceptionally early."

The reasons here given for postponing entrance at Oxford seem to have prevailed. For it was not till October 1883 that Leonard entered Corpus with a classical scholarship.

Mr. Llewelyn Davies tells me that there was some talk of his competing for a Balliol Scholarship, but that it was vetoed by his father, "who was already very uneasy about the trend of Leonard's thought on religious topics and who distrusted the Balliol atmosphere".

Of his college life Mr. Llewelyn Davies writes:

"He was very happy and congenially placed at Corpus,

where he found a small society with marked intellectual traditions and interests. For his first three years he was in college; during the fourth he and I shared lodgings near the Museum. It must have been during this period that his bent for philosophy became determined. Others better than I can say how much he owed to Fowler and Case, who set the philosophical tone in the college, and how far he was affected by the more idealistic tendencies then prevailing in the university in general. He played an active part, I believe, in the college literary society, the 'Pelican', and an elaborate paper which he read upon Mazzini stirred up much discussion, not confined to the undergraduates. In poetry, for which he had a keen liking, though rather on the intellectual than the æsthetic side, it was natural that Browning should be a predominant influence, as he was with all our generation. Many years later Leonard told me that M. Bergson had asked him where he could find the best writing on the theory of art in English, and he had replied that he knew of none better than in certain of Browning's poems.

"So far as I recollect, he took no active share in politics while he was an undergraduate." Other testimony, however, makes it clear that the radical opinions he expressed in his later schooldays were not suppressed at Oxford. In the debating society of Corpus this was certainly not the case. He writes to Miss Howard (now Lady Mary Murray) in December 1886, "The Tories in the College are very wrath at my carrying my anti-monarchical motion the other day. I hear that one of them is going to make a disturbance about it next Saturday." Nor were his propagandist activities confined to college societies. During his undergraduate days he was a frequent visitor at Castle Howard, where the influence of Lady Carlisle led him to join with other young Oxonians of his time, Gilbert Murray and Charles Roberts, in a temperance propaganda among the neighbouring towns and villages.

Another friend, Professor Oliver Elton, who came also from Marlborough to Corpus, though senior by several years, writes of his college life: "He was very frank and open, with a quick placable Cornish temper; he was emotional and un-British, but seemed always to keep his head; he was a youth of obvious natural integrity and high intelligence and ready humour. He was soon an enthusiast for philosophy. We had long discussions on causation and free-will; and at that date swore by J. S. Mill, with certain reserves. What with Thomas Fowler and Thomas Case, Corpus was then the natural home of the experientialist (if that is still the right word). I understand that Hobhouse may have been then, or later, attracted or influenced by the Hegelian-Oxonian school, but of this others will speak with authority. By nature a fearless mind, he took Mill's motto, 'Follow your intellect to whatever conclusions it may lead', and he was led to the left. In politics he was and always remained a firm radical. In religion he was an (if possible yet firmer) agnostic. I speak of college days without reference to further developments which can be studied in his books."

Another Corpus contemporary, a man of high distinction in the Civil Service, tells me that Hobhouse on first entering college life seemed irritated in mind and often moody, due partly, no doubt, to the recent unsettlement of accepted religious opinions. His recollection is that Hobhouse even as an undergraduate began the political activities of which I give some account later on, and that his early studies in theoretical and practical economics were carried on in two little societies, one termed the 'Adam Smith' society in Corpus, and another in which Arthur Acland, of Christ Church, was the leading spirit. Important Labour men, such as Mr. Burnett, were brought to Oxford to talk with radical undergraduates, and in other indirect ways the social unrest and ferment of the 'eighties began to rustle the academic groves.

His university career was one of great distinction. After winning a First in Classical Moderations and in Greats, he obtained a prize fellowship at Merton in 1887. Three years later he was appointed an assistant tutor in his old college, Corpus, where he was elected a Fellow in 1894.

The following recollections and impressions of his work and personality during this period of his tutorship at Corpus are contributed by Mr. H. M. Conacher.

"L. T. Hobhouse was 'Greats' tutor at Corpus in the 'nineties. He had already taken a prize fellowship at Merton, and this at least brought him into touch with Bradley and Wallace, the Scottish philosopher and authority on Kant and Hegel, who died tragically through being thrown from his bicycle against the stone wall of a bridge near Bletchington one afternoon in the summer of 1897.

"When Hobhouse came back to Corpus, of which college he had been a scholar, he took the 'philosophy' work, Professor T. Case having then given up all tutorial work except in Greek history. He lectured on the Ethics of Aristotle to Corpus and out-college men, and took a class of Corpus men on the Posterior Analytics.

"Of his Aristotle lectures one doesn't remember that he worked out any detailed schematism of the various virtues classified by Aristotle, but when he came to deal with the notion of justice in the fifth book, his interest was clearly aroused, and again he did not fail to impress on his hearers the view that though Aristotle raises the question as to what is the ὀρθὸς λόγος of morals, he hardly answers it.

"But perhaps it was in the working of the Oxford 'tutor' system that the best of Hobhouse came out for his pupils. They will probably remember the little room in the Fellows' Buildings in which he saw them for private work. Hobhouse, coming in from a lecture and throwing his gown off, would settle his long limbs in a low wicker-work chair and fill his pipe from a two-ounce tin of Player's Navy Cut. An interesting three-quarters of an hour would follow for anybody who cared for the problems of philosophy.

"His response to the individual pupil depended much on the effort and interest of the learner.

"Perhaps he wasn't too easy to know, and if any unsympathetic person were challenging beliefs dear to him rather irresponsibly, he would be met with a certain gruff asperity. And if a pupil did not take trouble with his work, he might expect to have some fragment of sarcasm jerked out at him, such as, 'If you must bring me a poor essay, it may as well be original.' But the victim did not seem to mind such rebukes, as he would repeat them to his friends, and another would be added to the stories gathering round a college personality.

"One doubts whether he was much in the Senior Common Room. The College was not his home. For these were the years of his early married life, and his children were born at Oxford. Still he would often come to the meetings of the Pelican Essay Club, where dons and undergraduates met, and when Arthur Sidgwick, the humanist, Frederick Pollock, then Corpus Professor of Jurisprudence, and Hobhouse were there, they were true 'Attic Nights'.

"Apart from philosophy, perhaps his chief interest was in politics, which for him merged in economics—and economics, again, was a case of γνῶσις ἕνεκα πράξεος the pursuit of distributive justice.

"Though he was usually supposed to have leanings towards collectivism, probably questions of machinery did not come first with him; and his attitude towards public questions and causes was determined by his intense humanitarianism. So he was a zealous advanced Liberal, and Arthur Sidgwick would say—speaking in days when Liberalism seemed to have lost its power—that Hobhouse was one who would always lead you on, i.e. as against half-hearted temporisers. Perhaps apart from Sidgwick, Sidney Ball, of St. John's, was the don with whom he had most sympathy."

But, though for the next ten years he lived in Oxford and performed the teaching duties attached to his post with zeal, he never felt himself cut out for the life of a college 'don'. He always wanted to get into closer grip with the practical affairs of life. In October 1889, shortly after he had won his Merton Fellowship, we find him writing to Miss Llewelyn Davies: "If I can get tutorial work at Oxford for next year, I think of coming to London for part of the interval before term. I want to see what life and work in London are like. I want to do some social and political work in a very small way, or at any rate to come in contact with those who are engaged in it. Oxford is rather a misty out-of-the-world place, and one wants a little knowledge of how things go on in the real centre of affairs."

This was not merely the occasional revolt of an energetic nature in favour of doing as against thinking and teaching—a certain *tædium academicum* fairly common in the donnish life. It was inherent in Hobhouse's conception of the philosophic task to which he had already consciously set himself, the study of the evolution of mind as the central process in history. In order to make this process real to himself and to others, he had to try to enter it, so to speak, at both ends, where it came out in present human endeavour and work, and where it first made itself manifest as a conscious process. I do not mean that the interest and attention he gave to the economic and political ferment of the 'eighties and early 'nineties were merely, or mainly, conceived as food for his philosophy. They gripped and held his personal sympathies as a new hope for humanity. For his emotions were deeply stirred by the struggle of the workers for social and economic justice, and for a fair share in everything that makes life worth living. In fact, though in the true sense he was always 'disinterested' in his pursuit of philosophic truth, knowledge and the life of reason were never conceived by him merely as ends in themselves, but as contributions to the wider purpose of a better human life. To this extent and in this sense he remained always a pragmatist. He sought to obtain a body of truth on the conduct of life in order that those who assented to it might apply it to human betterment. Indeed, he seems from early youth upwards to have been aware of a certain danger of excessive intellectualism. There is an interesting revelation in a letter written to Miss Howard in his early undergraduate days (December 1884):

"You know I am a little speculative by nature, and am always in danger of caring more for knowing truth than for doing good, e.g. for finding out what is the best reform to be carried than for the real effect on the happiness of the people that it will have when carried."

This body of truth could only be tested by contact with the facts of history. Hence the energetic support which he gave to the social movements of this time—the extension of Trade Unionism to the low-skilled workers and the agricultural labourers, the economic education of Co-operators, the contacts of educated men and women with the union leaders, the development of 'Toynbee Hall' and other university settlements—while it had its special and separate hold upon his sympathy, was also an integral part of his conception of human progress as an ordered and purposeful whole.

In 1889 and 1890, when the 'revolt' of the unskilled workers in the docks and elsewhere took shape, he was actively engaged in promoting an understanding of their cause in Oxford. He paid visits to Toynbee Hall in September 1889, and from there wrote to Miss Davies, "Everyone seems to agree that Burns and Tillett have come out splendidly. They and Tom Mann and the rest of them are coming here to-morrow for a sort of triumphal supper, but I shall unfortunately be gone. I think that the mere fact that the men have won is so good. It seems to me like a turning-point in the history of Labour."

In November of the next year he writes from Oxford: "We are organising a conference on Trade Union questions here for next Saturday. We have got representatives of many different points of view, old and new unionism, co-operation, capitalism, and socialism. Tom Mann, B. Jones, Graham Wallas, and others, and Acland to take the chair at one meeting and L. Courtney at the other."

His early activities outside his academic work were thus chiefly engaged in the Labour Movement. This continued to be the case during his years at Oxford, and inspired the writing of his first book, entitled *The Labour Movement*, published first in 1893, with a Preface by Lord Haldane. With several of his intimate friends, he was desirous to bring the Trade Union and the Co-operative Movement into closer relations with one another, and with the new social-economic policy of the National and Municipal Government which marked the early 'nineties.

At the other end of his working philosophy, we find him at this time studying physiology and bio-chemistry at the Museum Laboratory under the skilled direction of Professor J. S. Haldane. In December 1888 he writes: "I spend now from five to seven hours a day at the Laboratory, and have no strength left for anything else. I cut up frogs, and sheeps' hearts and brains, and now am working at chemicals. Haldane is a first-rate fellow."

These activities indicate the growing attention Hobhouse was giving to the physical basis of psychology, at a time when metaphysics still held the foremost place in his mind. His practice of the study of cognate subjects belonged to that sense of the unity of the world of knowledge which possessed him ever more deeply as he advanced in years and understanding. In later years he plunged into mathematical studies in order better to appreciate the revolution which Einstein and others were making in the foundation of scientific thinking, while his increasing additions to anthropology came to reinforce his earlier interest in instinct and heredity. It was this distrust of intellectual spiritualism, with its separatist tendency, that gave him the width of vision wherein lay his pre-eminence among the social philosophers of his time.

Of his outside social activities at this period of his life we get an interesting account from his correspondence with the lady who was shortly to become his wife, Miss N. Hadwen, of Halifax, whom he first met in Oxford in 1889, and whose closer acquaintance he made in a long vacation visit that year. In January 1890 he tells her: "Ll. Smith is coming to stay with me to-morrow, and we are both going out to agitate on Sunday afternoon at a village where they only get 9/- a week and very small highly rented allotments. To-morrow Hinds and I go to the scene of our accident to see a labourer who has all his accounts for forty or fifty years. I am going to get him to lend them to Ashley to publish them." And again in the same month: "Oh, we had a goodish meeting last night. About 100 men, women and children came, and we spoke from a wagon on the village green. Wages there average 10/- a week, and I told them that alone was a sufficient reason for our coming. Thirteen joined the Union, and a Branch was duly started." "I go out with Benson to-morrow. Markby takes the chair, and it will be an open-air meeting in Islip."

His early letters to Miss Hadwen sandwich these accounts of 'agitation' with philosophic disquisitions. A long letter of June 1890 opens: "I am very glad you find Aristotle really interesting", and proceeds to a long discussion of two difficulties raised by his correspondent. But for the most part his letters concerned themselves with the effort to stir up the village workers. "We had a grand meeting. Two hundred people all cram-full of enthusiasm. I like talking to the village people. I understand them, and feel *en rapport* with them. I feel friends with them, and it always makes me feel happy."

Other political causes appeal to him. There is the opening of his lifelong interest in Russia and a note of Dr. Watson's proposal to start a journal to record Russian atrocities. His economic views are visibly ripening towards Socialism, though he writes to Miss Hadwen (February 1890): "I don't go as far in Socialism as Webb does. I don't see my way with the same clearness, but we may come to anything. Think of the change of opinion in the last five years." "Webb", he adds, "is one of the most interesting men I have met. We simply sat and talked and talked and settled the affairs of the universe one after another."

Both Aristotle and Trade Unionism faded from this correspondence, as intellectual friendship passed into the closer personal bond of an engagement. The marriage, which took place next year, was the opening of a new and richer life for both of them, thirty-five years of a happiness of which his colleague Westermarck might well have taken note in his *History of Marriage*. The family had always had an unusually powerful hold upon the emotional nature of this sensitive being, and the devotion to wife and children, later extended to grandchildren, was in a very real sense his most absorbing passion, extending as it did to the most trivial incidents of the daily life of all the members of the family. This intense feeling for family life makes a definite mark upon the valuations which enter into a 'sociology' that links up so closely theoretic with practical interpretations of the evolutionary processes, and subjects them to the criterion of ethics.

Married life necessarily involved changes in exterior arrangements, and as children came Hobhouse settled himself down more closely to his teaching, and the slow preparation for the heavy intellectual tasks of production which he had undertaken, applying his leisure to the enjoyment and interests of his home. Not that he ever sank into the careful emotional economy that marks so many members of the sheltered academic world. But he had less time for external activities than formerly, and the very brilliancy of his teaching powers made larger demands upon his energy and health, which even in these early years were easily subject to overstrain.

I take the opportunity of giving here two vivid impressions of his Oxford life and teaching, one from a college friend of his own standing, Mr. H. M. Conacher, the other from one of his pupils, Miss Barbara Bradby (afterwards Mrs. J. L. Hammond). Though this latter part of Mr. Conacher's contribution may seem to trespass upon the field allotted in this volume to Professor Ginsberg, the exposition of Leonard Hobhouse's philosophic work, it is so intimately related to the Oxford thought of this period, and so illustrative of his reactions to that intellectual environment, that I have ventured to include it here as a brief independent commentary upon his early philosophic position.

Mr. Conacher writes:

"If his humanitarianism and love of social justice were his chief emotional motives, intellectually it was in reason that he believed both in practical concerns and in theory. All through his treatment of philosophical questions he was consistently rationalist.

"Hence though he respected William James as a psychologist, he kept well aloof from pragmatism. Similarly he could not accept Bradley's dialectics—too much was made of contradiction, and reason seemed to be baffled at too many turns. Yet he was not dogmatic, and nobody was less sectarian in philosophy. He was, as he said in the preface to the *Theory of Knowledge*, willing to learn from Lotze and Hegel as well as from Spencer and Mill.

"Reacting from the current idealism, he thought that the English empiricists had not perhaps enough justice done them; and though he could not accept Green's position, he recognised the brilliance of Green's discussion of the 'real' and of his analysis of the nature of 'the thing in itself', and said (as anticipating the turn of the tide) that he should set his face against Green being treated as Mill had been.

"Perhaps he did not attach importance to sheer erudition in philosophy, and so far as he concerned himself with the great names in the philosophical tradition, it was rather with those who had interested themselves in the theory of knowledge, Locke, Berkeley, Hume, and Kant, that he busied himself than with ontologists like Descartes, Spinoza, and perhaps one may add Leibniz, though he was something of both.

"It was during this time that Hobhouse wrote *The Theory of Knowledge*, published early in 1896, about three years after *Appearance and Reality*. Looking at the present movement in philosophy, one is disposed to claim that Hobhouse was a pioneer of the realism which seems to be the creed of Alexander and Broad, Russell and Whitehead. He reached his conclusions by a process rather different from theirs—so far as they have a common point of view.

"If we try to see Hobhouse's thought in the making, perhaps we shall take note that he is at some pains to challenge a set of views of which Bradley's *Appearance and Reality* and perhaps to some extent his *Principles of Logic* were the best exposition available. Anyhow, it is in the field of logic that Hobhouse was working. The time was one in which much work was being done in Logic, as by Bradley and Bosanquet in this country and Lotze and Sigwart in Germany. Generally Hobhouse was concerned to controvert the idealism which gave too much to the 'work of the mind' in knowledge. Green thus came in for a good deal of criticism.

"In the case of Bradley it was perhaps rather the tendency to see too many contradictions in the realm of 'appearance'. Hence Hobhouse shows a certain reaction towards the outlook of the English empiricists, but he does not go back simply to them. We may say perhaps that for them knowledge is considered mainly as a process, whereas for Kant the interest is in an analysis of the structure of the fabric of experience. Now Hobhouse seems to combine the two attitudes. As against the idealists he is concerned to extend the 'content' of data so as to include what he calls 'apprehension', memory and judgment. Beyond this there are two further stages—inference and knowledge. When he reaches inference (seeing that for him the mind does not guarantee its own operations, and yet reality is accessible to reason), he has to establish its validity. Here he did some of his most original work, working out the view that the validity of inference rests on coherence and the mutual corroboration of independent inferences.

"But he recognised that this implied that reality is a system—and here came in the influence of German ways of thought and of English idealism. The general belief in the uniformity of nature was now felt not to be enough.

"If it is asked how on the other hand he reached forward to the realism of our days, perhaps one may point to his steady insistence on the position that the abandonment of Hume's 'unrelated particular' made the Kantian reply to Hume irrelevant. So, too, we may say that Whitehead carries this line of thought farther. 'The philosophy of a generation back', he says, 'can be summarised as the belief that nature is an aggregate of materials, and that this material exists in some sense at each successive member of a one-dimensional series of extensional instants in time. . . .'

"It would seem that spaces would be as instantaneous as instants, and that some explanation would be required of the relations between the successive instantaneous spaces.

"It was a great achievement for a man in the early thirties —especially as he held that five hours a day was his limit for work. Unlike many British books, it was well planned, and there is a clear order and development about it. Perhaps Hobhouse would not have got through it in the time taken if he had not had the faculty of writing quickly; apparently he could keep up the effort of writing almost at the level of many people's power of sustained speech. Many passages of the work read like a lecture or a report of a discussion. Possibly this manner had its drawbacks. Hobhouse was not a pure scholar; if he had been he might have written at shorter length. Our modern mathematical philosophers write in a compact and direct fashion.

"A year after publishing *The Theory of Knowledge* Hobhouse left Oxford. To be happy in the life of a don perhaps needed a more placid disposition than his. Possibly he anticipated rather early the feeling that men are said to have in middle age after working on in Oxford through the twenties and thirties, that they would like a change.

"Probably he wanted to influence the great world of affairs a little more directly. And there was no doubt much in Oxford life with which he was impatient, and yet saw no chance of changing. 'A college is an organisation *pour rire*', he said once, thinking no doubt of its economic defects, such things, one supposes, as the gargantuan breakfasts and the sight of the scouts going out of college at eleven o'clock with great baskets of victuals. Then again he thought that there was a lack of earnest and stimulating fellowship in the learned community. 'A is afraid to write a book on this or that subject (of which he knew a good deal) because B will make fun of it.' Nor could one well think of him as a member of a group.

"There is no need to suppose he chafed at the conditions of tutorial work as preparing men for the schools, which he regarded good-humouredly. He said once of the examination: 'The questions may change, but the answers are the same.'

Mrs. Hammond writes:

"I find it difficult to detach the Oxford L.T.H. from the L.T.H. of Manchester and Wimbledon days, but looking back to the 'nineties of last century I see a tall, queer, energetic figure, striding through Oxford, dressed in homespun with a red tie. Oxford was in a very reactionary phase at that time; lost causes were disagreeably in the ascendant; and L.T.H. was restive in those surroundings. But his hostility never gave one the impression of bitterness and he was excellent company when he fulminated genially against the highly developed critical faculties of his fellow dons, and their hopelessly benighted political views. There were very few kindred spirits in Oxford then. Sidney Ball was his chief ally, and alone, I think, among dons shared his socialist views. Arthur Sidgwick, of the older generation, was a close friend.

"Though uncomfortable in the Oxford atmosphere, he was extraordinarily happy in his home life with his wife and small children, and his house in Park Crescent, where Nora Hobhouse, frail in body and indomitable in spirit, shared in all his social enthusiasms, was an exhilarating place where one felt that the world, bad though it might be, was going to get better. Then, as always, he was a brilliant talker, though brilliant is perhaps a misleading word, for it often means a talker who reduces others to silence. L.T.H.'s conversation never had this effect; nobody ever talked less for effect; his good sayings were tumbled out on the spur of the moment with a laugh, and his impetuous interest in a topic made others interested too and anxious to say what they thought about it.

"I was fortunate enough to have L.T.H. as my Greats tutor. In those days it was possible to pick and choose among the many enlightened coaches anxious to help on the cause of women's education. L.T.H., whom I had never met, was suggested to me as a suitable and congenial tutor, since he held odd, unorthodox political views. As a teacher he was remarkably stimulating; he was ready to help clear up the mental fogs left by undigested idealism, but his aim was always to make you think for yourself. He would take any trouble, provided you took trouble too, but I do not imagine he was adapted to administer knowledge by forcible feeding. I have heard it said that he did not suffer fools gladly. This, I think, is untrue. Not to care about the wrongs of the world was the unforgivable offence. Provided you cared, it did not matter how slowly or stupidly your mind worked. A pupil likely to do badly in the Schools to whom the wrongs of the Armenians, or Russian revolutionaries, or sweated workers, were real, was infinitely preferred to any brilliant scholar who cared for none of these things. He cared, indeed, so much himself that he was intolerant of Gallios, and I doubt whether he found many among his men pupils who came up to his standards of interest in social matters.

"The prevailing philosophical thought of Oxford was as uncongenial to him as its political tone. Idealism was the dominant doctrine, and every Greats lecturer who had nothing else to say could fill up gaps by pouring scorn on Mill, a practice which greatly annoyed him. He was fond of saying what he puts in his preface to *The Theory of Knowledge*, that Mill's fault was that, unlike other philosophers, he wrote intelligibly enough to be found out. Most of the time I was up he was working at *The Theory of Knowledge*, and when it came out in 1896 and received the cold welcome that was to be expected in that Idealist *milieu*, I think his restlessness increased. He felt that he had had his fling in that direction, and he longed to use his powers in the world of action."

CHAPTER II

MANCHESTER AND EARLY LONDON LIFE

HOBHOUSE's decision to leave Oxford and to throw himself
into active journalism and political activities was no surprise
to those who knew him best. His systematic thinking had
already framed itself on lines that demanded a closer contact with the external world than Oxford gave. The roots of
his social philosophy, his working-out of the evolutionary
principle in the growth of mind and its social institutions,
needed a fuller diet of personal practical experience than
was obtainable by occasional excursions from an Oxford
college. A certain restlessness of body accompanied this
restlessness of mind. Though still a young and in many
ways a vigorous man, he had already begun to develop that
nervousness about his health which dogged his life (as it
had his father's) before any patent symptoms of ill-health
appeared. The Oxford climate did not suit him. This was
the reason for wishing to leave Oxford that he himself gave
in his earliest communication with Mr. C. P. Scott. That
communication came about as the result of a letter written
to Dr. A. Sidgwick making inquiries for a good man to
join the staff of the *Manchester Guardian*. Mr. Sidgwick
approached Hobhouse, whom he describes as "quite the
ablest of our younger 'Greats' men and a strong Liberal
and progressive of the best type", and though Hobhouse's
first idea was to live in London and send articles from
there, he was persuaded by Mr. Scott to come to
Manchester and settle down as a part-time journalist
with sufficient leisure to pursue the philosophical and
sociological studies which he always recognised as his first
concern.

After a preliminary trial in the spring of 1897, during
which the matter of residence in Manchester remained
open, he decided to settle down in a convenient house in

Rusholme with his family and furniture removed from Oxford. This change was effected in the autumn of 1897, and Manchester became his permanent residence until the autumn of 1902. His life during this period was a varied and an arduous one. It combined continuous work in preparation of his *Mind in Evolution* (which appeared in 1901), with the active career of journalism that involved keeping himself in close contact with the political and economic movements of those eventful years. The actual writing of the numerous articles probably took less out of him than out of most of his fellow-writers. For his facility with the pen, transferring on to paper in fit shape the thought and knowledge he held in such complete control, was one of his most remarkable gifts. As soon as he was seized of his subject, he fell upon it with his swift and resourceful mind, transcribing with an almost automatic ease the opinions and judgments which the case evoked. But, even for his acquisitive intelligence, the labours of following in detail so many series of public happenings, in order to meet the sudden demands of the journalistic life, must have been considerable. Moreover, the intellectual facility of which I speak was not accompanied by that emotional ease or indifference so often attributed to the professional journalist. His passions and his conscience were profoundly stirred by the good and evil he discovered in current history, and his labours to help to make the right prevail carried a heavy emotional expense, especially during the later period, when the barbarities of the South African War revealed themselves in all their naked ugliness. Nor was he content to fight evil with his pen. His sympathy with causes that appealed to his passion for justice led him to take an active part in local organisations for their advocacy. So, for example, we find in the minutes of the Manchester District 'Protection of Native Races Society' early in 1898 the following resolution: "That Mr. L. T. Hobhouse is requested to approach Mr. John Morley and Mr. Leonard

Courtney, asking them to address a meeting in the Free Trade Hall, Manchester, in the coming autumn on the public action of the country towards weaker peoples, allowing them such liberty as they desire to treat the question according to the needs of the moment." The arrangements for this meeting first brought him into personal relations with the Liberal statesmen with whose position upon the outstanding issues of foreign and imperial policy he felt the closest sympathy, and the grave events of the next year strengthened his bond of sympathy and allegiance. When the Boer War broke out, a 'Manchester Transvaal Committee' was formed to protest against it, and Hobhouse took a leading part in organising the great public meeting in Manchester upon October 6th, when John Morley was the principal speaker.

The 'new Liberalism' whose meaning and distinctive qualities were his guiding principles for that interpretation of current events which is the rôle of the daily journalist, was for the time being concerned more with external policies than with the just dawning socialism of organised labour. While, therefore, we find Hobhouse in his Manchester period writing vigorous articles both on trade union policy and the new 'socialistic' trend in State aid to labour, as involved in Old Age Pensions, the main force of his pen was engaged in matters of foreign and colonial policy. In 1897–8 we find numerous articles dealing with China, India, the Greek War, Russia, Bechuanaland, Crete. The new imperialism, as expressed in Joseph Chamberlain's policy at the Colonial Office, especially in its growing concentration on South Africa, became, indeed, more and more the central theme of his journalistic pen, as the tacit conspiracy with Milner and Rhodes began to feel its way towards a forcible attack upon the Boer Republics. John Morley, writing to a common friend, Dr. Bridges, in 1899, says, "I cannot sufficiently admire the acuteness, industry, grasp, and power, with which Hobhouse has carried on this fight. It is one of the finest pieces of journalistic ability (in the highest sense) that I can remember."

But the burden and excitement of such a life took a great deal out of him. In the summer of 1898 he is complaining of 'nerve exhaustion' and a couple of years later his letters to Mr. C. P. Scott disclose several 'collapses', and a generally 'bad state of health', his doctor insisting upon rest and a long holiday.

Indeed, as time went on, his letters disclose frequent outbreaks of personal apprehension and unrest. In February 1900 he writes to Mr. Scott: "I am now pretty well convinced that I cannot *permanently* maintain the double work, and that philosophy has the first claim upon me." This restiveness is not, however, based entirely upon considerations of health, or even upon the prior claim of philosophy. For he adds: "Unless some great and unforeseen change occurs, the Liberal Party seems to me destined to futility, and I find more difficulty now in writing from any point of view but that of an avowed independent."

But this restiveness seems to have been occasional and not chronic. Nor did he contemplate any very early breakaway. For though a letter from Lord Morley in November 1901, offering him an introduction to Macmillans, shows that he had contemplated the post of a publisher's reader, this was probably attributable, at least in part, to temporary difficulties in the office relating to policy, selection, and treatment of subjects which seems to have caused him some irritation. At any rate, we find him writing with unabated vigour until September 1902. Considering that he was on a definitely 'half-time basis' his output was enormous. During the year before he gave up, the number of articles appearing from his pen was three hundred and twenty-two, at least half of which were 'longs' or else 'specials', involving full treatment of some intricate and important topic of the times, or full reviews of such books as Mr. Kidd's

Principles of Western Civilisation, or Mr. H. Samuel's *Liberalism: its Principles and Proposals.*

Though the Boer War bulked biggest through all these years and numerous articles dealt with the Mortality in the Concentration Camps, the suspension of the Cape Constitution, and the effects of Native Policy, home affairs were kept fully in view. The Education Bill now before Parliament was followed in detail and there was much to say about the Taff Vale case, the Agricultural Rates Act, Free Trade, the new Factory Bill, the Pottery trade, and the Yorkshire miners, not to mention topics outside the range of politics or economics, such as Holidays, the Death of Ruskin, the King's new title, the British Medical Association.

It is evident that from the early days of his connection with the *Manchester Guardian* Mr. Scott held the highest respect for his judgment and his intellectual resources, and a close correspondence was kept up between them. Mr. Scott was in Parliament during most of this period and Hobhouse furnished long reasoned opinions upon such issues as local taxation, the referendum, and trade union policy. His already clearly formed views upon the necessity of a reformed constructive Liberalism, involving an abandonment of the *laissez-faire* attitude of the older Manchester School, were impressed upon the paper, not only in his own articles but in the habitual policy it adopted in confronting the new social-economic issues of trade unionism and Governmental control.

It was, no doubt, the growing pressure of this arduous work that was the chief reason for his final determination in the autumn of 1902 to leave Manchester for London, where he hoped to have freedom to devote himself more closely to his philosophic work, and more particularly to the social implications of the theory set out in his *Mind in Evolution.* In one respect, at least, it was a fortunate moment for this resolve of his. For no sooner was he settled in his new abode at Wimbledon than a movement took shape in certain intellectual quarters for the formation of a Sociological Society. Hobhouse threw himself into this project with his accustomed vigour, and at a public meeting held in June 1903 seconded the resolution moved by Oscar Browning for the appointment of a committee to formulate the scope and aims of the Society and to draft its constitution. The Report of this Committee, which he took a large part in drafting, was adopted by a general meeting of the Society in November. He took an active part in the early meetings of the Society, which were mainly devoted to developing the significance of Sociology as a unifying science among the already recognised social sciences.

But while Sociology, both in its philosophic and historical aspects, was destined from this time forth to be the chief claimant on his time and energy, he did not find it possible to escape from participation in other causes of more immediate appeal. The heroic labours of his sister Emily in the restoration of homes and industry in South Africa engaged him more deeply than would otherwise have been the case in the whole problem of the African settlement, and brought him into personal relations with the Boer leaders when they visited England. To this period belongs the famous story of Botha and De Wet, who, while staying at Wimbledon, were taken by Mrs. Hobhouse to a livery stable to get a mount. "But can the gentlemen ride?" was the anxious question put by the manager to Mrs. Hobhouse.

A more serious interruption to his philosophic occupations, however, was in store. A heavy loss of the financial resources of the family which came unexpectedly upon him, called for redress by some income-earning occupation. So we find Hobhouse accepting the post of Secretary of the Free Trade Union, just formed to deal with the political emergency created by Joseph Chamberlain's protectionist campaign. This work, essentially propagandist in its character and demanding close office attendance, was not very congenial to him, and after a couple of years he resigned the post. Meantime he had been lecturing and writing. In 1902 he contributed to *The Pilot*, then edited by Mr. Filson Young, a series of popular articles on animal psychology, the product in large measure of his studies in the Manchester Zoo towards his *Mind in Evolution*. He wrote a good deal for the *Manchester Guardian* and from time to time put in spells of work in Manchester. In 1903 he gave a course of lectures at Birmingham University, which was to have been continued in 1904, had not ill health (the beginning of his slow breakdown) intervened. About this time friends suggested that he should enter a candidature for Deputy-Professor of Moral Philosophy at Oxford. But nothing came of this proposal. In July 1904 the University of London accepted his offer to give a course of lectures (without remuneration) on 'Comparative Ethics' in connection with the newly established Martin White benefaction. His notable little book *Democracy and Reaction*, a powerful protest against imperialism and the purely negative social policy of the Liberal Party, appeared in 1904 and was the subject of a eulogy by Lord Morley. In the winter of 1904–5 we find some correspondence regarding the offer of a Professorship by the University of Wisconsin, indicating the growing appreciation of his work in America. The University of London in the autumn of 1905 offered a lectureship apparently in continuation of the lecture work of 1904. But these projects for renewed and enlarged academic work were for a time set aside, in favour of the political editorship of *The Tribune*, which was to absorb his energies for the next year and a half.

CHAPTER III

THE "TRIBUNE" AND AFTER

THE *Tribune* episode was not a happy one in Hobhouse's career. It is strange that he should have thought it possible to make his political editorship of a large daily paper square with the declaration of views and principles set out by its founder and proprietor, Mr. Franklin Thomasson in a formal profession of faith submitted to him in the early summer of 1905. That document was in effect a statement of rigid adherence to the *laissez-faire* individualism of the old Manchester School, qualified by taxation of land values. Now, as a political thinker, Hobhouse had long passed out of the confined limits of the older creed and quite recently (1904) in his brilliant work *Democracy and Reaction* had urged with insistence the need of a constructive Liberalism, absorbing a considerable measure of socialism in the sense of organised collective action. "I venture", he wrote in his final chapter, "to conclude that the difference between a true, consistent, public-spirited Liberalism and a rational Collectivism ought, with a genuine effort at mutual understanding, to disappear."[1] This conviction, already deeply rooted in his political philosophy, had been sedulously nourished during his years with the *Manchester Guardian*, and was the prime *motif* in all the practical labours which he undertook in the field of politics and of industry during the quarter of a century that remained to him. It is possible that he was able to persuade himself that the immediate problems in the political field, largely concerned with the aftermath of the Boer War, and domestic issues, such as the new Education Bill and Reform of the House of Lords, need not bring into serious conflict the two schools of Liberalism, to which he and the proprietor of the proposed paper respectively adhered. But the fundamental divergence of political

[1] *Democracy and Reaction*, 287.

views was not the only obstacle to success in this experiment, nor was it the direct cause of the withdrawal of Hobhouse from the *Tribune* early in 1907. Two other difficulties arose. Though, as Political Editor, Hobhouse was placed in control of the Leading Articles, he was supposed to co-operate with the Managing Editor in dealing with non-political articles. But the latter, in control of foreign correspondence, reporting (which included Parliamentary debates), 'news', and special articles outside the strict diocese of 'politics', was bound to come into conflict with the Political Editor, if only in the allotment of space.

But by the summer of 1906 Hobhouse had become keenly aware of another divergence of views between himself and the management. Whereas he had designed to make the *Tribune* an intellectual instrument of what may be called the higher political education, the manager felt bound to play for a wider public, and in this view of his function had the support of the proprietor. For some time relations remained in a state of strain, and at the end of the year Hobhouse definitely resigned his post, severing his connection with the paper towards the end of January 1907. His own writing for the *Tribune* showed the same energy of mind, fertility of resource, and variety of knowledge which marked his labours in Manchester. His 'leaders' were largely addressed to subjects connected with the reconstruction of South Africa, legacies of the war, and to the new awakening of China. But his pen followed assiduously the domestic issues, both constitutional and economic, relating to the Reform of the Lords, the Trade Disputes Bill, and Mr. Birrell's Education Bill was supported in its parliamentary career by a series of brilliantly written articles. His versatility was displayed in dealing with such varied topics as Liberal Finance, Land Reform, Women's Suffrage, 'Poplar', and other issues forging to the front with the great Liberal revival, while he furnished an immense store of political powder and shot in columns entitled

'Facts and Comments'. Long articles upon Our Coal Supply, The Colour Line, Labour and Politics, The Party System, Imperialism, may be cited as marking his desire to expound the foundations of political and economic life, rather than to confine the paper to the passing show.

After his retirement from the *Tribune*, Mr. Scott tried to tempt him back to Manchester, but found that he was now too deeply rooted in London. But from this time on his contributions, both of articles and reviews to the *Manchester Guardian*, became a more or less continuous part of his work, and in 1911 he became a director of the Company. His refusal to return to Manchester was, doubtless, influenced by the new prospects of work in Sociology due to the foundation of a Chair by Mr. Martin White in that subject. Hobhouse was chosen in 1907 as a first holder of this Chair, thus drawn definitively from general philosophy into social philosophy and the social sciences whither his interest had for some time past been moving. With this new post he continued for a time the editorship of the *Sociological Review*, the newly established organ of the Sociological Society. After three years of this editorial work he resigned the post, partly from pressure of other work, but partly also from a divergence of view as to the conduct and contents of such a Review that had arisen between him and other active supporters of the Society.

His acceptance of the Martin White professorship in 1907 was the beginning of the distinctive contribution which he made, as teacher and writer, to Sociology. Up to this time the study had been suffering from the superficial generalisations with which Spencer had invested it, lacking a sufficient basis of historical research upon the one hand, and a close application of the evolutionary principle upon the other. The writer of the obituary notice of Hobhouse in the *Manchester Guardian* thus summarises his great intellectual achievement in this field:

"Hobhouse's appointment as professor of sociology synchronised with a new development in his philosophic work. He had long been dissatisfied with conventional ethical theories. He had seen that they are the natural reflection of a special environment and, as a sociologist, he was convinced that their evolutionary study was important. The publication in 1906 of his *Morals in Evolution* marked an epoch in the study of Sociology. Here Hobhouse revealed at their best the amazing range of his powers. A grasp of anthropological fact, of ethical theory, of the history of religions and institutions—all were combined to lay the foundations of a humanism never more impressively stated. The book made its mark from the start, and as far East as Japan, it has been recognised as a classic. It was the preamble to an even more imposing construction." "In three volumes (*The Rational Good*, 1921, *The Elements of Social Justice*, 1922, *Social Development*, 1924) Hobhouse outlined a sociological system as impressive as any in our time. Its root was the effort to harmonise the individual with his social environment, and it would not be an inapt description of the work to say that it brought all the materials of the social sciences to prove that ultimate good consisted in the liberation of the human personality."

Since a fuller exposition of his teaching follows from the pen of his colleague and successor, Professor Ginsberg, it may here suffice to stress the fundamental importance conveyed by his conception of 'the liberation of the human personality'. Social evolution consisted in the achievement of the latent powers of personality by means of organised social contacts and their institutions and corporate activities. These social structures were not ends, there was no such thing as 'a social mind', community was never conceived as an end, but always as an instrument for the enlargement and enrichment of personal mind. Probably he valued most highly (and there will be wide agreement with this valuation), as his richest contribution to the thought of his time,

Development and Purpose, published first in 1913, and largely rewritten for a new edition published in 1927. In this revision he received great assistance from Dr. Ginsberg. He writes to Miss Llewelyn Davies in January 1926: "Did I tell you that I provisionally completed 'D and P'? Ginsberg is reading it carefully and has already suggested one emendation which I have carried out successfully and which is an undoubted improvement. But he has not yet got to the critical part, which is near the end. He is awfully good, particularly for me, fearlessly conscientious in criticism, and knows my mind as well as I know it myself."

But, throughout his life, Hobhouse continued to concern himself with the practical issues of politics, both internal and foreign. His sensitive mind, earlier than that of more hardened politicians, was alive to the coming European conflict. In the beginning of 1911 (itself a fateful year) he took a leading part in the formation of a small group of men who called themselves 'A Foreign Policy Committee'. Mr. E. C. K. Ensor acted as its secretary, and its purpose was to feed a more continuous interest in current events outside this country, chiefly among Members of Parliament and journalists. It is a striking commentary upon the blindness of mind which afflicted even the leaders of opinion in these momentous years, that this Committee, after a serious endeavour to win attention to its work, was within a year forced to close down from sheer lack of membership and funds.

CHAPTER IV

1914 AND AFTER

THE Great War fell with a terrible impact upon a spirit so sensitive and so steeped in historical causation. We have seen how closely he followed political movements in other countries throughout his journalist career, and in recent years he had shown himself passionately sympathetic with the new dawning internationalism of The Hague. His pronounced anti-Imperialism was closely bound up with the cause of Arbitration as the pacific mode of settlement for all international differences.

In the last days of July when the war clouds were thickening, Hobhouse's sympathies were with the little Neutrality Group (including Lord Courtney and Lord Bryce) who had set themselves to oppose our participation in a European war, should it break out. The following letter from Lord Morley, dated August 5, 1914, makes this evident:

"I am grateful to you for writing. It is easy to advocate unpopular opinion, but to break away from a Cabinet with all the aspects and ramifications of such a proceeding, is about as hard a responsibility as a man can bear. I am glad you are so firm in approval. It is a vast relief, after two days of strain, to have washed my hands of their misdoing."

But as the significance of Lord Grey's committals, though unknown to Parliament, the people, or even to some members of the Cabinet, became manifest, and the policy of Prussian 'frightfulness' in Belgium was displayed in all its horrors, the attitude of suspense which Hobhouse, with many other Liberals, maintained even after the outbreak of hostilities, gave way to one of sorrowful acceptance of our obligation to join our Allies in resisting the German onset. Still perplexed by the secret diplomacy of Grey and his abrupt rejection of the final appeal made by Lichnowsky, he had accepted a *fait accompli* which compelled us to produce the necessary force to win the war.

Hobhouse was profoundly affected in his judgment of the war by what he held to be the philosophical and moral influence of the Hegelian teaching upon the political thought of Germany. As he says in the Dedication of his *Metaphysical Theory of the State* (published in 1917), he was for a time driven to abandon theory. The war must be won. "To each man the tools and weapons that he can best use. In the bombing of London I had just witnessed the visible and tangible outcome of a false and wicked doctrine, the foundations of which lay, as I believe, in the book before me (Hegel). To combat this doctrine effectively is to take such part in the fight as the physical disabilities of middle age allow." To his intimates he would regret his inability to be an active combatant, and he denied the moral right of a citizen to refuse combatant service in a just war in which his country had become involved.

But the acceptance was made with a heavy heart and with dismal forebodings which were only too well grounded. "The outlook", he writes to Mr. Scott on August 18th, "is more gloomy than ever. This secrecy means absolutism. We are utterly at the mercy of Kitchener and Churchill. We cannot so much as mention a fact without their concurrence. They or the Government have made Japan enter the war— a most serious step and no one knows to what adventures on the continent they will commit us. I see the gravest dangers to our most elementary liberties close upon us."

From the opening of the war to its close Hobhouse amid other activities kept in constant touch with the *Manchester Guardian* by private letters to the Editor, often containing memoranda of policy, and by leading articles. Mr. Scott writes to him in May 1915 in the following strain:

"I feel as if there were a far bigger work waiting here to be done by a man of your power—you know what I think of you, so I needn't spare your blushes—than anything you can possibly achieve directly in connection with the war. There is this whole vast question of national organisation and of the rousing and disciplining of the working class. The Government have no time and also not too much courage or statesmanship, and most of the thinking has to be done for them. Most even of the thinkers are serving in the ranks or serving tables, and on those who, like you, are left our destiny largely rests. I should like to see you giving your whole time and strength to the business. I don't mean necessarily in connection with the *M.G.*—that is as it may happen and no doubt it could be made a useful instrument —but in setting your mind on the whole complex problem and getting others to do the same—travelling about, seeing important people, inspecting works, and conferring with Labour leaders."

The munitions crisis was already opening, and conscription, industrial and military, was beginning to press for consideration. By May 1915 we find Hobhouse writing: "I agree with you that we shall have to accept a much more rigorous discipline if we are going to win, and it occurs to me possible that it may even involve a kind of conscription in which every man will be available for the Government for some work, soldiering or industrial, which will assist the prosecution of the war." He adds a little later on (September 3rd) that "if George is after effective industrial service"— "Labour cannot be put under discipline unless *works* are nationalised. Mistakes on this point greatly accentuated the S. Wales trouble."

How far he was temporarily carried away on the wave of war from his earlier Liberal moorings is perhaps best seen from a letter of January 1916, addressed to Mr. Scott before the Paris Economic Conference.

"My feeling is that there may be circumstances at the close of the war which will compel us to modify the Free Trade principle, but that we ought not to be prepared to

meet them half-way or to abandon F.T. on purely hypo-
thetical and problematic grounds."

From 1916 onwards for many years his attachment to
the *Manchester Guardian* was closer than it had been since
his residence in London. He not only contributed many
political leaders but took up a new line in 'back pagers',
essays which exhibit the wide range of his thought and focus
his wisdom in deeper commentary upon the issues of the
time. From the early part of 1917 his full force was devoted
to the conditions of an early peace, partly, to stop the fearful
waste of life, partly, because he took a somewhat pessimistic
view of the allied cause, with the Russian collapse and the
unpreparedness of America, whose 'associated power' he
rated below its intrinsic worth. Upon no part of his life-
work did he set greater value than upon this attempt early
in 1917 to get reason and pacific purpose into the war-mind
of England and Germany. Mr. Lloyd George was still in
favour of waiting and Mr. Scott was powerfully influenced
by him. Both, however, were brought over to the same view
by his powerful articles in the *Manchester Guardian* urging
the Government to a definite statement of peace terms.
These articles may be said to have influenced opinion in
Germany as well as England. They were widely quoted
there as evidence of a willingness to consider a negotiated
peace by a leading section of English thought. From May
onwards his correspondence with Mr. Scott shows an ever
stronger bent towards an allied statement of peace terms,
and the Lansdowne letter furnished new hope. In December
he writes in favour of a provisional acceptance of the German proposals for a Peace Conference, with no annexations
and self-determination as leading principles. His mental
powers were exerted to the full in the later war period. Such
exertion he seemed to require as a relief, especially as his
health inhibited activities of a directly practical kind. "One
has a strong sentiment for doing things as against writing,
but a night I had in camp a week or two ago and the two I

had in Flanders have sufficed to convince me that I could not stand the conditions."

But he underrated his capacity for 'doing things'. Apart from the teaching of sociology, which he continued through this period of public agony, he kept up various activities upon Trade Boards which he had carried on from 1909. He was a joint independent Chairman of the Co-operative Conciliation Board (with Sir Richard Redmayne and Professor H. J. Laski), and acted as arbitrator in various trade disputes. When the National Industrial Conference took place in the spring of 1919 he acted as Chairman of the most important of the sections, receiving the following letter from the Prime Minister:

"I have to express to you on behalf of the Government my great appreciation of the services you rendered as Chairman of the Sub-Committee of the National Industrial Conference which dealt with wages and hours. I know that the duties were very exacting and troublesome, and required not merely time and close attention, but also great skill in handling the different elements in the Committee. It was greatly due to your personal influence that so much was achieved, and the Government is very grateful to you for the work which you accomplished."

His work upon the Trade Boards ranks as one of his most valued activities in his later years. He took immense interest in mastering the details of the several trades in their bearing upon wages and other conditions of labour, and the quickness and essential fairness of his mind were recognised by the representative employers and workers alike. Not that this work proceeded smoothly at all times. Trade Boards were novel institutions, involving Governmental interference in the conduct of individual businesses, both in regard to employers' co-operation and the relations of the body of employers with a body of unorganised or ill-organised workers.

Mr. J. J. Mallon, Warden of Toynbee Hall, sends me

the following account of Hobhouse's work upon Trade Boards:

"Professor Hobhouse became interested in Trade Boards when, after the advent to power of the Liberal Government of 1906, the question of minimum wage legislation had been brought to the front by the advocacy of Sir Charles Dilke, Mr. Sidney Webb, and others and the work of the National Anti-sweating League. But Mr. and Mrs. Ramsay Mac-Donald, returning from Australia, opposed any legal regulation of wages, and their considerable influence divided the opinion of reformers. The MacDonalds had made a careful study of Wages Boards and the machinery of compulsory arbitration in Australia and New Zealand and they spoke impressively of the dangers and difficulties of the application of law to the regulation of wages.

"The MacDonald argument was in the main that the success of the Wages Boards in Australia was illusory, inasmuch as advance in wages had led to higher tariffs and higher tariffs to higher costs of living. The workers of Australia, they contended, had walked round a circle without any gain worth talking about and with the loss that they had compromised their socialism by supporting Tariffism. In a Free Trade country, the argument ran, wages could not be increased above their natural level by legal machinery. The conclusion was that Wages Boards were a palliative, or worse, and that the only remedy for industrial ills was in the progressive application of principles of socialism.

"Impressed by the MacDonald argument, Hobhouse decided thoroughly to investigate the subject for himself. After inquiry he concluded that the MacDonald pronouncements were too unqualified and that Trade Boards had great possibilities of usefulness in a Free Trade country. He expressed this view weightily in the *Tribune* and elsewhere.

"His interest in the subject grew after the passing of the first Trade Boards Act in 1909, and he watched the work of the pioneer Boards with close attention. Mr. Tawney's Studies on the results of the Trade Boards in the Tailoring and Chain-making trades confirmed the views he had already formed and encouraged him to emphasise the importance of legal minimum rates of wages in appropriate trades. In 1918 a second Trade Boards Act added to the power of the Boards and amplified the machinery for the extension of the Acts. Thereafter, in accordance with the recommendation of the Whitley Committee and other Reconstruction Committees, many Boards were established.

"The task which met these Boards of adjusting rates of wages to post-war conditions was not in every case easy and the part of the Chairman of the Board was one of exceptional importance. It was very much to the general gain that at this stage Professor Hobhouse was induced to interest himself actively in the work of the Boards. He accepted the Chairmanship of the Paper-box Board in 1918 in succession to Mr. Ernest Aves, who had been Chairman of all the Trade Boards up to the time of his death in 1917, and when, as quickly happened, he had shown that he possessed many qualities which were indispensable to good chairmanship, the Ministry of Labour made heavy claims on his services.

"In the big expansion of Trade Boards which followed the war, Professor Hobhouse was appointed in 1919 and 1920 as the first Chairman of a number of Boards on their establishment.

"Professor Hobhouse's services to the Trade Boards movement may be summed up under two main headings. He expounded with subtlety and persuasiveness the underlying principles of the Boards, and as Trade Board Chairman excelled in impartiality, in holding the sides of the Boards together, in clearing away misunderstandings, and in the inculcation of broad and philosophic views. The first of those services was rendered particularly in 1921, when at an early stage in the trade depression an attack on Trade

Boards, originating in certain quarters of the needlework trades, was fed by a number of well-known daily papers, and very rapidly developed. That the agitation was unreal, that the parties most active in it had no personal concern in Trade Boards and used them only as sticks with which to beat the existing Government and the Government Departments did not lessen its possibilities of mischief. The extension of the Trade Boards Act was suspended. Many Boards were in jeopardy. The then Minister of Labour was clearly prepared to buy off the agitation by any means in his power. In these circumstances Professor Hobhouse was invaluable. His influence in the Press and the Schools was fully exerted to resist the efforts of malicious or ignorant assailants, and he stood strongly against the policy dictated by the timidity of the Minister. On a Committee appointed by the Minister to report upon the administration of Trade Boards he urged a bold policy of enlargement, and at a later stage, when a nervous Government had conceded to the outcry against the Boards the appointment of another and more important Committee under Viscount Cave, his evidence constituted the main defence of the work of the Boards.

"About Professor Hobhouse as Chairman of Trade Boards it is possible to speak equally highly. The Chairman of a Trade Board is apt to be suspected by both sides. The representatives of the employers are apt to regard him as a theorist who knows little of the concrete operations of manufacture and trade. The representatives of the workers are impressed by the fact that he is the nominee of a Government Department, who as such is likely always, in their view, to play for safety and to exclude from his consideration the arguments which are addressed to him on the basis of the workers' poverty and needs. Professor Hobhouse was successful, as few men can hope to be, in removing both these prejudices. In doing this he was helped by the visible greatness of his personality, by his sincerity, by the purity of his purpose, by a wide knowledge of industry and affairs, and a rapid and understanding mind. He had indeed all the essentials and graces of good chairmanship. He was patient, but discouraged verbosity; he saw into the complicated arguments which occupy much of the time of Trade Boards Committees as to the scope of the jurisdiction of the Boards over processes and persons; he caught a meaning immediately, however poorly it might be expressed, and redressed it in appropriate phrases; his resources of draftsmanship were often the salvation of a Board when differences between the representatives of employers and of workers had brought its work to a standstill. Moreover, and this was his special distinction as Chairman, he was never satisfied to effect an agreement which was momentary or only on the surface. He strove, and induced his colleagues to strive, often successfully, for settlements which were founded on principles; he helped the Boards to feel that their decisions were moral acts; when he intervened in discussions the subject-matter was immediately dignified and enlarged. In the opinion of all who were in a position to judge he was the most eminent of the many distinguished men who have been connected with Trade Boards, and he communicated to their work something of his own sanity and serenity and wisdom."

To this testimony I may append the following note from an employer who had close contact with him on this side of his economic work:

"I have most pleasant recollections of a close association with Professor Hobhouse in Trade Board work for a considerable period, among other matters serving on a Departmental Committee on the organisation of that work of which he was Chairman.

"His was a most definite and most interesting personality, and his power of clear, logical, and forceful exposition of a subject really remarkable; at the outset, perhaps, one may have been a little apt to be conscious of 'The Professor', but this was early lost in admiration for his keen interest in and mastery of the many often delicate and difficult problems involved."

During all these years he never remitted the journalistic work, which expressed his interest in current politics at a time of critical eventfulness. His attitude towards the Labour Party was one of watchful favour, though he never formally detached himself from Liberalism, as he understood it. There is an interesting letter of November 1924 to the Editor of the *Manchester Guardian*, in which he proposes as a policy "to maintain principles, define views, advocate causes, and let party organisation adapt itself to them."

"But tradition and class distinctions kept many good Liberals outside Labour. Now Labour has grown so much that it tends to absorb them and to leave only the 'bad' Liberals who incline to the Tories, and a mass of traditional Liberals who can't desert a party of that name. This tendency received its first great impetus from Lloyd George in 1918, only that most of the 'bad' Liberals became Lloyd Georgites. The last two years has given it another shove. For a moment fate seemed to be avoided by the decision of the Liberals on the *Manchester Guardian* lead to support Labour. Labour responded badly, and the Liberals then drew away and inevitably gravitated towards the other side. They failed to present a third view because outside the enthusiasts there is really no third view. Liberals may be full of fight, but, as against the main body of Labour, what have they to fight for? Internationalism, Free Trade, Ireland, India, any particular kind of Social Reform? No, on all these there is agreement. There is really nothing, till you come up against doctrinaire Socialism, which is really outside 'moderate' Labour."

Although after 1920 he did little writing for the *Manchester Guardian*, he still retained his Directorship of the Company and assisted to mould its policy. His work at the London School of Economics was taking an increasing share of his time and energy. For in the autumn of 1920 he took over the Directorship of the Ratan Tata Department vacated by Professor Urwick through ill health. His work as part-time Professor of Sociology was taking an increasing part of his time during two terms of the year, owing to the growth of work and of the number of students, both English and foreign, who came to take advantage of his lectures and of the private instruction in which he excelled. At the close of 1925 the Martin White professorship which he had held since 1907 was converted into a full-time Chair, compelling him to confine himself more closely to this, the main work of his last years. Before that time he had been able occasionally to accept lecture work offered by other Universities, as for example the Muirhead Lectureship at Birmingham, where he gave the first part of a two years' course in 1923, abandoning the course arranged for the following year by reason of ill health.

In America, where, owing to the influential educational propaganda of Dr. Lester Ward and other pioneers, Sociology had gained an established position earlier than in this country, Hobhouse's writings had won a wide reception, various invitations came to him. As early as 1904–5 the University of Wisconsin sought to secure him as a professor. One visit to America he paid in the spring of 1911, delivering a course of lectures under the Faculty of Political Science of Columbia University, which was afterwards published in a volume entitled *Social Evolution and Political Theory* by the Columbia University Press. In 1912 letters from Santayana urged him to come to Harvard for the academic year October 1912 to June 1913, as a Professor of Philosophy at Harvard, doubtless with the hope of securing him as a permanent teacher in that great University. One of the latest of these invitations to America was in 1929, when Professor W. E. Haskins, of Harvard, invited him to undertake the William James Lectureship for 1929–30. During the same year Yale University also appears to have intimated a desire to secure his services. In 1929 he also received an invitation from the University of California to deliver a course of lectures. In America the study of Sociology was far better established as an academic subject than in England, and Hobhouse's contributions had far wider recognition. Almost the last work he did in 1929 consisted of two articles, one upon 'Aristocracy', the other on 'Christianity', written for the *Encyclopedia of the Social Sciences*, of which Professor Seligman of Columbia University was Editor-in-Chief.

Though he sometimes spoke in disparaging terms of the circulation of his books and of his influence upon the thought of his time, it is certain that, alike in the English-speaking world and in intellectual circles throughout Europe, his treatment of mind and its application to the social sciences from 1906 onwards (the date of the publication of *Morals in Evolution*) obtained a growing recognition as a seminal doctrine. While the older English universities still remained 'shy' of a study which they sought to compass and enclose under older orthodox categories, Durham and St. Andrews gave him honorary degrees, and in 1925 he was elected a Fellow of the British Academy.

CHAPTER V

GENERAL REFLECTIONS

A REMARKABLE consistency in the development of his mental life and activities is discernible as we follow his career from its conscious opening as undergraduate. Quite early a strong recalcitrance against the fetters of academic specialism displayed itself, and his earlier addiction to philosophic studies made it evident that he could never content himself with theorising even in the wide field in which his mind was roaming. To put clear reasonable order into an ever-widening field and to link logic with human action were equally potent urges throughout his life. This double trend almost inevitably led him deeper and deeper into sociology as the chief occupation of his later life. But here, again, while sociology, concerned with the correlation of the social sciences, itself registered a protest against a sterile separatism in politics, economics, jurisprudence, ethics, and the other studies of human conduct and institutions, this correlation could not remain for him a formal intellectual bond. It must be nourished by fresh contacts with living history, the distinctive movements of the day. Hence the active part which he took in the Labour Movement, in humanitarian causes, in internationalism, in constitutional reforms. These were no mere relief elements; they were incorporated in the very unity of his conception of 'a good life'. No man of our time has more fully vindicated the unity that underlies theory and practice. The organic conception pervaded his thought, his emotions, his external activities. If in the last resort it was his philosophy, his harmony of the many with the one, stability with change, in another sense it was the instinctive drive of his nature or disposition, a certain mental and moral restlessness combined with an exploratory experimental interest finding enjoyment in examination of the detailed works of nature.

Accepting this general statement one can best understand the wide divagations of his activities as teacher,
journalist, philosopher, politician, and social worker. His
main avenues of activity during the last twenty years of his
life were three: first, his work in the London School of
Economics, as Martin White Professor of Sociology, with
the books directly emerging from the studies which under-
lay this teaching; secondly, his journalistic work, for the
Manchester Guardian and the *Nation*; and thirdly, work
connected with the Trade Boards and other Labour activities
during the war and the post-war period. The two latter
activities were in a sense subordinate to the teaching and
writing of Sociology, and more sporadic. I have given
some account of the frequent contributions to the *Manchester Guardian*, especially during the latter years of the
war. But Hobhouse wrote frequent articles for the *Nation*
under the editorship of W. H. Massingham, and during
most of the years from 1907 to 1915 was a regular attendant
at the interesting weekly lunches, where unbridled discussion
on current themes of policy took place. In 1915, however,
the bitter divergence of views among members of this
group upon the origins and merits of the war and upon
peace negotiations caused him so much irritation that he
gave up his attendance at the lunches and wrote very little
more for the paper.

Something should here be said of the active part he took
in his last years in the foundation and direction of the
British Institute of Philosophical Studies, a society formed
in the spring of 1925 to foster the interest of a thoughtful
public in problems which hitherto had been too exclusively
confined in their appeal to the small body of expert teachers
and students of philosophy. With the Earl of Balfour as
President and Leonard Hobhouse as Chairman of the
Council, it attracted large membership, and its *Journal*
obtained very quickly an important place in the wider
intellectual life of the country. As an exponent of philosophic

thought, both with voice and pen, Hobhouse was of incomparable quality, and as a liaison between the academic world and the wider public he played a most important part. As in his distinctively political teaching he believed his audience and readers capable of digesting and assimilating reasoned principles, so he never acquiesced in the notion that philosophy was a sort of thinking reserved for a select erudite few. This endeavour to enlist the attention of educated men and women, whose main occupations lay in industry and commerce or in one of the professions, in vital questions relating to the nature and place of man in the universe, and in those problems which link up psychology and sociology with some ordered system of human history, was of profound interest to one who was ever more deeply impressed with the need for the dominion of reason in a life so confused and dangerous as that in which the world now finds itself.

His political and economic attachments became weaker in his later years. This was not because of any failure in interest, but from a certain disillusionment with existing parties, organisations, and methods. This appears in passages of the later correspondence with his lifelong friend, Miss Margaret Llewelyn Davies, who has placed many of his letters at the services of this memoir.[1]

Like many of the first brand of what are conveniently termed 'New Liberals', i.e. Liberals not contented with the negative *laissez-faire* and not averse from larger State intervention in social and economic reforms, Hobhouse looked early to some effective union of these Liberals with the rising forces of Labour. As early as 1902 we find him discussing with Miss Davies the desirability and possibility of such a union. Firmly convinced of the need of drastic reforms for a distribution of income and opportunities more equitable and more favourable to the poorer classes, he

---

[1] Except where expressly stated, all passages quoted from letters hereafter are from those addressed to Miss Davies.

thought he saw among middle-class Liberals a growing disposition to co-operate with Labour for these ends. But he was frequently 'put off' by what he deemed violent attempts to 'rush the pace'. With effective trade unionism and a popular franchise, he held that the workers ought by a union of collective bargaining and parliamentary power to make the needed improvements in their social economic condition, securing higher wages and other good conditions of employment, extending the range of public services for health, education, etc., and gradually socialising certain key industries by extension of public administration or controls. But such a policy could only be pursued in an atmosphere of peace and reason. He was alarmed, not at the prospect of any general spread of revolutionary doctrine (against which he thought English people immune), but at sporadic strikes and other unconsidered movements. As years moved on, the growing restiveness of Labour due to the hold-up of wage advances in the pre-war period, and conjoined with other policies of violence, syndicalism, the franchise extremists, Ireland, aroused his fears. I quote a letter written to Miss Davies in the February of that momentous year 1914, which gives expression to this feeling.

"Of course it is very nice for the few people who are very advanced to have a paper like the *Herald*, which forcibly expresses their sentiments. But what is the net result? These advanced people go on getting more and more confident that they are the people, while they are all the time getting farther away from the mass of the people. Our object,[1] on the other hand, is to address people of all views, and to try to reason with them. We may not make many converts, but we make some, and we mitigate opposition. If we went bald-headed for every strike that occurs, we should not have the slightest authority with anyone. As it is, what we say does carry a certain amount of weight, because

[1] Here he is speaking of the *Manchester Guardian*.

people know that we look at each question on its merits, and are prepared, if necessary, to admit faults on our side. If, indeed, Labour were always and necessarily in the right, this caution would not be required. But is not this dictum a confusion of two things? Labour is presumably suffering from the wrong of unequal distribution, and in all its efforts commands, therefore, a certain sympathy. It does not follow that every particular effort it makes to right that wrong is wise, or even fair; e.g. the coal-porters no doubt deserve their extra money, but were they justified, apparently with very imperfect organisation, in catching London out in a cold snap and hoping to force the public through its compunction for the poor, who could not get coal, to force the merchants to give in? Personally I feel convinced that these methods are putting people's backs up more and more, that in each case the well-to-do, if they sit tight, will find themselves able to tide through the inconvenience, that unorganised labour and the very poor will suffer, and that these classes will be quite prepared to help the rich in turning upon the union, which they now mean to do the moment they have the power.

"Well, you will say *vogue la galère*. It all brings us nearer to the great class war, nothing is to be got except by fighting. The moment you convince me of this I shall shut up shop as a radical or socialist or anything reforming, because I shall be convinced that human nature is hopeless, and that the attempt to improve society had better be left alone. Moreover, all that I see or read goes to convince me that if it comes to a class war, the class in possession will win hands down. Numbers are nothing. When it comes to force, organisation, drill, and tradition are everything."

But it was not only his hatred of force as a remedy that was troubling him. In common with many of his friends who had broken away from Liberalism during or after the war, he was distrustful of the undue influence of Trade Unionism, with its funds and its Parliamentary representa-

E

tives, upon the needed socialism of the Labour Movement. He writes in September 1926: "You will have understood that I have been getting away from orthodox Trade Unionism for a long time. This has been due mainly to Trade Board experiences, which have impressed me with the limitations of the Trade Union views. The fact that our" (*Manchester Guardian*) "action is resented by the Trade Union world therefore leaves me cold."

His general view of the relations of parties had assumed more definite form by November 29th, when he writes to another correspondent:

"My difficulty about the Liberal Party lies farther back than yours. I doubt if it any longer stands for anything distinctive. My reasons are on the one side that moderate Labour—Labour in office—has on the whole represented essential Liberalism—not without mistakes, but *better* than the organised party since C.-B.'s death. On the other side, the Liberal Party, however you divide it up, never seems any better agreed within on essentials. Of the present fragment, part leans to the Tories, part to Labour, part has nothing distinctive but is a kind of Free Trade Unionist group. The deduction I draw is that the distinction between the kind of Labour man who does not go 'whole hog' for nationalisation, on the one hand, and the Liberal who wants social progress on the other, is obsolete. I, anyway, have always felt that it was unreal and that, if we divided parties by true principles, the division would be like this:

| Communist | Ordinary Labour | Bad Liberal | |
| Theoretic Socialist | Good Liberal | Ordinary Tory | Diehard |

But traditions and class distinctions kept many 'good Liberals' outside Labour. Now Labour has grown so much that it tends to absorb them and to leave the 'bad' Liberals who incline to the Tories, and a mass of traditional Liberals who can't desert a party of that name."

In fact, he had by this time detached himself from all

party associations. Though he attended some meetings of the Liberal Industrial Council to discuss Trade Boards, "I told them I was not a member of the Liberal Party" (February 6, 1927). Of this Liberal Council he says: "I think they may stir up the Labour Party. —— in particular is much more of a Socialist than MacDonald or Snowden (which is not saying very much)." In another letter he adds: "I want to see whether individualism or the common good will get its way with these committees. I have an idea that they may wake up the Labour Party, which seems to make no constructive effort. On the other hand, if they relapse into opposition I can at once cut myself loose, as I have committed myself to nothing. They seem to present the usual mingling of discordant elements, people like E. D. Simon, of Manchester, whose sympathies are entirely Fabian, and people like Layton, who is a typical capitalist economist."

But while never joining the Labour Party, his sympathies continued to lean heavily in that direction. In his last letters to Miss Davies, written from his hospital in France in June 1929, he says: "This Labour victory is like the sunrise—only may the day be longer than it was in 1924. I was too despondent and never believed that Baldwin would be beaten, and, as you know, never cared who beat him if it could but be done. As it is, I am sorry the Liberals did not get more seats, as I think (I know it's blasphemy) they carry more brains to the square inch than Labour, most of whose men are merely dull and terribly afraid of their permanent officials. However, let us at least begin with every hope."

But while thus detaching himself more and more from 'party' in his later years, he lost none of his earlier passionate interest in the deeper issues of politics. Here is his comment upon the 'Arcos' raid of May 1927. 'Free Russia' had always been one of his enthusiasms, and his disappointment at the outcome of the 1917 Revolution did not abate his belief in free commercial and political intercourse with a great nation.

"The raid on Arcos is the most maddening or depressing thing that has happened. Evidently the Diehards have got the bit between their teeth, and as the Trade Union Bill is not doing well the Government and the Party are ready for another anti-foreign cry. If that kind of politics has come for good I shall have to give up my hopes for Democracy for good and all. Unfortunately minority government seems to be no better, and is bound to be more despotic. I don't regard our system as a dictatorship, because for generations discussion has been free and in the result decisive, and, if the 'classes' remain in power, it is precisely because the 'masses' don't take enough trouble about public affairs, and are uniformly ready to be swept off their feet by any anti-foreign scare—hang the Kaiser, or the Zinovieff letter, or next time something or other that they will find at Arcos. Also Labour would rather be damned by Conservatism than saved by Liberalism—party before country for ever!"

Many of his latest letters to Miss Davies are concerned with the mentality of the new generation as he saw them in the populous School where he taught and in his private social contacts. Of the students in the School he observes: "These generations are extraordinarily short-lived. I can count up the intellectual fashions that have taken and held my students for a brief space. When I began in 1907 there was a wave of social idealism. Then very soon came suffrage, then syndicalism, then the war, then Guild Socialism, then Freud. Freud, nothing but Freud, for three or four years; now, thank goodness, that is going out, and we have mostly Elliot Smith and the Diffusion Theory. . . . Each of these waves absolutely submerges everything for the time being; be the subject what it will, the students will always get it back one way or the other to the popular topic. It's lost labour to refute these things—they just die out in time."

Writing in December 1928, he expresses himself even more gloomily:

"The unmitigated selfishness with which Shaw has indoctrinated his generation isn't going to make them happier. It's probably going to lead to the final world catastrophe which a generation bent on pleasure will never take the trouble to avert."

It would be easy to argue from such utterances that Hobhouse, though still himself a believer in progress and the evolution of the rational good in the long run, was a pessimist for his own people and the short run. But such a judgment would be to misunderstand a certain element of impetuosity and moodiness that found expression in a conscious exaggeration of speech and writing. His remarkable facility of utterance in personal intercourse found vent and perhaps relief in words stronger than he seriously meant. It would, therefore, be unfair to take at its face value the rapid language of these letters. Though genuinely depressed and discontented by the happenings in this country and the world in the last years of his life, his real conviction was that we were 'going through a bad time', but that the permanent factors in the making of human history were unassailable in their working for a wiser and a better world.

The more sombre tone of his temperament in the last years was undoubtedly attributable to private calamities. The death of his wife in 1925, after an ideal companionship of over thirty years, fell as a crushing blow to his most sensitive spirit. For to him the loving life of the family was literally the holiest of things. I am permitted to publish the following letter written in reply to a letter of sympathy from one of his old students.

"Your expression of sympathy touches me very much. My wife made our home life so perfect that it was always the centre of my thought about all human things, and I am not surprised that it should have shown itself from time to time in my teaching, for I have aimed at realities, and this has been (and is) the greatest reality to me, and death does not destroy it." The recipient remarks: "Don't you think that this is a perfect letter for a philosopher to write about his wife?"

One who knew him well could trace throughout his judgments of our changing customs and institutions the determinant force of this religious feeling for the primacy of family life as the basis of a sound society. Though sustained by reason, it was derived from deeply personal emotions that resented all questioning. Thirty years of happy personal experience confirmed this conviction, and no one could understand his opinions and valuations who failed to take into account this potent element.

Only those inside this family circle could fully know the share which his wife took in every one of his activities. Her quiet influence was not confined to affairs of the home, though here he was singularly dependent on her for every detail of material arrangement. From the early years of their union she took an active share in the political activities into which they entered, relieving him of much of the secretarial work which was so irksome and yet so necessary. But behind all this lay a power of sympathy and inspiration which contributed to the very substance of his thought and teaching in the realm of ethics and philosophy. I cannot here forbear to quote a passage written shortly before her death, in the chapter which he contributed to a volume entitled *Contemporary British Philosophy*:

"There are those more highly privileged who have learned to know some nature crystal-clear compact of mother-love, with thoughts by instinct bent on other's needs, sensitively tender, yet of indomitable spirit, fearless, and believing no evil, through very selflessness enjoying and reflecting the charm of life. This, the sceptic may say, is to describe a woman as a man sees her in the hour of romance. It may be so, and it may be that in that hour some real things flash out that are afterwards obscured. Be that as it may, there are not wanting those who have put the vision to the test of lifelong companionship, only to find it gaining in clearness and truth."

His own ill-health, and its interference with his work and bodily activities, was another depressing factor of his last years. Despite a certain inherited disposition towards hypochondria, often associated with vigorous physique and high vitality, he pursued his wonderfully active career, with brief occasional breakdowns, until in 1924 the doctors found him suffering from an attack of phlebitis which, though curable, involved great care and imposed new and distasteful restraints. Part of several summers from 1925 onwards he spent at Bagnoles in Normandy under the care of a specialist who had won his confidence and from whose treatment he seemed to derive considerable benefit, although no complete cure was effected. Though this phlebitis caused him at times to 'lie up' and to receive students for special tuition at his own home, he felt that his teaching at the School had the first claim upon his energies, and even when he was due to retire in 1929 he consented, at the special request of the Director, to take on an extra year. "The fact is, I like lecturing. The didactic grows on me. A form of egoism cheap and easy compared with writing books—and I like my students."

While the phlebitis was a troublesome and hampering condition for some years, it was not considered immediately dangerous to his life. Indeed, the last time I saw him, shortly before his last visit to his Normandy doctor, Dr. Quiserne, he appeared to be in fair bodily vigour, and more irritated than despondent at the sort of holiday he was to have. Before his daughter could come out to him he wrote, indeed, a letter expressive rather of boredom than of anxiety.

"It's rather hateful here all alone, especially as Quiserne now forbids all walking. Tolerable when the sun shines and I can lie out in a *chaise-longue* in the 'forêt' which borders the house, horrid when it pours and there is nowhere to sit but my own room, intolerable when it's thundery, and the dining-room is like an American hotel room." Then follows a thumbnail sketch of the company—English, French, Norwegian, with none of whom he found himself particularly sympathetic.

Shortly after his daughter Marjorie arrived, he was stricken with a painful stomachic trouble, unconnected with the phlebitis, and not at once diagnosed or treated as dangerous. When he was removed to a hospital at Alençon it was too late. "His pain", wrote his daughter, "was terrible for a time, but fortunately not long-drawn-out, as he became unconscious many hours before he quietly stopped breathing."

He was laid to rest in the grave at Wimbledon where his wife was buried. A memorial service was held at the church of St. Martin-in-the-Fields, when an address was delivered by his friend and colleague, Professor Graham Wallas, and was attended by a large number of students and teachers from the neighbouring School of Economics and by many other friends.

So passed away one of the less known of the great men of our time. His more serious work, by its very quality, his lighter writing by its anonymity, his expressed opinions by their soberness, or sometimes by their unpopularity, kept his fame within narrow limits. Seldom seen on popular platforms, even in causes to which he gave his intellectual and moral support, not a good 'mixer' in the conventional sense of that term, his person with its distinction and its charm was only known to a comparatively small, though widening number of intimate friends, chiefly associates in his teaching and journalistic enterprises. Through his books, indeed, a larger intellectual public, both in this country, America, and Germany, was coming to regard him with reverence as one of the most powerful formative minds of his generation

It is difficult to assess the intellectual and moral influence of such a life. Though books are more abiding monuments than oral discourse, unless they reach a certain level, not so much of excellence as of significance, they are likely to be displaced by later writings that build upon them as foundations, following further the basic thought they contain. The very originality of much of Hobhouse's work in the new and plastic science of Sociology may lead to such displacement, leaving him to find his posthumous fame in the history of the growth of a science still in its infancy. This he would have regarded as his best achievement, viz. that he had incited and enabled others to move further in the untamed forests where he had been a pioneer.

In any case, great thinking bears its chief fruit in other minds, and there will be many thinkers who have gathered knowledge and stimulus from Hobhouse as oral teacher. Indeed, no attempt at a memoir could omit the striking body of testimony to this side of his career. I am fortunate in being able here to present several personal appreciations of his extraordinary powers as lecturer and instructor, from men and women who have studied under him. In quoting from them I shall cite passages that describe his method and manner as teacher rather than the substance of his teaching, which more properly falls under the part of this volume which Dr. Ginsberg has undertaken.

Though in his later years Hobhouse had little time for outside lectures, his Manchester life had put him into touch with surrounding centres of political and philosophical thought, and I have received several interesting testimonies to the impression made by his occasional addresses in these quarters. One of the most valuable comes from Warrington, where Hobhouse delivered lectures at long intervals of time to the Literary and Philosophical Society, and formed close personal attachments to several of the members.

I append some extracts from notes sent to me by a

student at Warrington, who received great gain from the teaching and personal friendship of Hobhouse.

"My first knowledge of Hobhouse was gained from his book *Democracy and Reaction*, a cheap edition of which I picked up on a railway bookstall. This book introduced me, so to speak, to a new world of thought. I was immensely impressed by a line of reasoning that was new to me in political thought, while the spirit of the book was sympathetic to my own.

"I had, of course, not been trained in political science, or I should have known where to go to get what I then wanted. It was hardly remarkable, therefore, that when I read Hobhouse's book on Liberalism I found it a revelation. Here at last I had found exactly what I was in search of, a body of doctrine, a set of principles that could be applied to any country and to any stage of development in which a society might be. I found no difficulty in accommodating my socialistic leanings within the walls of the new Temple. I found in Hobhouse as keen—if not a keener—desire as my own for all those social improvements and changes on which my heart was set. But I found, what I had not found elsewhere, that all the problems at which I had been slogging away in a hopeless kind of fashion, without any sort of guidance, in the twinkling of an eye, so to speak, were illumined so that, where before I did not see even darkly now it was clear noonday to me. I had now a gospel to preach. I felt as Mill said he felt after he had read Bentham. Things which previously had seemed to have no real connection, now fell into their proper place into a scheme of thought which ultimately became a philosophy of life.

"I had had bitter personal experience of the cramping effect of insufficient means, and of the bleak outlook for the vast mass of the people, and of the stunted lives bred under existing conditions.

"I wrote a short review of *Liberalism* for a local paper, and later a more extended exposition of its argument in a paper which I hoped to make use of in other ways. I sent the printed review and the MS. of the longer paper to Hobhouse, and asked him frankly for his views of the latter. He wrote me a very courteous and valuable criticism of the paper, a most generous appreciation of the review, and gave me much required advice on lines of further study. He was particularly pleased, he said, to find a response from youth; it was to the younger men that he had addressed his book.

"The kindly manner in which Hobhouse had treated me encouraged me to write to him again and tell him some of my intellectual difficulties. I had, at a very early age, come under the spell of Herbert Spencer and the agnostics, but I found, after some years of study, that agnosticism of the type I was familiar with led nowhere. Mostly the leaders of thought were unsympathetic to movements of social reform. A despairing acquiescence in admittedly evil conditions, and a hopeless attitude towards the future, characterised the thought which had become part of my mental make-up. Philosophical Idealism, which would have been the best antidote to the sceptical poison I was suffering from, did not make much appeal to me in the few samples of it with which I had made acquaintance up to that time. Hobhouse evidently understood my condition, and not only wrote to me some sound advice, and suggested a long course of reading in metaphysics and general philosophy, but he very kindly lent me his own copy of *Mind in Evolution*, with pencilled alterations and additions, which he was at that time reading with a view to a new edition that was not actually issued until 1915.

"*Mind in Evolution* was a revelation to me. It introduced me to a completely new line of thought. It corrected the tendency of Idealism to neglect the actual world of experience, and furnished grounds for hope of human progress which were entirely foreign to the agnostic philosophy of Spencer and Huxley.

"If the biologists' claim could be substantiated, of what use were the millions it was proposed should be spent on social betterment? 'Each for himself and the weak to the wall' became a social, as well as a moral, duty, if only by the intensification of the struggle for existence could the socially and biologically 'fit' be expected to survive. This problem Hobhouse tackled in the lectures which he delivered under the Beer Foundation at Columbia University in April 1911, and which were subsequently published under the title *Social Evolution and Political Theory*. In these lectures Hobhouse set forth what he called the 'harmonic' conception of human society, a conception he was to elaborate still further in *Development and Purpose*. It was through the reading of this book that my friend, Dr. J. G. Manson, of Warrington, at that time secretary of the local Literary and Philosophical Society, was led to invite Hobhouse to come to Warrington to lecture to the Society. I had kept in touch with him by correspondence, and he wrote to the gentleman who was to be his host at Warrington—who happened to be an old friend of my family—asking him if he would take steps to have me presented to him. Accordingly I was invited to this gentleman's house—together with Dr. Manson—after the lecture. The lecture was delivered on February 3, 1913.

"I well remember the impression the lecture made on me. Hobhouse was accustomed to speak without notes, and he was, without doubt, one of the most brilliant lecturers I ever heard. He had not perhaps quite the same control over his voice that a more practised public speaker usually has. He had none of the platform arts of the 'acceptable' orator, but he had an uninterrupted flow of language that must have been the envy of every would-be speaker who heard him. Lord Morley, in his *Life of Gladstone*, tells of a conversation he once had with Gladstone as to public speaking. Gladstone said it was his habit to steep himself in his subject until he had made it his own, 'and, as for the words, well, the words come'. Morley, commenting on this, said, 'The words don't come to everybody'. They came to Hobhouse, and they came so easily that he never seemed to be at a loss, he never hesitated, never corrected himself. The matter came forth, punctuated, ready for the printer, as if he had written it all out and learnt it beforehand."

But having regard to the fact that for more than twenty years he gave most of his time and energy to his post as teacher at the School of Economics, the testimony of those who were associated with him there as students or colleagues will have a unique value.

I therefore cite several tributes to his memory which have come into my hands. First, some passages from "An Appreciation" from the students' paper, *The Clare Market Review.*

"The second-year student, starting on his Sociological Honours Subject, was apt to be overwhelmed by the onrush of that course, 'Introduction to the Study of Society', which swept through Anthropology, Ethnology, Archæology, Comparative Social Institutions, Ethics and Religions, Social Philosophy, and Biology, to a last lecture or two on 'The Nature of Human and Social Development'. He never lectured from notes—not even in 1928–9, when the School suffered in a pandemonium of builders (though one saw how the strain told on him). He would often come in, ask a front-row student where he had finished last week, and then proceed at a prodigious pace. His hearers suffered a certain intimidation under this exhibition, which showed itself in a lack of originality in the ensuing classes; but he dealt with us sympathetically, and with no little patience in guiding discussion. In his Seminars we saw him at his best, trenchant in wit and criticism. Seated far back in his low chair with one hand in his white hair, smoking and watching the ceiling, he would listen to the paper under review; suddenly he would interject, 'No, no—surely! What do you mean by that? So-and-so never used it in that sense'—followed by a five-minute circular tour round definitions and implications. Then, 'However, I digress a little wide of the mark. Please go on. It's very interesting.' Or, in his magisterial chair at the head of the table, he would trace cabalistic patterns on the back of an envelope, with the pen trembling in his nervous fingers. He would say, 'It's like this. If this is your Idea, here are your Forms, but it doesn't follow that these lines, . . .' etc. One looked at the thin, mazy lines, and the anxious face searching one's own for signs of comprehension, and one concluded that behind the massive forehead there was a conscious pessimist—a pessimist because all his energies were concentrated on convincing others of the need and reason for optimism, development of potentialities, an ultimate Good, the 'becoming' of Mind. And yet—his Universals seldom seemed to beget their particulars in reality right! An intellectually courageous man! He looked far, like Moses on Mount Nebo. . . . '*Vidisti terram oculis tuis, sed non transibis ad illam!*' Well might he have said:

> Much have I seen and known—cities of men,
> And manners, climates, councils, governments.
> Myself not least but honoured of them all . . .
> I am a part of all that I have met,
> Yet all Experience is an arch wherethro'
> Gleams that untravelled world, whose margin fades
> For ever and for ever when I move.

"He stressed equally the needs for *a posteriori* work, and for that individual *a priori* foreshadowing which alone reveals the margin of the Untravelled World, and marks out the philosopher, attuned to 'the prophetic soul of the wide world'. Thus a profound harmony of (differing) spheres pervaded his work. Collation of facts, hypothesis, verification, modified hypothesis, new verification . . . so steadily emerged a system. And, to conclude—an anecdote which admirably portrays his scrupulous fairness and respect of opinions. The last Finals Seminar he conducted had been discussing a paper on 'The Philosophical Aspects of Private Property'. The writer had made an attack upon T. H. Green's inconclusive compromise and filed a plea for Communism, receiving support from other members of the Seminar. Hobhouse summed up: 'I think you're too hard on T. H. Green. He didn't dare say too much in those days, and hid a lot of good material in poor padding. But what pleases me is to see the younger generation in the School vigorously questioning Green's data and premisses. I had been led to believe that you were all individualists. I am relieved to find we may still expect Progress! You may be right. But I reserve my own view!'

"There are young men and women now in the School who will live to be very old, remembering Hobhouse. Just as he came to us—the plenipotentiary of a tradition of sound learning—so, one hopes, will those who are privileged to learn of him take their part in holding fast that which they have as the best of his tradition. On that basis they may pursue their studies with as sane and balanced a philosophy as the author of *The Rational Good* offered them."

Another student, afterwards a teacher in his department, writes as follows:

"I first saw Professor Hobhouse when I went to the London School of Economics as a Social Science Student in 1913, when I attended his Sociology lectures. The lectures lasted for an hour, and were followed by a class—in which there were long silences filled in with occasional questions from rather awed students—questions which led to explanations, amplifications, and discourses from Professor Hobhouse, with that amazing ease and fluency he always showed. In connection with these lectures Professor Hobhouse held a Seminar for students of Sociology and students in the Social Science course. The lectures covered a wide field of thought and fact and theory—they were above the heads of the larger proportion of his audience. At the Seminar that year we discussed concrete social problems. . . .

"Professor Hobhouse led us through new subjects—psychology, theories of heredity, types of social organisation, theories of society, theories of progress. I remember struggling to understand his extraordinarily eloquent disquisition on Hegel. They were subjects linked with others, a new subject emerging—sociology. We were a generation with our minds on concrete problems. I was told afterwards that my year was an able group of students. I think they were. Some of them were well above the average university age and experienced—some had done well at their universities before they came. In the Seminar that dealt with concrete problems the discussion went well, and Professor Hobhouse sat holding the strings of it, joining, directing, moderating, suggesting, amused by our furious zeal.

"Yet Professor Hobhouse's conception of society had a definite influence on his students—even if they were incapable of following it and understanding it in its entirety. It gave them a setting for their efforts in thinking out their particular social problems and showed them the interrelation and complexity of social subjects. To those who could follow further his teaching brought a great deal. The last time I was at the School he and I and a number of the Social Science staff discussed some of the students. Miss Haskins said that many of her students had told her that in their practical life and problems they had found Professor Hobhouse's teachings of value. He seemed pleased, and said that he had tried to put it in terms that would fit in with their experience. This is evidence of his real teaching interest and of its effect."

Another student writes:

"Professor Hobhouse, more than anyone whom I have had the fortune to meet, left an impression of greatness. To say that to have known him was an inspiration is not just an easy phrase, but does express a little of the very vital influence which he exercised, the incentive to strenuous endeavour, and the dissatisfaction with anything but perfection with which he in some measure filled us. I think that I count my relationship with him as the best thing that I got out of the School. I wonder if he knew at all how any of his students felt. He was always just a little difficult to approach, not because he ever in the slightest degree repulsed us, but because we always felt, at least I did, a little in awe of him, and because he was, I believe, just a little bit shy himself. There I may be wrong! But this is rather disjointed. May I try to give you just one or two notes on points that seemed to stand out?

"First and foremost was his extraordinary gentleness and courtesy. I can see him now—five of us used to come to a third-year Seminar in his room—sitting at the head of the table drawing cabalistic figures in front of him while one of us, I was rather given to it, struggled to express what we thought was a considered opinion of our own, throwing, as we fondly imagined, fresh light on some phase of conduct, or trying to re-express to him what we thought was his view on a subject in order to get him to re-state it again. And the marvel was that he always helped and was never impatient, and would sometimes even agree that there was something in what we said when it was a view of our own, or one that we had arrived at ourselves and one not held by himself.

"Another impression was that of his sense of humour. In one direction it was, it seemed to me, very simple and almost childlike. He obtained apparently infinite amusement from the wicked exploits of his jackdaw, who would remove all his precious papers and scatter them in the garden. On the other hand, he was amused at people. We had one student who was inclined to run a pet hobby-horse, and if he did not quite wink at us when she got on to it he very nearly did. But even then she would always have her say out and be encouraged to fully develop her ideas, which would be treated with the utmost respect.

"I have been looking through the essays which I did for

F

him to see if any of his comments on them are of general interest. Here are one or two:

" 'Why drag in the unconscious?' This is, I think, noteworthy. As I see it, Hobhouse disliked the so-called New Psychology as undermining moral responsibility and the trend of its teaching, which seemed to conflict with his own of the possibility of the rule in man of the Rational Will. 'Quantity cannot be measured against quality.' 'Suppression is not harmony.' 'Herd instinct—a degrading name.' 'Yes— but *how* does intelligence begin?' (no shirking in verbiage). 'Good'—against a quotation from Graham Wallas, where he says, 'Dr. Rivers seems to maintain that man controls his instincts by thrusting them into full consciousness.' "

Dr. Mitrany, who had a long acquaintance with him as student at the School of Economics and as worker on the *Manchester Guardian*, writes:

"Hobhouse, more than any teacher to whom I have listened, made one literally feel that one was sitting at his feet. His big stature (he always stood), the unhesitating flow of solid stuff (he never used notes), and his gaze, which generally looked over the heads of the listeners upon, as it seemed, a world which to him was familiar, but which was beyond our ken—all this contributed to create in us a feeling that we were indeed apprentices at the feet of a master. He impressed even those who could not follow his discourses. I have never once heard his lectures spoken of with the kind of critical contempt which students, and especially freshmen, so freely shower upon their teachers.

"As a teacher he had his defects; though they were really a reaction to the defects of the students, some of the students never recovered from the blastingly frigid tone with which he curtailed useless discussion. Graham Wallas once commented that 'the difference between Hobhouse and me is that he has no patience with young fools and I don't mind them.'

"His subject never was to him merely a dry academic

study. Invariably when discussing essays he would try to find out, for his own information, what kind of life the people led who were summed up in some statistics or sociological generalisations.

"He was anything but a party politician. But his humanitarian interests caused him to take a close interest in politics. One of his great disappointments was the neglect of the Labour Party to make use of his services. With him to believe was to serve. After the war he felt, like so many others, that the Labour Party had become the chief instrument for social progress, and he pressed upon the Labour Government of 1929 the desirability of expanding and strengthening the Trade Board system, offering his assistance in this work. For reasons which I do not know, this offer was simply ignored. I know that he felt this deeply.

"His facility in writing was truly amazing. At the *Manchester Guardian* I have known him write in one evening the long leader and two 'shorts' before the rest of us had fairly got going. During one of his spells of 'deputising' for C. P. Scott, in the summer of 1921, I remember that he revised in one week his *Democracy and Reaction* for a new edition, adding a fresh chapter and, I believe, a new Introduction, while giving most of the day and all the evenings to work for the paper."

In conclusion, I cite portions of a paper contributed by one of his latest students:

"It was naturally in his Seminars that we gained most. In my two Final Years (1927–9) the Sociology Honours students were about ten in number. Once a week one of us read a paper, one term in Social Psychology, one term in Comparative Social Institutions, and one in Ethics. It was arresting to notice how gentle, intellectually, he was with us. All that he required was intellectual honesty; given that, any opinion was worth examination by him. I can see him now, twisting his fingers or moustache or stroking one white lock at the back of his head, as the paper is read. His

fingers used to tremble increasingly as the match neared
the pipe; and, exhaling a cloud of smoke, he would interrupt before taking the pipe out, lest the thought escape him.
Very few crucial thoughts or criticisms ever did. The most
remarkable thing was his memory: he could quote verbatim
from everyone, not only from philosophical writers, but also
from Jane Austen, Dickens, the Brontës, Tennyson, and
German and French writers. I have always thought he had
a peculiar predilection, not so much for the ancient Greek
which he so often quoted, especially Homer and Æschylus,
but also for the Latin writers and the Latin of the early
Church and the Stoics. He used to quote Clement, Ter-
tullian, Epictetus, Seneca, Augustine, and St. Thomas
Aquinas regularly.

"There was a compelling romance about Hobhouse—the
romance of an intellectual pioneer. His personality was so
dominating, that it often intimidated pupils; and yet he
constantly stressed one's duty to 'the weaker brethren'. I
always had the idea that he concealed a wholly irrational
(i.e. non-amenable to rational analysis) 'Belief' behind his
brilliancy of analysis and interpretation. Otherwise it is
hard to explain his dynamic. But what that 'Belief' was is
difficult to say. It was wholly in the efficacy and ultimate
rule of harmony, achieved through sympathetic reason; and
to that extent it was a belief in man's salvation in Man.
Perhaps his concluding words of *Morals in Evolution* adum-
brate it:

" 'It is enough for the moment to reach the idea of a
self-conscious evolution of humanity, and to find therein a
meaning and an element of purpose for the historical process
which has led up to it. It is, at any rate, something to learn
. . . that this slowly-wrought-out dominance of mind in
things is the central fact of evolution. For if this is true it
is the germ of a religion and an ethics which are as far
removed from materialism as from the optimistic teleology
of the metaphysician, or the half-naïve creeds of the churches.

It gives a meaning to human effort, as neither the pawn of an overruling Providence nor the sport of blind force. It is a message of hope to the world, of suffering lessened and strife assuaged, not by fleeing from reason to the bosom of faith, but by the increasing rational control of things by that collective wisdom, the εἷς ξυνὸς λόγος, which is all that we directly know of the Divine.' "

CHAPTER VI

OTHER ASPECTS OF HIS LIFE

THOUGH most of this Memoir has concerned itself with his varied intellectual activities as author, teacher, journalist, and his extraordinary power of expressing with voice and pen the abundance of his knowledge and the originality of his interpretation, here and there a glimpse was given of what seemed to those who only knew him in these public capacities a quite different sort of man. While every student recognised his humour and the humanity in it, it was reserved for his closer friends to realise the lighter self of a personality which, as we see, was at first contact somewhat formidable.

While always subject, as we have seen, to periods of depression, his habitual mood within the family and in personal intercourse with friends was one of the keenest interest in personal affairs, a delight in gossip and a whimsical playfulness touching the people and events around him that endeared him the more to those who knew him, because it was not merely taken on as a 'relief' to his more serious tasks of life, but was of the very warp and woof of his subtly composed nature. The swift chaff and picturesque exaggeration of his talk on lighter matters was sometimes liable to misinterpretation by casual visitors, just as the occasional bursts of indignation that warped for the moment his more sober judgments. He knew men too well to entertain the facile optimism about their motives which goes to make the ordinary 'good-natured man'. But like Dr. Johnson, many of whose opinions he would have detested, but with whose essential make-up he had much in common, he loved to let himself down to frolic and levity upon occasions.

In his letters to intimate friends this spirit frequently took control of him. Here is a characteristic expression of it in a letter written at Christmas 1924 to Miss Davies, shortly after the formation of the Society for Cultural Relations between England and Russia:

"A noble box of apples has arrived. Whom are we really to thank? Well, I, of course, thank you. But who is the real donor? Never Trotsky or Zinovieff? Tell it not in Carmelite Street, or the *Daily Mail* will have us proclaimed debauched by Communist apples. It cannot but remind me of my aunt—do you know I have still an aunt by marriage, in her 101st year? In 1842 she lunched with her grandmother, who told her that she well remembered lunching with Dr. Johnson, when they had a dish of 'American apples'. Of these she partook so freely that Johnson remarked, 'Let us hope, madam, that these will not rebel.' "

In the relaxation of his summer holidays this genial attitude prevailed. In his frequent summer visits to Patterdale he was the life and soul of the party, consisting mostly of young people, whom he would regale with comic performances and imitations of people, with droll Cornish stories and vivacious leading of choruses.

His son gives an entertaining picture of this aspect of his life, adding some graver comments upon aspects of his character only revealed within the intimacy of the family which help us to a better understanding of the riches of his nature.

"My earliest recollections of my Father relate to the games he used to play with me on the drawing-room floor of 4 Park Crescent, Oxford. Though many people will have similar recollections, there are not so many parents to whom the companionship and amusement of their children was so essentially a part of their own enjoyment of life. In those days we had scientifically fought battles, the chief feature of which that I remember was a large glass marble which when discharged from a cannon did great execution with the opponent's fortifications. Then there was an elaborate cardboard model of Oxford station which occupied evening after evening. Father had a passion for railway trains which I inherited, and we used to go to Port Meadow of an afternoon to watch the expresses. 'Dear Daddy, Have you seen any of those funny little shunt engines?' is the context of one of my earliest preserved letters.

"Later I remember particularly the holidays at the sea and the building of elaborate waterworks and the damming of streams. Then when my sisters grew older came the regime of round games in the evenings, which always developed into a rag. Father would make a complete buffoon of himself for our benefit, both then and long after, up to quite recent years. His dramatic rendering of 'Tit Willow' will never be forgotten: his final dive on to the floor when 'he threw himself into the billowy wave' was masterly, and incidentally shook any normal building to its foundations.

"Additional features of the nightly entertainment were his songs, most of them Cornish, sung with great gusto but not too much tune, and his repertoire of impersonations and Cornish and Oxford stories. His representations of the old Warden of Merton, Mr. Spooner, Hinds the chimney-sweep, and Old Snow were classics. He had a regular cycle of Cornish stories, and could speak the dialect of North Cornwall to perfection. On the great occasion of my grandfather's jubilee he told a Cornish story to the assembled parishioners as his contribution to the entertainment. The local comment was: 'It was a brave good story that Mr. Leonard did tell, but it warnt *Cornish*, my dear, it was just like us folks do talk around here.'

"Father had a kindred gift of parody and doggerel. His Homer might well pass for the original, and contained long accounts of holidays and adventures and 'catalogues' of friends and relations. One poem dealt with his bicycling adventures, and how he was held up by a policeman:

πλῆσμεν ἄντιον ἧκεν
Βοβεὺς Πηλιάδης.[1]

[1] "A policeman encountered them, Bobby the son of Peel."

Another poem contained a dramatic account of a journey to Switzerland with Harold Spender (εὐπλόκαμος Σπινθῆρος), and the adventures which befell him.

"Father certainly owed a great deal to his marvellous memory. He could quote Homer, Virgil, Browning, Shelley, Pickwick and C. S. Calverley by the yard. The lines that he learnt at school he never forgot. When he was quite a small boy he would retail to his dormitory *in extenso* the stories which he had read in the holidays, and it was, I believe, a ritual that he should recount an instalment each night after lights out. Such a memory must have been an enormous asset in his research work, and was equally of service in politics and argument. He would always remember and quote a case or fact or statistics to support his point, to the exasperation of an unfortunate opponent relying on generalities. He might have made a good debater in the House, but he would not have liked the life. He was several times asked to stand, and a safe Liberal seat was offered him, but he would not undertake the necessary subservience to party principles.

"Although, like most of us, there were occasions on which he did not relish a joke against himself, or more particularly against something for which he cared, he had a very keen sense of humour of a genial, not a dry kind. In the obituary in the *Manchester Guardian* his humour was described as ironic: to my mind that was utterly incorrect. I should regard it as thoroughly mellow.

"The *Manchester Guardian* also stated that he did not suffer fools gladly. Of his manner in dealing with people generally I cannot say much, but certainly in the circle of his immediate friends he could put up with many a remark which must have been irritatingly fatuous to him, with courtesy and interest. I must admit, however, there were certain types of people of whom and whose pursuits he was absurdly intolerant. For many years motorists were anathema to him, even to some extent after he bought a car

himself: before then he would hardly talk rationally about
them. The dust, smell, and the destruction of the country-
side on the part of the rich (as it was in those days) roused
him out of all proportion to the offence. Even so he was
amenable to being well chaffed about this idiosyncrasy.
Perhaps what he resented most was being driven off the
roads on which for so many years he had delighted in
cycling.

"Until those days cycling was a great stand-by in the
way of exercise. He had started early in the art, and was
once the possessor of an old high bicycle. Father was not
unathletic for his size, and had he not had poor sight and a
weak heart he would have been keen on many games. As it
was, he delighted in sculling, and played an excellent game
of tennis for many years. He was very fond of skating and
tobogganing, and on various occasions we had some glorious
weeks in Switzerland. But Switzerland lost a little of its
glamour when ski-ing came in, which was really beyond
him at his age. Moreover, Father was immensely conservative in some ways, and would not take up with a reversal
of the old order of things. Thus, though he was very fond of
whist, he refused to learn bridge, and he despised golf.
He had the traditional instincts of a conservative county
family, and these not being allowed to intrude upon his
thought, used to come out in little ways in his habits.

"He hated all forms of sport which involved taking life,
and he could not bear to see an animal ill-treated. He was
extremely fond of the various dogs and other animals that
lived with us from time to time. One of the time-honoured
jokes against him was that when he used to work in the
garden of our home at Highgate the jackdaw could and did
steal his important papers from his table and litter them
about the garden with impunity, interrupting the train of
philosophic thought in a manner which would have called
dire wrath down upon any human.

"The underlying basis of Father's thought was optimistic, yet he was often a victim to pessimism and depression. Much of this was due to ill-health: it was only when I came to read his early letters that I realised how early in his life he had come to suffer from chills and dyspepsia. At an age when most people never give their bodies a thought, he was dieting and liable to constant trouble. In his later life he suffered a great deal from these ills, which brought with them the plague of insomnia. When I realise how much he was worried in this way I am astonished at the fortitude and good-humour which he nearly always maintained. He also suffered from what passes over most of us lightly, the tragedies of public events. These he felt with such an acuteness as to make them almost personal. The Great War was a shattering blow to him. It struck directly at the whole foundation of his thought, and I am sure that it and its consequences were very largely responsible for the break-up of his health in 1924 and his early death.

"His comparative attitude to the Boer War and the Great War illustrates the essential balance of his mind. Because he thought England was in the wrong in the Boer War, he was not afraid to say so and to face the consequent obloquy: because he thought England was in the right in the Great War, he was as anxious that we should win as anybody, though he was always hoping and working for peace. If his sight and health had been good enough he would have volunteered; as it was, he knew that he would be of no use, but I am sure that he envied and would have changed places with his old friend, C. E. Montague.

"As to Father's relations with Mother and ourselves, I can only say that he was the most devoted person imaginable. Our welfare was always his paramount consideration. He was always our dear friend and companion, and considering the ways of mankind where the generations are different, the camaraderie between us was very close. He really excelled himself in the manner in which he cast off thirty odd years and became one of us. He brought us up to appreciate and enjoy the great works of literature, from the *Uncle Remus* which he read to us in our early days to Aristotle, which he read with me in the Oxford long vac. For years and years, in fact up to the end, he regularly read aloud every night to those of us who were at home. How many times he has read to us *Pickwick*, *The Three Musketeers*, or *Pride and Prejudice*, I should not venture to say, and there were certain poems of Browning which he read us countless times. He found something essentially kindred in Browning: they had the same breadth of outlook and sympathetic qualities, while the Epilogue to *Asolando*— the third stanza—might have been written of him and for him: at least that is the way I feel."

The variety of high gifts which Leonard Hobhouse possessed and so freely gave will be manifest from this brief record of his life and the testimony of those who shared his many activities. But in gathering these contributions towards a portrait of the whole man we are confronted by more than the usual difficulties. His strongly pronounced qualities of mind and character, which seem to reveal so much, rest on a background which is very difficult to fathom.

The most distinctive feature is the union of a powerful intellect with a profound emotional nature. It is the quick and continual interaction of these powers that seems to govern all his thinking processes and his exterior activities. There is little attempt to 'dry' his logic, or to expel feeling from what are primarily intellectual judgments. In a system of philosophy pervaded and moulded by 'purpose' this union of thought and emotion, indeed, found its reasonable justification. But the union lay deeply embedded in his personality. I would say it constituted his greatness. It had its difficulties. It made him impetuous and sometimes intolerant. But he had a better comprehension of himself than the ordinary man. Though not, I think, unduly introspective, he early acquired a habit of allowing for his passions, and of correcting what he knew to be first and not best judgments.

Next I should place the wide range of his interests, extensive and intensive. Though his intellectual life necessarily concerned itself with abstractions and large generalisations, he was never content to work long in this rarefied atmosphere. His discontent with the idealist philosophy dominant at Oxford in his day is largely traceable to this natural craving for actuality in knowledge and in conduct. We have seen how his social psychology led him to study bio-chemistry in the Oxford Museum and zoology in Manchester, in order to get hold of the workings of the pre-human mind as preparatory to the study of its evolution in man. His nature was exploratory, curious, not merely among the wide fields of theory, but among the by-paths and recesses where the exceptional and the unique in shape and action lurk. It was this urge which in his later years was driving him ever deeper into the study of primitive man and his ways of going on.

Indeed, it may be said that his passage from general philosopher into sociologist was attributable chiefly to his refusal to make the usual amount of severance between the life of thought and the life of action. His political activities, conducted through participation in 'causes' or through journalism, were part and parcel of his sociology, which was never merely a disinterested study of how human institutions arose and worked, but embodied a desire to help in moulding institutions so that they might work better. In other words, he realised politics and economics as living history, embodying a 'purpose' which he by his fine understanding and energetic action might make somewhat more effective. I do not mean that he held this view of his activities as a 'call' or a 'mission', but that the union of thought and 'humanity' within him led to this use of his powers.

How far his Cornish blood and upbringing were respon-

sible for his quite un-English measure of active emo-
tionalism, showing itself alike in the intensity of his feeling
about public affairs and in the intimate absorption of
family life, it would be idle to discuss. Throughout his life
there were periods of immense and enthusiastic activity,
broken by periods of moody depression and slackness of
will. Sometimes these diverse moods came and went very
quickly. One illustrative incident occurs to me. When we
were working together on the ill-fated *Tribune*, I asked
him to walk with me from Fleet Street to the National
Liberal Club, where we would dine. Though apparently
in good condition, he refused to go so far, on the plea that
he might be physically unable to get back to Fleet Street.
After dining at a restaurant near at hand, we returned to
the office, and he set to work at once with his usual celerity
and vigour upon the ordering of the editorial matter and
the performance of his own evening task. It was a sudden
brief collapse of confidence. These bouts of moodiness and
slackness, however, did not seriously interfere with the
immensity of his intellectual output, or with the abundance
of his services to the causes to which he attached himself.
For the affluence of his mind was wonderful, and was easily
and equally available for speech and writing. Upon his feet,
impromptu he could set his mind to discuss a theme of
which he would unfold the numerous implications, with
no apparent searching and with no discernible effort of
expression. So with a leading article, his facts and opinions
were waiting at the gateway of his mind; with his swift-
moving pen he could summon them and place on paper
an almost faultless record in less time than most journalists
would require to clear their minds and search their memories for action. Even in the more studied writing of his
books this unusual speed and facility of thought gave him
an immense advantage over the slow plodding industry of
others. I do not mean, of course, to imply that he was not
industrious. No feats of memory and no pace of acquiring

knowledge can account for the performance of so many
and so varied tasks as those which he carried to completion.
His was distinctly a life of toil, somewhat lightened by his
variety of interests and undertakings, but a life which
took much out of him for the benefit of others. In nearly all
men the intellectual life involves nervous depression and
some irritability. Colleagues in his journalistic life sometimes
found him inconsiderate and not easy to work with. This
perhaps was inevitable in a nature whose moods of personality were so pronounced, and under the circumstances of
journalistic work. As has already been said, he was not in
temper a freely sociable man. He did not care for clubs
or social functions, nor easily make acquaintance with
strangers. This misled some into thinking him self-centred
or somewhat arrogant. But this is a complete misunderstanding. What aloofness he sometimes showed was in reality
a diffidence, a natural shyness, a distaste for obtruding his
personality or his views. As appears from the testimony
of his friends, he was always ready and eager to enter into
the interests and to share the activities of his circle, and
to make real friends of his students and others to whom he
was drawn by some common interest or some claim to help
which he was in a position to give. The more public services he rendered, as for example on Trade Boards, were
not the dictates of cold duty, but were inspired by a genuine
sympathy, not merely with a 'cause' or 'movement', but
with the particular men and women with whom such work
brought him into contact. Many men go through life
with many friends whose regard for them, quite genuine,
never rises to affection. All who became friends of Leonard
Hobhouse came to feel for him an affection which deepened
the longer that friendship lasted. They not only admired
his qualities, but conceived a deep and growing regard for
the excellent being that inhabited his bulky, shaggy frame,
with features so expressive of tender emotions and a brow
so powerfully knit for thought.

THE WORK OF L. T. HOBHOUSE

BY MORRIS GINSBERG

CHAPTER I

INTRODUCTORY

A JUST appraisement of Hobhouse's contributions to science and philosophy is a task which should be more fittingly undertaken by a band of specialists than by a single writer. He was one of the pioneers of comparative and social psychology. He developed a technique of the greatest value in handling the vast and chaotic data of anthropology. He laid the foundations of a scientific sociology. In the field of philosophy proper he made extensive and original studies in logic and the theory of knowledge, and was one of the founders and most systematic expounders of modern critical realism. In ethics and social philosophy his writings constitute perhaps the most important attempt that has been made recently, at any rate in England, to work out the implications and possibilities of the Rationalist point of view. In his metaphysical writings, he has attempted a comprehensive synthesis, impressive alike for the vastness of the empirical data which it handles and the freshness and comprehensiveness of his deductive arguments. The range of his work is thus encyclopædic. A detailed critical account of it is certainly beyond my power. The task I have set myself is more modest. It is to give a brief account of his fundamental ideas with the object of bringing out the relations between his various studies and the essential unity and systematic character of his thought. There is no doubt that quite early in his career he formed a fairly clear idea of the main trends which his inquiries were to take, and that throughout his life he adhered steadily to the plan thus early formed. There can be few people indeed to whom it is given to carry out with such success so comprehensive and vast a scheme. It is particularly noteworthy that, ready as Hobhouse was to revise his views in the light of advancing knowledge, he found in the main that the fundamental decisions reached in his earlier work stood the test of time, and that the great changes in science and philosophy which occurred during his lifetime served rather to give point and added significance to his principal conclusions than to necessitate radical reconstructions.

To understand Hobhouse's scheme of work, it is necessary to consider briefly the formative influences to which he was subjected in his early career. Among these the most important were the evolutionary philosophy of Spencer, the Positivism of Comte (especially as interpreted by Bridges), and the social philosophy of Mill and Green. From Spencer he inherited the ambition for a philosophy which should rest on a synthesis of all the sciences, though he soon came to see that such a synthesis does not exhaust the field of philosophy, which, in his view, should include not only the scientific interpretation of reality, but also every sort of appreciation of the real which conformed to rational tests. Like Spencer, too, he was impressed with the value of the idea of evolution as a key to such synthesis, but again soon discovered that a much more thorough examination of the results of the evolutionary sciences than was achieved by Spencer would be required before they could be made the basis of an evolutionary philosophy. He felt, in particular, that Spencer's application of the idea of evolution to the problems of social life and development revealed fundamental contradictions, necessitating a radical reconstruction of the whole theory, and that the appearance of minds in the evolutionary order was a decisive phase of the process of evolution, and, in the history of humanity, involved a gradual curtailment of the sphere of natural selection and the emergence of rational and directed control over the conditions of development. The rôle of mind in evolution thus became for Hobhouse a central problem, and, in dealing with it, he was led to define his attitude to the idealistic philosophers and the Positivists, and he came to the conclusion that Hegel's conception of a self-conscious spirit and Green's conception of a spiritual principle should be tested empirically by a study of the evolution of mind, and related to the notion of a self-directing humanity which the Positivists employed in their interpretation of the course of history. We may now consider this double influence a little more in detail.

The influence exercised by Positivism on Hobhouse was profound. Like Comte he stresses the inter-connection of social phenomena, and the consequent need for a science of society which should give a *vue d'ensemble* of social life. Like Comte he regards the idea of development as central in sociology, and like him again he came to formulate a generalisation expressing a relation between the growth of mentality as exhibited in science, art, and industry and the various forms of social organisation. With Comte he considers the emergence of sociology as a positive science as a crucial point in the history of man which, as it matures, should render increasingly possible an expansion of the area of conscious control over the trends of human development. He shares with Comte again a kind of religious humanitarianism. Humanity, not as a collective concept including all men and women, but as a spirit working in them, a spirit of harmony and expanding life, shaping their best actions, appeared to Hobhouse as it did to the best Positivist writers, as the highest incarnation known to us of the Divine. Yet despite all these resemblances the differences are no less profound, and necessitated indeed in Hobhouse's view a complete transformation and re-interpretation of the Comtean philosophy.

These differences can only be understood in the light of Hobhouse's attitude to the philosophy of the British Idealists which was dominant at Oxford and in the English and Scottish Universities generally in the 'eighties and the early 'nineties. While sympathising with the Idealist school in their emphasis on spiritual development as a fundamental principle of the world order, while agreeing with them in

stressing the organic nature of society as against the barren
individualism of Spencer and his followers, he was never
able to accept the view which reduces all reality to forms of
the spiritual. "When everything is spiritual", he says, "the
spiritual loses all distinctive significance", and he felt in
particular that the idealists never faced the central difficulty
of the existence of error and evil. The spiritual principle
could not, he thought, be regarded as co-extensive with
reality, nor even as the ground of reality. It is rather the
principle of orderly development within the world order, a
force making for growing harmony but limited by the
material it works upon and closely conditioned in its purposes by the existence of conflict and indifference among
the elements of the real in so far as they are unco-ordinated.
These convictions led Hobhouse to epistemological investigations (*Theory of Knowledge*, 1896), which resulted in
what may be termed an organic view of rationality that
was to be the basis of all his future work. This has affinities
with idealist metaphysics (especially as worked out by
Bosanquet), but is essentially realistic in its interpretation
of the nature of knowledge. Accordingly, though Hobhouse
was impressed by Green's notion of a spiritual principle
realising itself in the finite consciousness, he was unable
to accept the epistemological arguments upon which
Green based his view. Green was led to his conclusions
by a reconsideration of the Kantian theory of knowledge.
He argued that our knowledge of objects implied the
reality of some unifying principle amidst the flux of
fleeting impressions, something permanent amidst the
variable manifold of sense experience, and he maintained that this permanent was essentially a system of
relations, which again in his view was unintelligible except
on the assumption of a combining or relating activity, a
single eternal consciousness, of which particular existents
were limited manifestations. This reasoning Hobhouse was
unable to accept. He was convinced that the idealists in

their development of Kant's theory, in their insistence that even in sense awareness relations were already involved, had cut the ground not only from Kant's feet, but from their own. If the relationless sense datum was a figment, there appeared to be no reason for ascribing relations to the work of the mind. The whole notion of knowledge as a making or constructing appeared to Hobhouse fallacious. In knowledge we recognise things as combined or related, but we do not create the relation through the act of knowing. But though Hobhouse repudiated Green's epistemological arguments for an eternal and timeless spiritual principle, it yet appeared to him that an empirical study might be made of the growth of mind, with the object of determining its rôle in evolution, and that this might lead to a transformation at once of the Hegelian view of development and of the evolutionary theories of the scientific naturalists, and to an empirically founded conception of a self-directing humanity akin to that held by Comte and the Positivists.

But if Hobhouse's realism separated him from the Idealists, it separated him equally from Comte. He recognised that Comte's repudiation of metaphysics as merely a transient stage in the growth of thought, valuable only as a solvent of theology, was not only based on an inadequate notion of the function of metaphysics, but itself implied an unconscious metaphysics. For the distinction between phenomena and reality, the denial that ultimate causes can be known, the repudiation of problems of origin and purpose really rested on metaphysical considerations due to Kant and Hume, and were, therefore, themselves not exempt from metaphysical scrutiny and criticism. The positive method, in other words, should be applied to knowledge itself, and all concepts including epistemological ones be referred back to experience and tested by their power of correlating and co-ordinating the empirically given order. Knowledge based on such "experiential reconstruction", in Hobhouse's view, gave us information of the real

world, not of mere appearances. This position Hobhouse
was prepared to defend not only against the relativism of
the Positivists, but also against the destructive attacks of
the Idealists, notably Bradley. He argued that the contradictions which Bradley alleged beset the categories of
science and common sense, arose from an undue hardening
of the concepts and their application to the real world
without the necessary qualifications, and he was prepared
to show their validity if correctly formed and legitimately
applied, and that not as mere elements of uncertain value
merged in higher concepts but as actual expressions of some
part of the truth.

The stage that Comte called metaphysical Hobhouse
preferred to call dialectical, which proceeds by analysis
and co-ordination of concepts. This stage, of course, has
its value in the history of thought, but also its dangers.
These arise from the tendency of concepts to form a world
of their own, remote from the experiences from which they
were originally crystallised, a world which may come to be
regarded as independently real, or at any rate independently
valid, and one which is set up as a standard to which the
world of experience must conform on pain of being pronounced unreal. The positive phase, on the other hand, or in
Hobhouse's phrase, the stage of experiential reconstruction, refuses to rest content with the ideal of an internally
consistent conceptual order, but seeks constantly to refer
back concepts to the facts of experience and to criticise
them in the light of our growing knowledge of the conditions which determine the development of thought
itself. In this sense Hobhouse would agree with Comte
in saying that in proportion as the treatment of a subject
becomes scientific, its method ceases to be purely dialectical
and becomes positive. He would, however, deny that positive thought is debarred from dealing with ultimate questions, and he would insist that though Comte was right in
stressing the fact that all knowledge is historically or

sociologically conditioned, yet the positive method is capable of correcting to an increasing extent the errors arising from this circumstance, in proportion as it succeeds in unravelling the conditions under which thought develops and embodies this growing knowledge in its reconstruction of experience.

In the light of these considerations we can now understand Hobhouse's attitude to science and philosophy. Throughout his work he insisted on the close relation between them. One of the weaknesses of at any rate some of the idealist systems of thought was, in his view, that they tended to regard the work of science as secondary in importance and to think that metaphysical analysis and construction could be carried out independently of any particular scientific scheme. The true function of metaphysics was to co-ordinate the underlying ideas of the sciences and of experience generally. In his earlier work, however, he eschewed metaphysical construction on a large scale and looked to philosophy rather for criticism and analysis. But he always felt that the physical sciences at best formulated only one aspect of reality, and that there were other orders of experience, æsthetic, moral, and religious, which had just as much claim to be taken into consideration in a synthetic account of the whole of reality. Already in an early paper he showed that so-called mechanistic explanation which generally pretends to keep close to experience affords in fact an excellent illustration of the evils of abstract dialectics, of what Comte called metaphysics. In its revolt against vagueness the mechanical mind seizes eagerly on those concepts which appear most easily verifiable, and then mistakes these luminous bits for the whole. It treats concepts quite in the dialectical spirit as independent quasi-entities, which can be combined, separated, and recombined, forgetful of the fact that elements conceptually distinguishable do not in fact operate separately, but determine and modify each other and are affected by the whole of which they form parts. In his view of the limitations of the natural sciences in relation to a complete world order he was confirmed by the recent developments in the physical sciences themselves. Yet he did not share the belief of some recent exponents that the newer theories tended to a subjective interpretation of nature or to destroy the idea of universal causation. While repudiating subjectivist interpretations, he did, however, think that the effect of the recent discoveries was to do away with the notion of matter as a permanent substratum of all change, and this confirmed him in his view, reached by a different road, that what we call matter is a rough formulation of one aspect of the real, while the term mind refers to another aspect of experience equally characteristic of the real, and he came to conceive of reality as a developing order whose fundamental characteristic is the interweaving of the mechanical and the teleological.

The general outlines of Hobhouse's scheme of work may now be briefly stated. His first inquiries were epistemological (*Theory of Knowledge*, 1896). These were in the main concerned with the validity of the postulates of empirical knowledge, and resulted in an organic view of rationality which was to inspire all his subsequent work. He then turned to the study of mental evolution in the animal world (*Mind in Evolution*, 1901). Five years later he published *Morals in Evolution*, in which he traced the growth of moral and religious ideas, utilising the data of anthropology on a big scale. The results were frequently revised by him, as is clear from the changes he made in later editions, in which he embodied results reached by workers in animal psychology and comparative ethics, sciences which have made great advances since his works were first published. In these works he reached a conception of development as the extension of harmonious correlation, and traced its principal stages. Next he turned to problems of value, and showed that the goal of the process of development was the harmony of all human experience. This conclusion, together with his other results, suggested the application of the notion of a limited teleology to the wider whole of reality. The ethical conclusions reached in the *Rational Good* (1921) were applied by him to the problems of social and political organisation in *The Elements of Social Justice* (1922), and the whole of his sociological work was summed up in his *Social Development* (1924). These works, together with his *Metaphysical Theory of the State* (1918), in which he criticised the Hegelian social philosophy, formed a series entitled collectively *The Principles of Sociology*. Finally he resumed his metaphysical investigations and attempted a synthesis of his philosophical and scientific work in his *Development and Purpose* (first edition, 1913; revised and largely rewritten, 1927). In this book his fundamental conception of a conditioned teleology is examined both from the point of view of the logical requirements of systematic explanation and its value as an instrument in the scientific handling of empirical facts, and it is claimed that both lines of inquiry lead in the main to the same conclusion.

Hobhouse's studies may be conveniently arranged in four parts. The first is an examination of the empirical facts of mental evolution in the animal world and in man, and will here be discussed under the headings of Comparative Psychology and Sociology (Chapters II and III). The second is an inquiry into the goal of development in the light of criteria deducible from the conception of a rational order. This will be dealt with in a section on Ethics and Social Philosophy (Chapter IV). The third is a logical and epistemological investigation into the validity of thought and the possibility and reliability of a rational reconstruction of experience (Chapter V). The fourth is a metaphysical synthesis in which Hobhouse seeks to determine the position of mind in the structure of reality, and to apply the notion of development to the whole world order. This will form the subject of Chapter VI. In a concluding chapter it will be shown that the conception Hobhouse formed of rationality inspired all his work and served as a connecting link between his scientific and philosophical studies. In my exposition I shall not seek to follow the development of his thought chronologically, but rather to present it in its mature and final form, ignoring the fluctuations and divagations inevitable in so long a period of work. The material upon which my account is based is derived from his published writings, from notes which I took myself as a student attending his courses, and above all, from discussions with him which I was privileged to enjoy over a period of nearly twenty years.

CHAPTER II

COMPARATIVE PSYCHOLOGY

HOBHOUSE's first systematic inquiries were, as we have seen, in the domain of logic and epistemology. These suggested to him a view of reality as a system of mutually related elements in which the whole sustains and is sustained by the parts. At this stage of his work, however, he was not prepared for metaphysical constructions on a large scale. He felt that categories such as those of mechanism and purpose, though valid within the domain of partial experience, broke down when applied to the interpretation of reality as a whole. Mechanical explanation in the long run traces back one *de facto* collocation of elements to another, and so *ad infinitum*, but affords no method of explaining collocation itself, and thus points to the need of a principle of inter-connection of a different type. The category of purpose, again, seemed to imply a distinction between a mind forming a plan and the means whereby it is realised, and thus could not be applied to the whole. The appeal to a pseudo-teleology in which the distinction between preconceived plan and its gradual realisation was blurred seemed to Hobhouse futile. "To assume, as some teleological systems seem to do, that it (i.e. Being) has value because it is perfect, i.e. complete, seems to reduce teleology itself to the level of mechanism. There is an attenuated teleology which sometimes takes on itself the function of copy-book piety. Things are because they are good, and are good because they are. This kind of thing had better be left to the copy-books" (*Theory of Knowledge*, p. 589). The notion of the organic seemed more fertile, at any rate as a starting-point for further investigation, but the organic appeared to be distinct both from the mechanical and the purposive. In any event, Hobhouse felt the need of an empirical study of the operation of these principles in the

organic world and in human societies before their bearing
on the interpretation of reality as a whole could be usefully
attempted. He turned accordingly to comparative psychology and sociology, avoiding controversies of ultimate
causation. His method broadly was to establish what may
be called a morphology of mind, that is, to examine and
classify the various forms of mental activity and social
groupings and to trace the stages whereby they have been
successively evolved.

In this chapter we are concerned with the study of the
growth of mind in the animal world and the transition to
human faculty which was embodied in *Mind in Evolution*,
1901 (Third Edition 1926. Compare the summary of his
principal conclusions given in the earlier chapters of
Development and Purpose). Animal psychology on strict
experimental lines was in its infancy when Hobhouse
began his work, and he is now generally recognised as one
of its pioneers. He carried out experiments on cats, dogs,
monkeys of several species, a young female elephant, and
an otter. He introduced new and ingenious tests, for
example, the draw-in test, the lock-and-key test, the box
and pole test, and others, which have since been used by
several other investigators of primate behaviour. (Compare
"The Development of Modern Comparative Psychology,"
by C. J. Warren, *Quarterly Journal of Biology*, December
1928.)

His method may be described as behaviouristic, that is,
it is based on an interpretation of the observed behaviour
of animals. This point is brought out clearly in an article
written by Hobhouse just before his death for the new
edition of the *Encyclopædia Britannica*, and though expressed
in a form which perhaps he would not have employed when
writing his *Mind in Evolution*, may yet be quoted as expressing the real spirit of his work. "In all fields the principal
data are contained in behaviour. . . . In the last analysis
the phenomena of our own consciousness are also the

behaviour of those complex wholes which are ourselves and this Radical Behaviourism is the one and only method of all psychology. It is also the one and only method of physical science, for if mind is the unity which we conceive to run through certain forms of behaviour, so matter is the unity which runs through other forms of behaviour. This truth is now fully recognised in physics, which conceives matter as a form of energy. Radical Behaviourism applies impartially to matter and mind. The world of our experience is material in so far as it acts in certain generic ways known roughly to common sense and more elaborately to physical sciences. But we also find many objects which, while behaving in some ways like matter, being, for example, visible and tangible, nevertheless reveal differences which are the more striking the more rigidly physics delineates the material world as essentially indifferent in all its changes to the later outcome of such changes. For throughout the world of living things we find Behaviour so correlated with circumstances as to contribute to the maintenance of an individual organism and its race, and among many organisms we find a correlation wider, more efficient, and making not only for racial life but for certain qualities of life. The factors at work in this correlation are many, but there is something running through them all which stands in marked contrast with our conception of matter, and we call it generically mind. It is still for psychology to give more precision to that term, as it is for physics to give precision to the conception of matter, and it is for philosophy to explain how the one and the same reality can exhibit these differences of aspect. What is at present known as Behaviourism would sweep the whole field of direct consciousness out of psychology in the name of the strict requirements of observable fact as a basis of science. We do not know what facts we observe more directly and immediately than that, for example, we are sometimes cold or hot, angry, pleased, grieved or joyous, but, says the Behaviourist, all these are physical states. That is a confusion between, for example, a sensation and its stimulus. Science has only two rules about observation. One is that our inductions must be founded on it, and the other is that we must treat all observations impartially." (Article on "Comparative Psychology," *Enc. Brit.*, vol. vi, p. 168.)

The basis of Hobhouse's classification of animal behaviour is to be found in the notion of correlation. This is not to be identified with the conscious co-ordination of elements. As Hobhouse uses it, it includes the relating of elements to one another or of all to a whole, whether the elements be parts of a physical structure, or mental processes, or social groupings. His method is to study the forms of correlation inductively by an analysis of our own experience as we know it in its mature form and a comparison of the activities of animals. The result is to show that there are forms of correlation in which the psychical factor is absent or unimportant, while others can only be interpreted in terms of conscious processes of varying degrees of complexity.

In the following account I propose (*a*) briefly to describe the principal stages or phases of correlation distinguished by Hobhouse, (*b*) to discuss their diffusion in the animal world, (*c*) to bring out the bearing of the results arrived at on the wider problem of the place of mind in evolution. It will be convenient to set out the phases of correlation in the form of a table.

FORMS OF CORRELATION

I. Correlation by Heredity.

    (1) Structural Activity.
    (2) Reflex Action.

II. Correlation by Co-existent Conditions.

    (1) Equilibration.
    (2) Sensori-motor action.
    (3) Instinct.

III. Correlation based on Experience.
  (1) Enduring organic effects.
  (2) Acclimatisation.
  (3) Inarticulate Correlation.
    (a) Selective Modification.
    (b) Assimilation.
  (4) Articulate Correlation.
    Co-ordination of Concrete Elements.
  (5) Correlation of Universals.
  (6) Correlation of Governing Principles.

By structural activity Hobhouse understands modes of action which depend directly on the inherited structure of the organism, for example, the correlated action involved in digestion or respiration, which go on in normal conditions of themselves, and are not dependent on special stimuli. Though admitting of a certain variation from case to case, the elements of the combination are type reactions laid down in the congenital structure. Since these type reactions are regarded as having been established by natural selection in the course of the struggle for existence, they may be considered as methods correlating the response of the individual with the previous adaptations of the race, and thus, in a sense, to embody past experiences. Closely related to this type of response is the reflex, which is a uniform response of pre-formed structure to stimuli. Reflexes are in general adaptive though not purposive, and they do not, as such, provide for variation in circumstances. The distinction from structural activities is not always easy to draw, as these, too, may need something external to act upon. In any case we are dealing in both with responses in which the correlation between response and the requirement of the organism is fixed by the inherited structure. Next, we find cases in which action is maintained but with repeated reversals and variations until equilibrium is restored; for example, "Paramecium in normal conditions swims gently forward, absorbing food by whirling its cilia. If it encounters a solid body it backs a little, then swings round through an angle of varying magnitude and advances again. If it strikes again the process is repeated and various directions are tried so that in the end if there is any egress it is found. The animal swims in a fashion to explore the object, but the exploration is indirect and persists through the inhibition of repeated errors." In this and other examples (compare Jennings) we have at a minimum a series of varying reflexes with rejection and selection determined, as it would seem, by a disturbance of equilibrium seeking relief. Here is the germ of effort or conation, that is, action dependent on its own tendency to bring about a result. At the lowest there are involved suppression and adjustment of type reactions which imply a persistent uneasiness demanding a change from the present situation.

Next, in what is designated sensori-motor action, we have a variation and adjustment of type reactions guided by a sense synthesis of the objects calling forth the response. Animals following the turnings and twistings of a prey combine and adjust their reactions in relation to the behaviour of the object. It is claimed that even the lowest grades of animal life, e.g. the amœba, must be credited with such powers. The responses are adapted to the situation as it changes, and this implies that the changing relations are somehow grasped and correlated in the act of attention, and that some sense of approximation to the results guides action and inhibits deviation.

In instinct we have a type of behaviour which may be described as a correlation of sensori-motor, structural and reflex acts by a persistent tension of feeling determined by hereditary structure and guiding trains of acts towards ends of racial service without prevision of these ends. The notion of instinct is properly applicable, as is illustrated best, perhaps, in the case of the most developed insects, where we find trains of adjusted actions adapted to secure definite ends but performed in circumstances in which, in the absence of experience, there can be no foreknowledge of the end nor conscious contrivance on the part of the organism. In such circumstances we impute a felt need governing a train of adjustments. Since these are of the sensori-motor type they are not explicable merely as compound reflexes, but are held to involve consciousness. Instinct thus interpreted is the highest form of correlation effected by heredity and co-existent or present conditions combined.

A radical difference is to be noticed when we find correlations effected as a result of the individual's own experience. Hobhouse first notes cases in which what has happened previously to an individual affects his present conduct without, however, producing specifically new types of correlation. Such are the effects of the condition of the organism at the moment of stimulation. For example, an animal sated with food will react in a different way to food than an animal hungry. Again, there are effects of experience which may be roughly called acclimatisation. Thus all organisms adapt themselves to unusual conditions, such as heat or cold, and stand them better after a certain amount of exposure. We have here an instance of general organic adaptability, or plasticity, and so far we need not attribute the change to any appreciation of the results of action on the part of the organism.

The case is different in what is termed Selective Modification. Here, as a result of experience, one of several possible type reactions, that, namely, which is most effective in a situation, comes to be preferred. This sort of "learning" is amply verified for protozoa, and for several of the lower metazoa. Thus a stentor touched with carmine will bend aside. If again molested it will reverse the movement of its cilia, and if the annoyance persists it will contract strongly upon its stalk and finally uproot itself and swim away. Now when the stentor anchors itself again it has apparently learned something, for if touched again it does not go through the whole series of type reactions but at once contracts and moves off. Here, as a result of experience, one type of action has been given preference to another. In our own experience we are familiar at a higher level with this type of correlation in the acquisition of skill in which, by inhibition and encouragement, certain responses become preferentially established, while others are eliminated.

A step further is taken when an animal learns (*a*) to inhibit a response to which it is at first impelled, or (*b*) to respond to a stimulus to which it was originally indifferent. This process Hobhouse calls assimilation. Examples of the former are Mr. Lloyd Morgan's chicks learning to avoid small bits of orange-peel or the cinnabar caterpillars. Or again, the burnt child dreading the fire. Examples of the latter are cases in which, for example, fish come to the surface for food when someone approaches them, or any animal getting to know its master and its feeding-time. The essential point in the explanation of such phenomena in the lower animals is that a sense stimulus assimilates to itself, or becomes infected or charged with, the feeling which is the natural consequence of the response to the stimulus. The process may be thus illustrated.

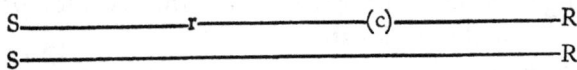

$$S\text{————}r\text{————}(c)\text{————}R$$
$$S\text{————————————}R$$

Here the feeling (c) consequent on r, the response of pecking, has come to quell the original response r, and the effect persists in the sense that in the future reactions are more easily inhibited till a point comes at which they wholly cease, and S is met with the avoiding reaction R. The excitement S takes unto itself or assimilates something of the character (c). It "means" in Stout's language the experience which in the first instance followed it. Similarly, the sight of the keeper means the sight and smell of food. Here the excitation assimilates to itself the motor tendencies and feelings with which it is intimately associated. The correlation is thus effected by consciousness, but is not itself an object to consciousness. The elements that enter into the correlation are not sorted out or disentangled. What happens is that the psycho-physical structure is so modified as to give directly a result which at first was reached indirectly through the experience of feeling. In higher phases the "meaning" will become disentangled and form an idea, but at this stage we need not impute more than a massive or inarticulate correlation of repeated experience. The conscious element is an impulse feeling attached to a sensory excitement as a result of previous experience. The biological significance of this process is that through it habits are formed out of random acts.

So far we have been dealing with modifications of primary behaviour by experience, in which terms in certain relations operated upon consciousness, but in which the related terms are not brought explicitly to consciousness. Thus, for example, a reptile stimulated to come forward for food on the approach of food has learned something as the result of several previous experiences, but there is no ground for thinking that it analyses the situation and deliberately adapts means to ends. Further development implies (*a*) a growing distinctness and comprehensiveness of perception capable of apprehending related objects distinctly and yet together, and (*b*) the power of going forward beyond the present and of guiding conation so as to bring about something that is anticipated in "idea". It seems pretty clearly established that ideas primarily arise as subsidiary to conation, and that their function is to guide conation. Let us consider how this might happen. Suppose an animal in order to get food has to operate on three objects A, B and C in definite space and time relations. Then such a series of related elements will, in accordance with our previous account, be stamped in by agreeable feeling and will form a complex which is capable of being revived as a whole. Suppose then that A alone be given; then if the conation persists (for example if the animal is hungry) action will be directed to B and C. The animal will "look for" B, and its action will be directed to something not given. Here is the germ of the "practical idea". The further development of this requires the disentangling of the idea (1) from the direct conational interest, and (2) from the definite order of past experience, and this happens in the main because desired objects appear in different contexts so that their attainment involves different procedure in different cases. The direction of action involving a combination of efforts to effect a definite change in the perceived situation is the "practical judgment". We may say that a consequence is anticipated on the basis of a parallel experience, but there is no explicit analysis of elements or generalisation. The argument is, as a logician might put it, from particulars to particulars.

So far the ideas, even when operative, are, to use Stout's terminology, at most explicit but not "free". Animals at this stage do not seem able to disentangle or free their ideas from the actual perceptual context. The next stage implies the development of analytic comparison, resulting in the recognition of elements of affinity between different portions of the perceptual world. The data of perception are broken up into distinct elements and recombined to form new wholes without reference to the order in which they were perceived. Hobhouse calls this "cross-correlation" on the ground that it cuts across the order in which experience comes to us in perception or practical activity. The terms in this correlation are concepts which enable us to deal with experience in masses grouped by continuity and affinity of character. Thus it becomes possible to distinguish the permanent elements in changing things and the common or universal in varying forms of experience and to formulate general rules applicable to classes of objects. Here we have the chief differentiation between man and the animals, for there appears to be no evidence of the use of general ideas by animals. The growth of conception is, of course, intimately linked with the development of social life and of language. Animals do indeed use symbols in the sense that they are capable of employing signs which evoke a response or stimulate action, but it is not clear that they can combine signs and so form new collocations capable of expressing varying individual situations through a combination of general terms.

The development of language fundamentally transforms the course of subsequent evolution, for it makes possible the growth of a social tradition which embodies the collective experience and gives the individual a sense of his continuity with others in the social group, and of membership in a larger whole having its roots in the past and looking forward to the future. Experience is thus indefinitely widened in scope, and it comes to be organised into bodies of thought and action held together by general principles, while it becomes possible to formulate ends, personal and social, going beyond immediate impulse as fixed by heredity, and to regulate behaviour in accordance with general and standardised rules. This stage may be characterised as the correlation of universals, disentangling the common elements and the relations of continuity and permanence underlying variations. In the sphere of practice it correlates the ends of the impulses into wider purposes embodying the more permanent interests of the individual and society. Yet at this stage the work of correlation remains partial and uncertain, for the methods of correlation are as yet unconsciously moulded by the massive forces of heredity and social tradition. It remains to subject the process of correlation itself to a critical analysis, to disentangle the categories, principles and methods which thought employs, to evaluate the part played by heredity in the moral consciousness. This is the last phase distinguished by Hobhouse, and is described by him briefly as the correlation of the governing conditions of the life of mind, that is, of the methods and aims of correlation itself—a correlation of correlations.

It should be explained, perhaps, that the method which Hobhouse follows consists essentially in an analysis of human experience and a comparison of the stages thus arrived at with homologous elements in the animal world. Whether the stages represent the actual order of evolution, either in the history of man or of the animals, is a question which he does not attempt to answer, but he points out that the evolution is hardly likely to have followed identical lines in different species. With this proviso, we may briefly summarise his conclusions relating to the diffusion or distribution of the various grades of correlation in the animal world.

Traces of conation are found in very low stages of the animal world, and it is probably co-extensive with animal, if not with all life (*Mind in Evolution*, p. 397). Behaviour of a sensori-motor type, which, in Hobhouse's view, is the first indication of consciousness, can probably be asserted even of the amœba, so that consciousness must be carried down to the lowest animal types (*Development and Purpose*, p. 61). The persistence of organic effects and acclimatisation seem established for protozoa (*Mind in Evolution*, p. 109). The evidence for selective modification among protozoa seems also clear while that for true assimilation is very doubtful (*Development and Purpose*, p. 72; *Mind in Evolution*, p. 141). On the other hand, there is evidence for the power of learning by experience for fish, reptiles, and amphibia; for many insects and crustacea, and among molluscs, for the cephalopoda (*Mind in Evolution*, p. 140). On the basis of his survey of the available evidence, and of his own experiments, Hobhouse thinks it highly probable that the kind of correlation designated "practical judgment" is reached by the higher animals, very probably indeed by the apes, possibly also by some other mammals. Into the nature of the evidence it is not possible to enter here (compare *Mind in Evolution*, chapter 12). On the whole, investigations undertaken since Hobhouse wrote in Europe and America seem to confirm his views. Koehler's work on the apes conclusively shows that a stage of conscious correlation is reached by the chimpanzees, at any rate. Whether it can be asserted below the anthropoids is, for the present, somewhat doubtful. The two final stages are peculiar to man. The correlation therein achieved is a social product, and its nature will be more fully dealt with in Hobhouse's sociological work.

The conclusions which suggest themselves on the basis of the preceding survey of the forms of mind in the animal world may now be indicated, though we must bear in mind that Hobhouse proposes to supplement and amplify them in the light of his survey of social evolution, and the rôle played by the human mind in that evolution. The essential function of mind is correlation, that is, the relating of the elements of experience to one another and to the requirements of the whole of which they form part. Correlation can be classified into several forms on the basis of the scope comprehended, and the methods employed. As mental development proceeds, the factors correlated become increasingly conscious, and the scope of correlation widens. In the course of this development several turning-points may be distinguished which, though continuous with what precedes them in evolution, amount to a real change of quality. This is in particular true of the stage in which the mind begins to criticise its own procedure, to determine the conditions of its own development, and to guide its future evolution in the light of a rational system of purposes. The appearance of these specific forms of correlation gradually increasing in scope and articulateness, is what Hobhouse terms (after Sutherland) orthogenic evolution, of which the essence is, in his judgment, progress in organisation. His argument is that the higher phases of this movement are the work of mind. If conation is, as he believes, co-extensive with life, there is at least a germ of mind in all life. If so, it is at least a possibility that conation plays a part even in building up organic structures, not only in the sense that it modifies individual structure, but that indirectly it may, through its effect on the environment, act on the racial type. In what way the relation between the mind and the biological forces is to be conceived remains for further inquiry. Meanwhile the facts of orthogenic evolution suggest the operation of a principle essentially conational in character, gradually achieving increasing correlation as it progresses from its earliest manifestations in the gropings of unconscious effort to the clearness of articulate purpose, and that the development of not "a side product of natural selection but the central fact in the history of life upon earth". The further growth of mind, as expressed in the collective achievements of mankind, forms the central problem of Hobhouse's sociological work, to which we now turn.

CHAPTER III

SOCIOLOGY

WHEN Hobhouse approached the study of sociology he found that, broadly speaking, four tendencies could be distinguished in the study of human relations. There were, firstly, the treatises of the political philosophers, which though in many instances worked out in relation to urgent problems of an actual political situation, yet in the main proceeded in the dialectical manner by an analysis of conceptions and ideals and presented accordingly the characteristic virtues and vices of the dialectical methods. There was, in the second place, the attempt made by Comte to bring social science into relation with the general conditions of human development, to disentangle the trends and laws of social evolution. Fundamentally, in Hobhouse's view, Comte's method, which insisted on combining critical analysis of conceptions with a comprehensive grasp of historical fact, was sound. But unfortunately the lead given by Comte was not generally followed. Sociological investigation was diverted into other channels. This was in part due to a certain over-rigidity of Comte's system, but more fundamentally to the development of biology and the efforts made to apply the new biological conceptions to social evolution. These tendencies, exemplified by Spencer and others, Hobhouse regarded as in the main of the nature of a reaction. His view was that important as were the contributions which the biologist could make to the data of sociology, nothing but confusion could result from the efforts to apply biological principles uncritically to the interpretation of social evolution. "The last word of biology is the first of sociology." A great deal of Hobhouse's teaching both in his lectures and his books (compare especially *Social Evolution and Political Theory* and *Social Development*) was devoted to a searching examination of biological theories

of human progress, though the lessons he has taught us in
this connection do not seem to have received the attention
they deserve. Fourthly, the latter half of the nineteenth
century saw the emergence of several special social sciences,
such as comparative religion, comparative mythology, comparative law, and comparative institutions and morals, to
which later the teachers of sociology at the School of
Economics, Westermarck and Hobhouse, themselves made
magnificent contributions. Hobhouse's ambition was to link
up these varied approaches to social science, and to effect a
vital synthesis between them.

To appreciate his point of view it is necessary to consider
on the one hand the relation between social philosophy and
sociology, and on the other the relation between the latter
and the special social sciences. Social philosophy concerns
itself primarily with the analysis and criticisms of conceptions and categories, and with the problems of values; social
science adheres to a description of facts as they are or have
been, and to a determination of the agencies involved in
social persistence and change. Yet clearly the two studies
are closely connected. For in the first place ideals and values
may and do themselves act as forces determining or conditioning changes and to that extent they belong to the
"facts" of social life and their mode of genesis and development may and indeed must be studied by the methods of
social science. Neglect of this consideration has often led
to an unduly fatalistic view of the nature of social processes.
In the second place, it is important for the philosopher
engaged in the study of ethical ideas to keep in touch with
historical fact. As Hoffding pointed out, what is ethically
obligatory must be sociologically possible. But though the
studies are closely related they must none the less be kept
distinct. It was perhaps the essential weakness of some of
the Hegelians that they blurred the distinction and thus
tended to confuse the ideal with the actual, while some of
the Evolutionists made the converse error of confusing the

actual with the ideal and attempted to deduce ethical criteria from the mere facts of evolutionary process, forgetful of the fact that if it is untrue that whatever is is good, it is equally untrue that whatever comes to be is good. It was necessary, therefore, to keep the study of values and the study of actual development and its conditions distinct. A complete account of social life would involve a union of the two studies.

In applying the notion of development to social change Hobhouse eventually found the means for effecting this union. For development may be studied both as a question of historical fact and from the point of view of ethical valuation. The scientific problem is to correlate the several aspects of social change and to measure the kind and amount of growth in the light of criteria not necessarily ethical but analogous to those that might be employed by the biologist in dealing with organic evolution. The ethical problem is to determine whether the development thus established, if it be established, satisfies ethical standards of value. The former type of investigation leads to a comparative study of culture deriving its data from anthropology and history, and seeks to discover whether there is a thread of continuity running through the tangle of the countless processes convergent and divergent which make up the life of man on earth. The other presupposes an ethical theory and a method of applying ethical criteria to the phases of historical development.

This ambitious programme occupied Hobhouse for many years. In *Morals in Evolution*, 1906, he made a comprehensive study of social institutions and moral and religious ideas. The later editions of this work embodied researches on the primitive peoples carried out by Hobhouse in collaboration with Dr. Wheeler and the present writer and published in 1915 under the title *The Material Culture and Social Institutions of the Simpler Peoples*. In the years 1918–24 appeared *The Principles of Sociology*, a series of works which provide a comprehensive synthesis of Hobhouse's philosophical and scientific work in the field of social studies.

Hobhouse's methodology consists essentially of the following stages:

(1) He attempted to provide what may be called a morphology of social institutions, including moral and religious ideas. It should be remembered that this part of his work does not necessarily imply an evolutionary theory. Already in the preface to *Morals in Evolution* he explains that the results of such a comparative study would remain standing even if the theory of evolution were shattered. At the same time, of course, a social morphology might form the basis of an evolutionary theory and acquire new significance if interpreted in the light of such theory.

(2) He has devised methods for correlating various aspects of social change in the light of their contribution towards the general advance of the community. This necessitates an analysis of the notion of development as applied to communities and the elaboration of criteria of advance of a non-ethical character. In the light of these criteria he seeks to effect a transition from morphology to development.

(3) He inquires into the conditions of development which he groups under the headings Environmental, Biological, Psychological, and distinctively Sociological.

(4) This leads him to put forward the hypothesis that there is a broad correlation between social development as measured by his criteria and the growth of mind. The method here is to distinguish phases or stages of the growth of mind and to relate these phases to the growth of the social fabric. In short, he argues that there is orthogenic evolution, and that it is the work of mind.

(5) He seeks to determine the relation between development, as thus measured, and the standards of ethical valuation as laid down in his ethical works. This is essentially

an inquiry into the possibility of progress and its relation to human thought and will.

(A) THE COMPARATIVE STUDY OF INSTITUTIONS.—Hobhouse made very extensive studies into the principal forms of social institutions, and no summary or outline could possibly do justice to the wealth of the material he amassed, or to the critical acumen and thoroughness with which he handled it. Here we can only sketch some of the main lines of his argument and only, as it were, in illustration of the methods he employed.

(1) *Forms of Government.*—The chief result that Hobhouse arrives at in dealing with government is that in political evolution three main phases may be distinguished. In the first we have forms of grouping resting on the ties of kinship and neighbourhood, often attaining high solidarity but limited in scope and incapable of much expansion. In the second we find larger and more differentiated communities attaining greater efficiency in organisation, but the principle of organisation is force and authority, and there is hierarchical subordination. This type of organisation is found among the simpler peoples, but is predominant in the periods of expansion and consolidation. It has been embodied in many forms of society, including absolute monarchy, feudal monarchy, and empire. In the third we have the civic state in which the idea of government is fundamentally transformed, and in which the common life begins to rely on moral force and the willing co-operation of free men. This phase is to be noticed in rudimentary form in the small kindred groups of the simpler peoples, but is first realised on a scale wider than that of the kindred or local group, in the civic state of antiquity and medieval Europe, on a still larger scale in the Western nation states, and in the efforts at international organisation of the modern period.

The simpler peoples, especially those of the lower stages of economic development, live in small communities. Very often the little groups are of the nature of "enlarged families". A little farther up the scale we hear of small villages or bands. Contact between such small groups is dependent largely upon whether they are exogamous or not. Generally these little societies rest largely upon kinship, fortified no doubt by magico-religious ideas. In the lowest stages these little communities form the effective social unit. Nevertheless, they may well have more or less definite relationships with neighbouring groups. A number of such groups may inter-marry or co-operate for purposes of common defence, or for certain religious or ceremonial purposes. In such cases the aggregate of groups may be spoken of as a tribe, though frequently it will have no common government. In dealing with the problem of government among the simpler peoples it is therefore necessary to distinguish between what may be called primary and secondary social groups, meaning by the former the smallest organisation above the family which has a recognised unity and a measure of independence (enlarged family, clan, or band), and by the latter an aggregate of primaries. It is often found that while there is a fairly well-developed system of government within the primary group, there is little or no government beyond it. Higher in the scale of development we find societies which are no longer merely tribal, and which approach what may be called national governments. That is, we find centralised forms of government with heads of districts appointed by a king or national council

It may be of interest to add the following points: Government is frequently in the hands of chiefs. These may owe their power to prowess in war or the hunt, or to wealth or to personal attractiveness; or else they may be hereditary. Upon the whole, there are as many cases of chiefs who owe their power to personal as to hereditary qualifications. Frequently in early society the power of the chief is not of a formal and decisive character, but varies with his personal influence. In a large number of cases there is government by means of "councils". It seems that even in the simplest societies, government by discussion is as familiar as that by the "strong man". Cases occur in which there appears to exist no coercive authority at all, or in which the power of government is very slight. It can be shown that there is an advance in organised government as peoples advance in economic development.

Upon the whole we may say that there is a tendency both to the consolidation of government and to the extension of the area of organised society as we advance in the economic scale. As we move from the lower hunters to the higher agriculturists we find more evidence of the existence of government both in primary and secondary groups. In the lowest societies there is in nearly half the known cases no organised government at all, and in three out of four no government beyond the primary group. In the highest pastoral and agricultural peoples there is organised government in all cases, and often the organised government includes more than one primary group, and extends to a large village, a tribe, or even a "nation".

The movement described may be summed up in the following table, which gives the percentage of cases of effective government enumerated in each grade of economic development distinguished among the simpler peoples.[1]

	In the Primary Group.	In a Wider Community.
Lower Hunters	53	25
Higher Hunters	75	30
Agricultural I	73	22
Pastoral I	87·5	62
Agricultural II	90	45
Pastoral II	100	78
Agricultural III	100	77

When historical records begin we find communities resembling those of the more advanced among the simpler

[1] For a further explanation see *Simpler Peoples*, Ch. 1.

I

peoples. The invention of writing and the improvement of communications make possible an expansion of the area of government and the growth of increasingly centralised administration, with the result that the principle of authority has deepened and widened. In the Eastern world the beginnings of polity are connected as elsewhere with tribal organisation, but this grows into large organisations of cities and states. They are essentially theocracies going through various phases of centralisation and decentralisation varying with the efforts of kings to create large monarchies and empires. In all cases the structure is hierarchical, and based on subordination. All power has its source in the king, and there is no notion of self-government by a free people.

It is not to be supposed that the elements of reciprocity and spontaneous solidarity characteristic of the simpler societies completely disappear in the authoritarian phase. On the contrary, they may well operate in the actual life of the people despite a superimposed authority. Nevertheless, as principles of government, they do not receive embodiment apart, as it would seem, from some constitutional experiments in the early tribal republics of India (*Social Development*, p. 253), till we come to the civic states of Ancient Greece. There we find the notion of organised government and settled law as resting not on authority, but on the free or rational acceptance of loyal citizens. They failed, however, to carry out the principles of civic life consistently, for they rested largely on slavery and the conflict of rich and poor was a source of continual strife. They were, moreover, limited in size, and unable to devise any effective organisation for dealing with inter-state affairs. Rome developed the idea of consolidating conquest by the extension of citizenship, but the mechanisms it employed were inadequate for this purpose, and it lacked the unity of spirit which alone can give a large-scale organisation sufficient plasticity and adaptability to meet emergencies. The civic principle came to life again in the medieval cities, but they suffered from the same defects, internal faction, and external exclusiveness, as beset the city states of antiquity. On a larger scale the experiment of freedom is first made in the modern world, and is still in progress. It is still hampered by what are essentially the same difficulties in a new form, difficulties of effective organisation on an international scale, of overcoming racial and national antipathies, and of making the legal equality which has been generally attained, into a greater reality by the removal of economic inequalities.

(2) *The Growth of Justice.*—From the general character of the social union we may proceed to a study of the evolution of the methods whereby obligations are maintained. Here Hobhouse gives a masterly survey of the tangled motives which are, and have been, involved in punishment, of the psychology of custom, and of the differentiation of law out of custom. I can only attempt an outline of his study of the gradual establishment of an impartial authority for punishment and reparation. His work is based, in the main, on data derived from anthropology, but also, though on a smaller scale, from civilised codes. In this development there is, as in other aspects of social evolution, no single and consistent order, yet certain phases may be distinguished through which the movement apparently proceeds. In the first place, the development of the social order, both in extent and in internal quality, is roughly correlated with advance in economic culture. For the simpler peoples it is found that as we ascend from the lower hunters to the higher agriculturists, we find both larger societies and better provision for the maintenance of order, accompanied by the decline in the number of cases of self-redress or retaliation. The following table shows the percentage of cases in each grade of economic development in which the principle of public justice preponderates:

	In the Primary Group.	In a Wider Community.
Lower Hunters	18	2
Higher Hunters	16	16
Agricultural I	34	31
Pastoral I	44	40
Agricultural II	49	47
Pastoral II	61	61
Agricultural III	74	71

In the second place, it seems clear that order is first established within the little group and then gradually extends itself to the wider society. Self-redress would appear to be, in the main, the initial stage of development, and public control is superimposed by successive stages. In general self-redress is limited by custom prescribing the character and degree of revenge, and is further qualified by the fact that the individual does not stand alone but is entitled by custom to the assistance of his kindred. Gradually the community may intervene through its elders or chiefs by endeavouring to settle disputes through methods of conciliation, or it may take drastic action on special occasions such as repeated murders, or other particular crimes that arouse special resentment. Again, the public authority may "assist" private justice. The injured party may, for example, get the chief to help him to find the stolen goods, but he initiates the proceedings, decides whether to accept compensation, or exact life for life, and he executes the sentence. In other cases vengeance may come to be "controlled", or allowed only under certain conditions; while there are others in which public justice and recognised customs of self-redress exist side by side. Hobhouse follows up in a detailed and careful study the various ways in which public offences come to be defined, sanctions provided and formulated, and administered by an impartial authority. He shows that the establishment of a more or less fair and impartial law with executive and compulsory power may be said to be the contribution of the authoritarian form of society, but the latter tends to give rise to great social and even legal inequalities and punishment is at first unnecessarily severe and ungraded. With the emergence of the conception of citizenship a more humane view of justice comes to prevail, formal equality is established, at any rate in theory, and the retaliative and repressive elements are gradually eliminated. The idea of justice is more consistently carried through, and is brought into relation with the growing knowledge of the conditions of social life.

(3) *Forms of Economic Organisation.*—The economic structure is conditioned by the nature of property, especially property in the means of production. We must therefore consider the general nature of property and the forms in which it appears in social evolution. By property is meant the system of rights in the exclusive use, control, and enjoyment of things. For the purpose of comparative study several forms may be distinguished, but it must be remembered that the terms employed to describe these forms may have different implications when applied to societies differing widely in cultural evolution. To begin with, there is common property; by this is meant (1) that over which several individuals have rights, but (2) which, taken together, they hold collectively as against others not belonging to the group. Here the individuals have rights to their shares, but the apportionment is supervised by the community. From this must be distinguished collective ownership, where the owner is a defined corporate entity; and individual, or private, property. The results of comparative study do not justify any generalisations of unilinear evolution. We can only indicate what forms of property preponderate at different stages.

In general, private property in personal belongings, such as clothes, implements, ornaments, etc., is recognised among the simpler peoples, but in regard to land a great variety of systems is to be found. For the Lower Hunters Hobhouse's detailed investigations show that the small group of nearly related individuals, which constitutes the social unit, occupies in common a defined territory. In some the group land is practially exclusive; in others it is preferential, that is, other groups of the tribe may also have rights. He notes communism in the sharing of food in a few cases only. The custom of sharing it (though not always equally) is found often. All individuals have access to the land. Evidence of private ownership in land is, however, found in some few cases on this level; for example, among the Veddas; but the communal principle in the sense defined clearly predominates among the hunting peoples in respect of land. In the lower phases of agriculture also we generally find tribal or gentile property in land. But with more settled agriculture individuals or families acquire "occupational" rights which often harden into permanent ownership. The community may, however, retain rights in various forms, such as the right of redistribution, or the power of preventing alienation, or the control of the admission of aliens. The detailed study in *The Simpler Peoples* (chapter iv, sec. iv) shows that on the whole the communal principle, whether in the form of tribal or gentile, or local grouping, loses rapidly in the agricultural stages, but not so much in the pastoral. It does not, however, lose to the purely individual or "several" form of property, for the proportion of "several" ownership is nearly constant through the different grades apart from a drop among the Higher Hunters. The gainers are the chiefs and nobles, who rise from almost zero in the first three stages to over 30 per cent. in the two higher. The communal principle, in short, loses to the signorial. At the stage when barbarism passes into civilisation, the communal, individual, and signorial are interwoven, and the signorial and the communal are fairly balanced. The tendency is then for the preponderance of power to pass to the chiefs and nobles, leaving the commoners in an increasingly precarious and dependent position.

These facts may be indicated briefly in the following table, which gives (1) cases in which effective property in land may be called communal, (2) cases in which it might be called several, and (3) cases in which ownership is restricted to the chief or the nobility. The cases under each head are reduced to a fraction of all the cases analysed. (The pastoral peoples are omitted as the numbers under each grade were too small.)

	Communal.	Several.	Restricted.
Lower Hunters	0·69	0·30	—
Higher Hunters	0·80	0·11	0·08
Agricultural I	0·64	0·36	—
Agricultural II	0·54	0·34	0·12
Agricultural III	0·29	0·34	0·37

Hobhouse does not attempt to deal in detail with the complex questions of the origins of the various forms of feudal tenure and the relationship between lords and vassals, or with the forms of capitalism in modern civilisation. He notes, however, certain distinctive features of modern industry which have a bearing on the general lines of economic development. By capitalism is meant "the employment in the production of goods for sale of those who have not the means of production by some who have or can command this means" (*Social Development*, p. 290). In this sense capitalism is found in different forms in ancient, medieval, and early modern times, but it receives its first real impetus with the mechanical inventions of the modern era. What is called "the capitalist system", however, is not a fixed entity but a complex of institutions continually being transformed. Its conditions are the elaborateness of the apparatus of industry, the existence of large aggregates of workers, the specialisation of industry, and the consequent concentration of power in the hands of those who can control the means of production. The forms which it has taken depend upon a complex interaction of economic and political factors which we cannot here attempt to disentangle, but we note that the effect has been for capitalism to move away from the system of free competition towards one of combination in many shapes and forms. Simultaneously there has been an enormous extension of legislative regulation, administrative control, and fiscal measures designed partly to mitigate the gross inequalities that had arisen but partly also adapted to the needs of an imperialistic nationalism. There does, however, emerge the conception of industry as an organisation in the service of the common good, and the problem is beginning to be faced, of building up a system which shall reconcile high specialisation and large-scale production for a world market with freedom and independence for all those who share in it.

On the whole the general line of economic development may be described as passing through three phases; in the first, there is little economic differentiation, the means of production being accessible to all. This soon passes into a differentiated system of rich and poor, and the economic organisation, like all else, comes to rest upon the principle of subordination. The later phases of this stage are characterised by a tremendous extension of scale, and a gain in efficiency, and theoretically, the system is based on free contract, while the conditions are often unequal and subordination remains. In the last stage, of which we can as yet only see the beginning, efforts are made to combine the requirements of high industrial organisation with the demands of social freedom.

(4) *Class Differentiation.*—A somewhat similar line of development can be traced by following the general trends of social differentiation revealed by comparative study. In the simplest communities there are, apart from the distinction between members of the group and strangers, and the distinctions of age, sex, and marriage divisions, within the community, no differences of status. But this rudimentary equality soon gives place to differences of rank. One of the clearest correlations established in *The Simpler*

Peoples is that between economic advance and the appearance of nobles and slaves. This will be readily seen from the following table:

	Serfs and Slaves.	Nobility.
Lower Hunters	0·02	0
Higher Hunters	0·32	0·11
Agricultural I	0·33	0·03
Pastoral I	0·37	0·02
Agricultural II	0·46	0·15
Pastoral II	0·71	0·24
Agricultural III	0·78	0·23

The gradual emergence of difference in status out of a more primitive equality can be traced also in China, India, and the Graeco-Roman civilisation. We cannot here follow the investigation into the multitudinous variations of class distinctions which Hobhouse undertakes. In general it is clear that up to the middle civilisations social divisions tend to increase rather than diminish. The Universalist teaching of the higher spiritual religions and of ethics were not on the whole strong enough to counter the powerful economic and political factors making for class differentiation. In the modern period the principle of equality before the law gradually gains ground, but can hardly be said to have been accepted by the Western world as a whole before the revolutionary period. Modern communities in general secure to all individuals equal protection under the law in respect of fundamental rights, and such restraints as are imposed are conceived as necessitated by the requirements of the common good and are at any rate not the expression of arbitrary fiat. Some progress is also made through the extension of social services in securing a measure of equality of opportunity. Upon the whole there has been sustained, though not uninterrupted, advance in this direction; the most serious exception to the fundamental equality of rights and obligations is the colour barrier.

(5) *Relations between Communities.*—The development here is extremely complicated and difficult to summarise.

Broadly, Hobhouse notes three phases. In the first, "the relations of small communities are external"; in the second, "such communities are either amalgamated under a super-incumbent power, or the weaker are reduced to dependencies and the stronger quarrel over the question of their disposal". In the third, "there are rudiments of legality and equal treatment for the group and communal as well as for the personal life" (*Social Development*, p. 299).

The simplest societies, for example, the Lower Hunters, live in small groups moving about on friendly terms but without political union among similar groups with whom they constitute a tribe. Many of these peoples live a peaceful and undisturbed social life, and on this ground it has been claimed by some recent authorities that they afford good evidence for the view that peace is the typical condition of early man. Hobhouse's very minute and careful investigations show that though these peoples cannot be said to carry on organised warfare, they are, with one or two exceptions, familiar with reprisals developing into feuds. Regular organised warfare implies a social organisation which these peoples do not possess, and to deny war of them in this sense is almost meaningless. But fighting does occur in several instances between groups or between members of different groups on questions of trespass and personal injury. As Hobhouse neatly puts it, "To show that war is not primitive is quite a different thing from showing that peace is primitive" (*Development and Purpose*, p. 208, note). The figures in the *Simpler Peoples* (p. 228) suggest that while there is no association of peaceful propensities with the lowest stages of culture as such, there is for the primitive peoples evidence of the growth of warfare with the advance of industry and of social organisation in general. Private feuds were eventually suppressed by the growing power of the centralised states, but on the other hand, the rise of authoritarian states is accompanied by an enormous extension of organised warfare. In the early stages war is waged not merely against communities, but against the individual, and the conquered stand at the will of the victor to be disposed of. The figures in *The Simpler Peoples* show that in general the practice of killing some or all of the vanquished predominates (with the exception of the Lower Hunters), and is nearly constant till we reach the higher agriculture, where its fall is the reverse side of the equally marked rise in the practice of enslaving prisoners (p. 233).

Hobhouse notes here and there among primitive peoples cases of chivalry in war and the existence of customs of truce and peace-making. It remains that in the majority of cases the conquered are treated as rightless and defenceless against those who conquer them. In this respect the character of war is not fundamentally changed in the early civilisations. Ideals of peace and of humanitarian universalism are indeed preached by the world religions, but on the whole these ideals do not receive embodiment, and as states grow stronger they assert increasingly their illimitable sovereignty. Yet gradually the conception emerges that war is not waged indiscriminately upon individuals, but is a "contention of states through their armed forces", and from the seventeenth century onwards codes gradually grow up protecting individual rights in and after war. Slowly, too, there emerges the notion that the principles of morality apply to collective entities, whether organised in states or as dependencies, or as subject groups within states, and that they are to be treated on a basis of equality from the point of view of the common good of humanity. It is to be noted that the mere fact that the problem is now at least formulated in terms of world relations is an indication of development, though just at present it is certainly impossible to predict whether the tendencies making for universal world order will prevail or whether the opposing forces will triumph and perchance lead to the entire collapse of modern civilisation.

(B) SOCIAL DEVELOPMENT AND ITS CRITERIA.—We have

now illustrated Hobhouse's method of handling the study of institutions. How is the transition to be effected from morphology to development? What is to be understood by development as applied to human society? These questions occupied Hobhouse's mind throughout his sociological work, and he has attempted to answer them in many of his writings. In what follows I will seek to render his thought, as I understand it, without necessarily following the lines of his own exposition.

In the first place, the process of social evolution is made up of innumerable different processes which, at any rate in the lower stages, may not be merely independent but even antagonistic or indifferent to one another. Yet just as in organic evolution we may speak of a general evolution, meaning by that the sum of the countless processes of evolution going on in separate species, so the development of humanity may be regarded as a sum of countless movements proceeding in many centres, propelled in each case by inner forces, yet not wholly independent and owing much to contact and interaction. Further, if there is no initial unity, there is ample evidence of a growth of unity in humanity, a trend toward wider and wider synthesis, and this raises the question whether this growing movement does not point to a permanent driving-force in human history lying behind the various forms of union and inspiring every effort of co-operation. The study of this wider synthesis, however, presupposes a knowledge of the partial syntheses of which it is the union. We may therefore begin with an analysis of the nature of development as applied to communities. Here it is important at the outset to insist upon "the organic characters" of communities. The community may be described as a self-maintaining structure of which the parts, though always in movement, are yet in relatively permanent and defined relations to one another, so that the whole is maintained as a whole. The degree of intimacy between the parts and the methods of mutual adjustment vary from case to case. Cohesion may be precariously achieved by the application of force or measures of repression, or it may be the expression of mutual needs harmoniously fulfilled. In short, communities differ from one another in their degree of "organicity", and it is by the character of such differences that we measure their development. In the article on sociology in Hastings's *Encyclopædia*, Hobhouse enumerates three criteria, but in the later exposition in his *Social Development* he gives four. These may be derived from the nature of development. They are: scale, efficiency, freedom, and mutuality. By scale is meant, firstly, quantity of population, and secondly, scope or range and variety of the activities comprehended in the life of the community. By efficiency is meant adequacy of organisation and differentiation and co-ordination of functions relative to the ends which the community sets itself. By freedom is meant scope for thought, initiative, and character. Societies differ from one another according as they maintain themselves or realise their purposes by methods of repressive subordination, or by methods which call forth the spontaneous response of their members and their willing co-operation in the service of ends in which they can find fulfilment of their own nature. Freedom in this sense is intimately related with mutuality; that is, willing co-operation in the service of a common good in which all participate. Social freedom is only attainable through a harmonisation of purposes, in other words, through the bringing of purposes into a relation of mutual or organic support. The four criteria may be briefly summed up in the words "energy, organisation, and vital harmony" which Hobhouse shows to be the marks of development in general (*Social Development*, p. 84). It is important to realise the relations between these different aspects of development in the history of humanity. Increase in the scale of organisation has often been achieved by means of repression and constraint, and thus at a cost to freedom and mutuality. On the other hand, expansion may enrich life by the introduction of new and more varied elements, while the larger the community the less perhaps the danger of external aggression, and the greater the security within. It is probable that ultimately development in scale will reach its final point in a world organisation. So again efficiency of organisation may be attained in the sense that certain ends are adequately realised by the society as a whole, but the ends may not spring from the will of the majority of the members, who may then be confined to inferior functions. Even mutuality and freedom, which, as we have seen, are intimately connected, may clash, for there may be mutual co-operation in the service of narrow ends which will therefore in the long run not afford scope for initiative or outlet for character. At the highest remove all the criteria would meet, for both logical and historical analysis suggest that efficient control over the forces of external nature and of the inner nature of man must rest upon an organisation on a world scale and on methods calling forth the spontaneous response of all its members in the service of common ends. In actual fact the development is partial and one-sided; there is growth in size but perhaps no increase in efficiency, or in efficiency without more freedom, or in freedom without more efficiency. In the present stage of sociological knowledge the application of these criteria to actual communities is extremely difficult, the more so as it may in any case be hard to estimate the probable consequences of any one partial development on the potentialities of further development. Nevertheless, for the purposes of a broad survey, the criteria may perhaps serve.

If now we revert to the brief survey of the development of institutions given above we may summarise the general trend of development somewhat as follows: When the life of humanity is considered as a whole and a comparative study is made of the various forms of institutions, a certain net movement is to be traced amid great variations in methods and rate of change. In the first place, there is ample evidence of the extension of the scale of organisation. Among the simplest peoples the groups are small and relatively homogeneous. There are indications even at this stage of a larger unity—the tribe—but it is ill-defined and loose. By fusion, by interrelation through marriage, conquest, or natural increase, larger aggregates are formed, and among them a similar process of extension goes on until, in our own time, there are even efforts towards world organisation. In general the extension of the area of social organisation is accompanied by a liberation of expanding human energies, and so by greater efficiency. This is first achieved on the basis of authority and subordination, as will be evident from our account of the growth of government, the administration of justice, economic and social differentiation. In the higher phases the principle is accepted that government does not rest on authority, but on its function as an organ of the common good, and some measure of political freedom is the norm for the more advanced nations. In the realities of freedom there has been in the modern era substantial advance, both in the removal of barriers and in the positive provision of the conditions requisite to initiative and the growth of character. Despite serious difficulties in the way of economic freedom, it cannot be denied that modern society has made considerable advances in generalising and extending effective partnership in the elements of a civilised life. Thus in the later phases there is both a larger scale of organisation and a fuller and more vigorous liberty, and with it, nevertheless, a greater efficiency in the control of the conditions of life, external and internal, than can be traced in the earlier phases. The authoritarian phase loses something of the original spontaneity and mutuality of the simpler phases, while it gains in scale and efficiency. The later phases witness an effort to reconcile mutuality and freedom with efficiency on

a large scale. The synthesis is effected through a very complicated double movement in which liberty and order from
being opposed come gradually to be recognised as both
essential to the common welfare. At first the movement is
directed towards the emancipation of the individual from
the bonds of his status in the authoritarian society. This
is the phase in which the rights of the individual are asserted
as against the claims of traditional authority. This can be
seen also in the increasing importance of individual ownership. But on the other hand, it soon becomes clear that the
rights of the individual must be conditioned by the common
good, and that absence of restrictions does not secure equal
freedom in a world in which economic power is very
unequally distributed. It becomes necessary to define
individual rights in terms of the common good and a common responsibility. This is the problem which confronts
the modern world, and it cannot be denied that a substantial
advance has been made in dealing with it.

(C) THE CONDITIONS OF SOCIAL DEVELOPMENT.—
Broadly, we may distinguish four sets of conditions which
determine social change—environmental, biological, psychological, and distinctively sociological.

(a) The physical environment sets to every society the
problem of meeting its physical needs, and the economic
structure is the solution, good or bad, of this problem. It is
now widely held by biologists that the environment does
not directly affect the inherited structure or racial quality
of organisms, but rather acts indirectly by favouring the
perpetuation of some types and eliminating others. Similarly it would seem that the environment does not directly
act upon the social structure, but the social structure must
either adapt itself to the environment or adapt the environment to itself. Both methods occur, and the latter is the
more prominent as the power of man over nature increases.
In this sense the environment may condition the direction
of human energy and the survival or elimination of types

of institutions. In particular, situation relative to other communities, political as well as physical conditions being considered, is perhaps in many cases the explanation of individual differences among peoples of nearly similar culture. Further, culture contact to some extent dependent on geographical conditions is among the most pervasive and well-established influences in civilisation. In general the most important influence of geographical conditions upon social development is to be found in its effect on intercommunication and defence. In all cases it should be remembered that the relation between societies and their environment, physical and political, is in the nature of a true response and not of a passive reaction to an external force. It is a genuine interaction determined by the character of the society in question as well as by the forces acting upon it. Hence the results are not unvarying, and they do not permit of ready generalisation.

(*b*) *Biological Factors*.—Hobhouse has given a great deal of attention to the biological aspects of sociology. It was largely his conviction that, on the basis of the biological theories which were dominant in his youth, it was impossible to account for, or indeed attach intelligible meaning to, any upward process in evolution that led him to undertake his comprehensive studies of the function of mind in the evolutionary process. He noticed early that Spencer's chief critics in biology—the disciples of Weismann—were more Spencerian than Spencer in their dealings with social progress, and he soon came to the conclusion that though biology might furnish much of value to the student of society, yet what was needed above all was a direct study of institutions themselves, and an analysis of the interactions which determined changes in them.

There can, I think, be no doubt that Hobhouse succeeds in showing that the conception of natural selection, whether as applied to struggle between individuals or groups, cannot fruitfully be used in dealing with human values.

K

Human progress, he shows, involves the continual restriction of the sphere of the struggle for existence upon which natural selection depends, and the substitution therefor of a conational principle operating through trial and error, and in the higher phases through conscious purpose. This is directed at a fuller organisation of life through rational control of its conditions, and continually endeavours to replace the rude and haphazard efficacy of struggle by an intelligent apprehension of the possibilities of organisation, in the light of a fuller grasp of standards of value.

On this fundamental issue it is perhaps not necessary to dwell further, but a word must be said on the more guarded forms which biological theories of society have assumed in more recent times. In a valuable chapter of his work on *Political Theory and Social Evolution*, 1911, Hobhouse discussed the value and limitations of eugenics, and he returns to the subject again in *Social Development* (chapter v). His position may be thus summed up:

(i) It is clear that the inherited characters, physical and mental, of the individuals composing a society must be of importance to the society of which they are the constituents. Society can only work with the material available in its stock; and it will not survive if it puts too high a demand on them or fails to provide the conditions for the fulfilment of their deeply rooted dispositions. Further, if accurate knowledge is available of what to breed for and how to breed for it, there is a case for rational selection. In particular, if there are radically bad tendencies in a stock so vicious as clearly to outweigh its merits, it is desirable that the stock should not be perpetuated. There seems, for example, to be a clear case for the prohibition of parenthood to certain types of the feeble-minded. Thus far Hobhouse would go with the Eugenists, but he warns us that this policy is hardly likely to affect the elements most dangerous to society. "We might eliminate the feeble-minded, but who would ever eliminate the too strong-minded? The superman type, the Junker, the profiteer, the soulless efficient, are between them the scourge of the earth. The rest of us who want to live in peace and get on with the work of civilised life may well feel that if it comes to elimination, we are much less likely to eliminate than to be eliminated by them" (*Social Development*, p. 116).

(ii) There is, however, no case for the argument often implied or assumed in Eugenist literature that social progress or deterioration is reducible to racial progress or deterioration. That these processes cannot be identified is clear from the fact that with relative constancy of racial qualities enormous social changes can nevertheless be effected, and that the rate of social change in no way corresponds with the rate of racial change. The argument, moreover, is based on an extremely crude view of the relations between human character and the environment. These are, in fact, extremely subtle and complicated. Man's inherited propensities are potentialities of extremely wide range, the conditions of whose manifestation are supplied by the social environment and by the individual's own experience. The very same propensities can lead to entirely different results in different settings. Accordingly, through the subtle interplay of forces outer and inner, changes in the social environment can bring about changes in human behaviour in a manner independent of alteration in race qualities. Human quality does not differ profoundly from period to period. Social problems are essentially problems of organisation, of so adjusting the elements of human nature as to make possible harmonious fulfilment instead of conflict and frustration.

(iii) A good deal of Hobhouse's argument is directed against what may be termed biological justifications of caste, and the hostility to measures of social amelioration with which these are often associated. Here his contention is that there is no ground for suggesting any permanent disharmony between the demands of social justice and the

requirements of biology. We may first deal with the alleged
evil consequences of the difference found to exist in effective
fertility between different social classes. Such differences,
it is often maintained, must result in race deterioration,
since they involve the increasing recruitment of the race
from inferior stocks. Associated with this contention is the
further argument that a prime cause in differential fertility
is the deliberate limitation of the family among the more
educated classes, and that this limitation is the result of the
burden of taxation, imposed on them, moreover, for the
benefit of the inferior classes. Hobhouse points out, firstly,
that this view of the incidence of taxation will not bear
criticism. The great burden of taxation is due, not to the
maintenance of the poor, but to military expenditure which
is "imputable in the last resort to national passions and
to the failure of the wise and eminent to control them".
Secondly, as to the failure of the "better" classes to reproduce
themselves in sufficient numbers we must distinguish.
In the first place, position in life is not necessarily an indication of good biological heredity. In the second place, in
so far as success is determined by an unusual and inborn
capacity to succeed, the qualities summed up in this phrase
are not necessarily all socially desirable. Indeed, family
limitation itself may to some extent depend on qualities
socially undesirable, such as preference of luxury to family
affections and a preponderance of cold calculation over the
warmer feelings. It is arguable that the elimination of the
bearers of these qualities may be no great loss. On the
other hand, in the case, for example, of the professional
classes who cannot afford large families, the trouble is in
the social system, which fails to reward their functions
adequately. This failure, in turn, is not due to the need of
maintaining the poor, but to the demands of militarism and
the grossly unequal apportionment of the rewards of professional life. A juster economic system would here be the
most eugenic of agencies.

Thirdly, as to the multiplication of the unfit we must also distinguish. The fertility of the mentally defective is a question by itself, and society is entitled to prevent their reproduction while it must provide them with the necessary care and provision. For the rest, we must refrain from taking poverty as a test of fitness, and here again the remedy would seem to be primarily social, and equalisation of opportunities and a general rise in the level of life would tend to reduce differences in fertility. In general the teaching of comparative sociology is against rigid castes. "Endogamy belongs to the backwaters of cultural history", and the most successful societies are likely to be those who encourage free social mobility and the greatest wealth of diversity. From the eugenic point of view, then, what seems to be important is that we should have a social system in which success would go to the socially fit, and this is only possible in proportion as the social order is based on justice and equity.

In sum, Hobhouse does not think it probable that the causes of human development will be found in biological conditions. They explain at most the peculiarities and interrelations of the various aspects of change and persistence at given stages of development. The general course of social development is, in his view, to a much greater extent prescribed by the nature of mind, and the causes of growth he finds in the efforts of the mind towards order and correlation. The study of the psychological conditions of social development is therefore of primary importance, and to them we now turn.

(c) *Psychological Conditions.*—Put in general terms, the problems that come under this head relate to the mental elements which govern human interrelations, whether by way of co-operation or antagonism, and conversely to the reactions of the social formations upon the tendencies of the individual. Hobhouse has attempted answers to these problems in many of his works, and in a sense they form the essential core of his sociological and even metaphysical constructions. In what follows I shall try to present the essentials of his social psychology as briefly as possible, and without necessarily adopting his order of exposition.

We have already discussed the general problem of the relation between the inherited propensities and the modifications due to experience in dealing with comparative psychology. Here we are concerned in particular with the inherited framework that we find in man. To begin with, there are the mechanisms, automatic or reflex, fully determined by the hereditary structure though not always operating from birth. There are, secondly, what Hobhouse calls root interests, or permanent needs, the basis for which is laid down, so to speak, in the ground plan of personality, and which underlie the whole course of life and give it direction. There are, thirdly, determinations of these general proclivities to specific objects operating in their pure form through specific mechanisms. These are the instincts. These more specific propensities are generally subservient to, and under the control of, the root interests. Further control and governance require the co-ordination of impulses and interests, and this is effected in man by intelligence, which, in turn, has an hereditary basis, but which, of course, depends upon experience, individual and social, for its manifestation and growth. An example will illustrate the relation between the root interests and the instincts. The drive of hunger is instinctive, but it is only one of a number of similar limitations or specifications of a more general root interest—the supply of bodily needs, namely, thirst, excretion, exercise, rest, sleep. In addition to these needs of the body there are other fundamental needs in relation to other human beings and to external nature. Each need is served by a variety of special forms. Without pretending to completeness, we may set out the relations between them somewhat as follows:

Fundamental Needs.	Special Forms.
Supply of bodily needs	{ Hunger, thirst, excretion, exercise, rest, sleep, etc.
Relation to Physical Environment:	
Mind making itself at home in the world	{ Avoidance of injury. Investigation. Construction.
Relation to other life	{ Response and craving for response specialised in: Dependence and protection. The sex relation.

The impulses of the first group relating to bodily needs are pretty definitely prescribed by the inherited constitution, both in respect of the drives and the mechanisms employed in their satisfaction. Their control and appropriate subordination, however, come within the scope of reason. The needs of the mind are served by the impulses to experience, to understand, to construct, and to appreciate. The cognitive interest is, however, extremely variable in strength, distribution, and liability to atrophy, but it cannot be reduced to any of the other impulses, and appears to be a root impulse. Hobhouse suggests (*Social Development*, p. 166) that it is phylogenetically a late development. To the constructive interest Hobhouse is also inclined to attribute true independence, while he leaves it an open question whether the æsthetic impulse is equally independent or a fusion of the constructive with other emotional impulses.

The social need is, put in the most general terms, the need of intercourse and response, of giving and taking, of fellowship, or, as Hobhouse also puts it, "that which asks for response from others and gives the response which is invited". This craving for response holds even of antagonistic impulses; anger, for example, dies if there is no response. When the response is roused by another's need we speak of sympathy. Affection is the concentration of the social impulses on some particular person to whom we come to stand in a relation of intimate and individual responsiveness. In sex love there is a fusion of the sex instinct in the strict sense, namely, as a drive with determinate stimuli and responses, with the craving for mutual response due to the social root interest. It may be said in passing that the sex impulses also, as is obvious, affect and pervade the relations between men and women in a variety of ways in which the instinct proper is not called into play.

The parental feeling, too, is regarded by Hobhouse as a special differentiation of the general social proclivities, defined and concentrated on the child. In actual development it is possible that maternal love was the first step in altruism, but it is a mistake to seek to derive all altruism from this or other specific instincts. Rather must the specific social impulses be regarded as limitations or differentiations of the wider root interests concentrated on specific objects. One further point must here be noted: the social impulses, fusing with the constructive, may, when the higher level of reflection is reached, inspire social ideals covering the whole of life. At the lower level they account for much in the attitude of respect or regard for society and its traditions; in other words, the embodiments of traditions, for example, ceremonials, are charged with the meaning of social life and evoke social feelings.

Self-regard is also a root interest. Hobhouse's exposition is somewhat difficult to follow. (Compare *Social Development*, pp. 159–162. It is not clear whether this is a sentiment, as some of his remarks suggest, or a root interest.) As I understand his view, it amounts to this: self-regard is our attitude to the feelings and impulses *qua* parts of the self, with their objects, so far as these are to be found in a sphere other than themselves, thrown into the background. Some of our feelings have no object, but only a stimulus (notably the bodily feelings). Others, for example the emotions of hope and fear and especially the impulses, normally go beyond themselves, and are directed to objects outside the self. In these cases especially self-feeling concentrates on them as acts of the self or as manifestations of its power. The interest is then not so much in the object as in impulse fulfilment. With due limitations it is clear that this is not an unhealthy element in life, though, as there is hardly need to say, it is easily capable of becoming a disruptive force. Social impulses, of course, may come into conflict with other impulses and a wider social impulse with a narrower. Sociologically it is the latter, that is, group egoisms, which give rise to conflicts often the most difficult to resolve.

Ill will Hobhouse takes to be not primary but a secondary consequence of exclusive egoism, individual or collective, fostered and defined, especially under conditions of antagonism or ignorance or misunderstanding. He notes further that pain as an excitant may come to be an object of desire, and many forms of cruelty are probably to be explained as a perverted form of sympathy which the sight of another's pain produces. The morbid interest in punishment is not infrequently to be referred to a desire for excitement satisfied by this sort of inverted sympathy which the suffering of others affords.

The interests enumerated underlie the whole mass of impulse-feeling, and with the growth of intelligence and will come to be concentrated upon pivotal objects round which life is organised. To follow this development we must consider a little more in detail the nature of the drives to action, and especially the relation of impulse to feeling and interest

As against the theory of psychological hedonism, Hobhouse asserts emphatically that in the main impulses to action are not dependent on previous experience of feeling. On the contrary, in their primitive form they operate without foreknowledge of consequences. At the same time it is not true to insist with some of the opponents of hedonism that all feeling of pleasure and pain has as its necessary and invariable condition an antecedent effort. A feeling of pain may clearly initiate effort, for example, withdrawal, and a feeling of pleasure may certainly maintain or sustain the experience which it accompanies even when there was no prior impulse. For example, in the contemplation of a beautiful view we yield ourselves to the experience until a distraction occurs, or strain ensues. It would seem then that it is sometimes the impulse and sometimes the feeling that comes first. The relation between impulse and feeling is, moreover, extremely close. In the first place, as we have seen already, the experience of pleasure and pain supervening upon actions tends to confirm or inhibit the impulses which initiate them. In the second place, apart from the cases in which feelings initiate action, they tend to prompt and sustain the impulses while in operation. Thus anger sustains and prompts the actions which relieve it and the impulse is maintained until the feeling is satisfied.

The common element in impulse-feeling, which may be described, perhaps, as a feeling of tenseness or excitement, is the interest in the situation, the abiding mood, guiding and directing appropriate responses. In more complex behaviour there are interests belonging to the situation as a whole which persist amid the variation of the component impulses feeling—which the organism experiences in the process of attaining the object of the interest. Innate interests, guiding impulses towards determinate ends are instincts, and we have seen that these are subservient to the root interests or fundamental needs which thus constitute the ground-plan of life. These are much wider than the specific instincts, and they persist when the organism has learned to vary its behaviour or to attain satisfaction of them by means not specifically provided in the hereditary structure.

Feeling, then, sustains impulse. In general, it has an optimum point of intensity, at which it gives the greatest reinforcement to action. When the impulse is obstructed, or when there is an overplus of excitement which action does not satisfy, the feeling is intensified and we have emotions. Their function is to impart further energy and to maintain action until the tension is relieved. In accordance with a now well established theory, clusters of emotions centring round a pivotal object come to be formed in connection with our enduring interests. These Hobhouse, following Shand, calls the sentiments.

In the course of our experience the objects of our interests emerge into consciousness. Thought gradually enables us, more or less imperfectly, to understand our interests, to relate them to one another, and to the objects in the attainment of which they can be satisfied. In following this development of rational will we may avail ourselves of the scheme given above of the levels or stages of correlation. Thus impulse-feeling in the narrower sense is characteristic of the level of instinct. At the stage of the practical or concrete judgment, we may speak of desire which is impulse defined by an idea of the end now seen in anticipation. The emergence of universals and general principles enables us to correlate partial desires into purposes and schemes of purposes. At this stage we may appropriately speak of will whose function it is to subordinate passing impulses and desires to large and comprehensive aims. The will is thus not a new entity with energy of its own; it is the synthesis of the impulses, and derives its strength from the impulses as connected. The will is the unity of the self in its conational aspect. This, however, is not to say that the will is moved mostly or especially by the idea of the self or the self-regarding sentiment. It is moved rather by the principles on which the organisation of the self as a whole depends, and these of course relate to objects or ends which, though they interest the self, are not the self. Be this as it may (compare important note in *The Rational Good*, p. 50), it follows from the above brief sketch that the function of rational will is not to override the impulses, but to harmonise them by a progressively articulate formulation and co-ordination of broad and pervasive ends in which they can find their appropriate if necessarily controlled satisfaction. Its strength at any stage is that of the root interests with their impulses in so far as they have attained unity and stability.

So far we have spoken of the make-up of the mind as discovered by analysis of the individual mind, but it is obvious that the development of the mind, especially in its higher phases, implies a social *milieu* and is socially conditioned. We may now indicate briefly, first, the psychological elements which determine interaction, and secondly, the converse reaction of society upon the individual.

Individuals are related to one another not only through the social interests and the impulses which serve them, but also indirectly through the other interests. For these, as they mature, become matters of collective endeavour and cannot be fulfilled without co-operation. The ties which bind an individual to his society, psychologically regarded, thus rest on a fusion of the social interests in their collective form with other root interests such as the constructive, the cognitive, and the egoistic; and his relations to the society vary according to the ingredients which enter into the mixture.

We turn now to the second part of our problem, namely, the manner in which social formations act upon the individual. Briefly, the influence of society upon the individual may be summed up under the heads of selection and mutual stimulus. The social environment acts selectively upon mental development in that it encourages some impulses while it inhibits others. Thus the phenomena of repression and sublimation alike depend on social influences. It also to a great extent determines the growth of thought by providing a medium for its expression, and so moulding the thought itself. Further, both thought and action are influenced by mutual stimulus, and more broadly by the responses of others. In the less rational forms of these responses we have the phenomena of crowd psychology, which, however, are not so important as the regular and normal interchange of ideas upon which the more rational element in the life of society depends.

Hobhouse uses the term social mentality to indicate the kind of conditions which result from the interactions of minds in society, and which give it a certain unity. By this term is not meant a unitary mind analogous to that of the individual but rather, as Hobhouse puts it, a sort of network or web of relationships woven into a pattern in some aspects, and merely a tangle in others. If we analyse the methods by which the life of a community is maintained, and by which changes are brought about, we can distinguish the following elements. In the first place there is an unconscious correlation brought about by the fact that the individual has to adjust himself to a working scheme that no one has worked out in its entirety, and of which no one may even be aware as a whole. Thus, for example, in the economic field individuals find the channels of their activity determined in greater or lesser degree by the prevailing economic system. In the second place, there is the more direct control of custom. Custom operates quasi-automatically upon individuals, but its effect none the less is to make the individual aware of what is expected of him, and what he may expect from others, and in this sense its guidance is conscious. In the third place, there is an apprehension by individuals varying in range and articulateness of the good of others, and an effort of varying conational level towards its realisation. Every individual has some interest beyond himself, and this brings him into relations with others of like or complementary interests. Thus purposes common to a group are formed and apprehended with varying degrees of clearness by different members of the group. In large communities there are innumerable partial common purposes, and these are often, as is natural, more fully grasped by individuals than the vaguer and relatively dim larger purposes of the whole community. The formation of a true public will is a complex process, and is often impeded by the growth of partial public wills which develop a collective egoism of their own, and which are only with difficulty brought into harmony with the larger requirements of the wider community. In general, in large communities only very few individuals have anything like a clear conception of a consistent public policy. Others perhaps have only a general but vaguer desire for the well-being of the group, but very ill-defined notions of the policy needed for its attainment. On the other hand, subordinate groups within the whole may not infrequently attain a more developed common will which then comes into relationship with other sectional wills, and with the vaguer conational forces of the larger whole which they seek to influence and direct.

The most common method of operation in large groups is strictly comparable to what in individual psychology is called trial and error. The accommodation of partial purposes to one another, their interrelation or correlation, is brought about by a series of efforts at adjustment within which the external observer may perchance detect a principle which the agents themselves certainly could not formulate. There is, in short, a point by point adjustment but no comprehensive or settled purpose. In the course of these efforts a single impulse may be widely operative among the members, and even a clear volition for a particular object, but a system of purposes is rarely of sufficiently wide diffusion to enable us to speak of a true common will, at any rate in large communities. Nevertheless, the growth of a common mind and will in respect of range, partiality, and generality is a necessary factor or condition in development as judged by our criteria. To determine its true rôle in the history of civilisation it is necessary to inquire into the way in which the growth of mind is reflected in social evolution. This brings us to the study of the distinctively sociological conditions of development.

(*d*) *Social Factors.*—So far we have been dealing with factors which, strictly speaking, provide the raw material for social interaction. Here we are to deal with the interactions themselves. The method is to mark out phases or stages of development in the different aspects of social life, and then to study their interrelation. With the development of institutions we have already dealt. We must now follow Hobhouse's study of intellectual development, of the advance in material culture as measured by the control man attains over natural forces, and finally, of the religious, ethical, and æsthetic outlook.

Phases of Intellectual Development: On the cognitive side Hobhouse distinguishes four stages: (*a*) an incipient phase in which the rudiments of articulate thought are still in process of formation; (*b*) a second in which what may be called the common-sense or empirical order is built up; (*c*) a phase of conceptual criticism and reconstruction in which thought systems are elaborated, largely on a dialectical basis; and (*d*) a phase of experiential reconstruction in which efforts are made to relate the thought structure itself with its conditions in a developing experience. We may now describe these phases briefly.

The mentality of the lowest phase is obtained by an analysis of modes of thought that we find in the untutored mind of to-day, and by abstracting from the more developed forms of thought and regarding them as they would be apart from the checks which are due to a cumulative social tradition. To some extent our inferences in this connection may be corroborated by a direct examination of the ideas of peoples in the lower cultures as described by the anthropologists. We must note that even amongst the most untutored peoples we already find a body of empirical knowledge dealing with matters that are very close to practical experience in a manner which does not differ in essentials from the methods employed by more mature minds. But outside this limited area, though also to some extent interpenetrating and colouring that area, we find a mass of ideas, methods, and attitudes which give to primitive thought a distinctive character. Briefly, the leading characteristics of early psychology are (i) a blending of what for more reflective thought are distinct categories; (ii) a loose application of unsifted generalisations, and a failure to criticise generalisations in the absence of logical checks; (iii) an incapacity to detach belief and disbelief from the requirements of emotional conditions—the dominance of impulse-feeling in determining the current of thought; (iv) the necessity of formulating in some manner, however crude and perverted, of rationalising, as we say, the various acts which feeling prompts. These characteristics can, in Hobhouse's view, be shown to underlie magic, animatism passing into animism, and the mythology based thereon. They persist also in the higher stages, and are only just beneath the surface of our own thought.

In the second stage, considerable advance is made, firstly in the organisation of ideas, secondly in the differentiation of belief from feeling. It is essentially the stage of general ideas in which thought operates distinctly in accordance with the categories, though the categories themselves are not as yet disentangled or named. Similarly, common sense employs practical tests of truth, though as yet it has no abstract logic. In doing so, it acquires some power of subjecting make-believe under the sway of feeling to the test of experience. Common sense even before the stage of science employs synthesis, analysis, and generalisation, and has sufficient insight into the nature of inference to distinguish between a grounded truth and one resting merely on fancy and make-believe.

The transition to the higher stage is inspired partly by the requirements arising out of the practical life. As the mechanical arts improve they give rise to problems the solution of which involves more consecutive effort and methods of analysis going beyond those which are at the command of common sense. In this way, for example, attention comes to be given to more exact measurement and calculation, and gradually more exact concepts and more rigid deductions are insisted upon. But a more far-reaching impulse leading to further development is rooted in the spiritual needs of mankind. There is always a recognition, however dim, of the fact that things do not explain themselves, that behind the appearances of ordinary experience there is a deeper reality. Further, the common-sense order fails men in dealing with the fundamental problems of life and death. Magic and animism, and the traditions embodying them, are in answer to these problems, and for long remain unquestioned, but eventually the demand for greater consistency and the craving for deeper spiritual satisfaction are expressed in the movement of reflective religious and philosophical thought, and the problem arises of reconciling the tangible results of the empirical order, further systematised by a dawning science, with the vaguer if deeply felt ideas of religious experience. Here we are concerned only with science and philosophy. In brief but masterly manner Hobhouse sketches the rise of the sciences in the early oriental civilisations (compare *Development and Purpose*, chapter viii), and the development of a systematic critical method among the Greeks. The main work of the Greek thinkers, in Hobhouse's view, was the construction of a conceptual order and the critical analysis of the structure of thought. It is true that in astronomy they laid the foundations of the union of mathematical reasoning with exact observation, and in biology and politics they made searching and systematic observations. Yet in the main observation is restricted and direct experiment rare. Their success in this field cannot be compared with their achievements in elaborating an order of thought which was to be the basis alike of mathematics, ethics, and metaphysics.

The phase of experiential reconstruction belongs essentially to the modern world. It owes its success, in Hobhouse's view, to a combination of three factors, the systematic pursuit of observation and experiment, the provision of instruments of precision, and the development of new methods of mathematical analysis which made possible the expression of continuous processes in conceptual terms. The essential characteristic of this phase is that in it concepts are brought to the test of experience and criticised from the point of view of their adequacy to interpret experience. On the other hand, experience itself, the nature of its data, and the processes by which results are obtained, are subjected to analysis, and efforts are made to estimate the strength of the subjective factors and the influence of the particular stage of development through which thought is passing. It is admitted that thought is relative, yet it is claimed that it is capable of transcending its own relativity through self-criticism and the study of the conditions of its own development. Thus, in Hobhouse's view, the notion of development is integral to this phase. Its work is, of course, not accomplished and its aim, the critical reconstruction of experience, is the problem of thought in our own times.

The development traced is not continuous, yet on the whole the movement is more regular and definite than any other collective achievement of mankind. With this movement we may next compare the advances made by men in the control over the forces of nature. Here, also, there is no law of automatic progress. There are many breaks in the process, yet on the whole there has been a net advance of which we may now indicate the principal stages. Broadly put, human control over the environment passes through a stage of semi-dependence upon nature in which the gifts of nature are used with a minimum of transformation. The lowest hunting peoples rapidly become extinct, and probably the peoples of the Paleolithic age approximate with this. In the next phase natural materials are more deliberately shaped towards human ends, and use is made not only of the products of nature but of the productive powers of nature, for example, in the breeding of animals and the cultivation of the soil. This phase is characteristic of the untutored contemporary life of the simpler peoples and of the period just preceding the beginnings of recorded history. In the third phase the overt forces of nature, such as wind and water, are utilised in the transformation of natural resources both in kind and direction. It is marked by the introduction of writing, the use of metal, and the formation of settled states of some extent and population. There is intensive agriculture, irrigation, manure, rotation of crops being employed. The early oriental civilisations also built up the first elements of systematic knowledge in mathematics and astronomy, together with a rough and empirical knowledge of chemistry and medicine. They also had knowledge of all the elementary machines, for example, the wheel, the pulley, the lever, and screw. The development of conceptual thought which was discussed above and is contemporaneous with this phase, has had little effect on the industrial arts. The reason for this discrepancy in the general correlation is partly to be found in the nature of the dialectical interest in its early forms which diverted attention from practical applications, partly in the slave system which diminished the need of mechanical aids or substitutes. Finally in the fourth place, efforts are made to disentangle the hidden or underlying conditions of life and development, and to utilise the knowledge thus gained in an attempt consciously to direct social evolution. Industrially this stage is definitely reached in the middle of the eighteenth century, though some of the inventions which made it possible go back to the Middle Ages, and even to Greek science. Its essential characteristic is that industry obtains from science the power to go behind phenomena to the unseen forces of the physical world, of life, and of mind, and to use these powers for the purposes of man.

In his richly documented studies of religious develop-

ment Hobhouse also distinguishes four principal phases.
By religion he understands the service of the spiritual
order, the sense of those deeper realities which enables man
to be reconciled with his place in nature, which gives meaning to his life, consolation in grief, guidance and encouragement in the perplexities of life. Religion grows up in
response, perhaps primarily, to these emotional needs, but
as thought advances the demand arises for intellectual and
speculative coherence, and the higher religions work out
a reasoned theory of the place of man in the world and of
his relations to his fellow-men. The conception of the
spiritual comes to receive more definite meaning in the
course of religious evolution by being contrasted with
the mechanical, the self-centred, the partial; and it is not
to be expected that the terms of these antitheses should be
fully formed in the earlier phases. But even in the simpler
societies there is some conception of the spiritual, of
agencies directing the human body and other spheres of
nature. In the cult of the dead and the fear and regard
for some natural objects which prompt men to treat them
as alive and so to think them alive, we find the elements of
the belief in spiritual beings characteristic of the first phase.
The notion of spirits, however, is the psychologist's way
of describing what is implied in acts of service and cult
when the ideas underlying them have undergone considerable development. In accordance with the teaching of
modern psychology ideas arise primarily in the service of
conation, and in the case before us it is likely that what
comes first is not the belief but the action. The emotions
of love and awe, hope and anxiety, prompt to acts, and
these acts engender the notion of a Being that can respond
to them. In the lower phases of thought this Being is very
obscurely conceived as something which is human and non-
human, animate yet inanimate, intelligent yet insensate.
This animism or animatism interfused with magical ideas
and practices and the cult of the dead appear to form the

working creed of the first phase. Hobhouse carefully reviews the evidence for the alleged existence of a belief in greater gods, creators, transformers, originators of tribal custom, and concludes (*Morals in Evolution*, p. 396) that, firstly, in general these beliefs are not of independent origin; secondly, there are some cases even in low grades of a conception of a creator and of a supreme sun or sky god; but thirdly, these are rarely the objects of a cult. These conclusions were confirmed by Hobhouse in a more recent investigation into the religious beliefs of the Lower Hunters, as yet unpublished.

In the next phase reached by many of the simpler peoples and in archaic civilisation the spirits of animism are replaced by the gods of polytheism. They are beings with definite personality directing natural objects but separate from them and presiding over them. They are human yet superhuman, and at their best embody ideas of beauty and goodness. They are related to one another, and in a variety of ways come to be systematised, identified, and fused or put under the presidency of a supreme god. Animistic and magical practices persist. In these endeavours after interconnection there is occasionally a dim prevision of a higher unity and a deeper spirituality, but in polytheism proper this prevision is expressed in figurative and mythical language, and falls short of the deeper insight which is the basis of the world religions.

In dealing with intellectual development we have seen how the discrepancies and failures of the empirical order give rise to a demand for critical reconstruction. The movement of "reflection" which expresses this demand does not always follow the same lines, yet all the spiritual religions have, logically regarded, something in common. They bring clearly into consciousness certain fundamental conceptions which, in the lower stages, operate in an inarticulate and unconscious manner. Such are the antitheses between reality and appearance, the permanent and the changing, the eternal and the transitory, the universal and the individual. The methods of handling these antitheses vary, and they are inspired not only by the requirements of dialectic but of a profounder individual and social experience and feeling. They are guided by the search for unity in face of the incoherence of the world of experience, by the need of reconciling the demands of the dawning ethical consciousness with the actualities of life. The tendency in the monotheistic religions is to find a solution in the conception of a transcendent deity and of a divine order over and above, and so outside, the world of experience. In the Indian metaphysical systems generally the tendency is towards a pantheistic interpretation according to which reality is one and unchangeable, and of which the world of space and time and of finite experience is a delusive appearance. In Buddhism the theological element is unimportant and ultimate reality is held as unknowable, yet it formulates the notion of a spiritual order as a guide for practical life, and so may be grouped with the spiritual religions. It is clearly impossible here to follow Hobhouse's analysis of these rich and varied movements of reflective religion in all their ramifications and modifications. We are concerned here mainly with the points of advance which they make as compared with previous stages, and these may be indicated briefly. They are all conceptual religions, using categories of thought explicitly and deliberately which are only implicit in the earlier stages. In them the demand for unity in experience comes to clear consciousness. They all formulate a conception of the spiritual clearly demarcated from the sensible and claiming domination over it. Further, with the conception of the spiritual a new set of ethical ideas is connected. The spirit in man must enter into relationship with the universal spirit, or at any rate must get rid of its finitude; hence self-suppression, subdual of the senses and of all that makes for self-assertion: hence also universal love and benevolence. In Hobhouse's view the elements of truth in these systems may be justly termed true scientific discoveries as important as any of which the physical sciences can boast. Their limitations were rooted in the over-emphasis of the antithesis between the world of the flesh and the world of the spirit, and the fact that while insisting that there is only one real world they failed to throw light on the relation between this one spiritual reality and the world of experience. True, that in mystical experience, or in moments of religious exaltation, spiritual insight claims to transform ordinary experience. It remains that no real unity can be achieved until the empirical order itself is reconstructed and a deeper synthesis effected.

This deeper synthesis is the work of the fourth phase, which, of course, is yet in the making. The history of the relation between science and theology on the one hand, and between ethics and religion on the other, cannot here be traced. In Hobhouse's view (*Social Development*, p. 241) the main tendency of modern religious development has been "to emphasise the immanence of the spiritual principle in the minds of men, to identify the spiritual with the ethical at their roots, and both of them with the law of love, to recognise frankly development in the spiritual world and to distinguish the permanent significance of religion from the forms of belief". Putting our results together, we may thus say that in the development of religion we may distinguish a phase in which the spiritual is wholly confused with the material; a second phase in which the spiritual stands out as an anthropomorphic and even superhuman personality; a third phase corresponding to the phase of conceptual reconstruction in which the spiritual is interpreted as an embodiment of ethical and intellectual ideals, that is, as the perfect and absolute whole, but in which the antithesis between the spiritual and the empirical is drawn in a manner which makes them essentially irreconcilable; and finally a fourth phase in which the spiritual comes to be conceived neither as the whole nor as an unconditioned

creator of the whole, but as a dynamic principle or element
in reality, the source of order and harmony progressively
revealing itself in nature and man.

In ethical development proper, of which Hobhouse has
made the most extensive studies, he distinguishes the stage
of primeval custom, of moral common sense, of ethical
idealism, and of realistic humanitarianism. An examination of the codes of conduct prevailing among the simpler
peoples points to a stage in which ethical conceptions
are confused or only half formed. In all known societies we
find some sense of mutual obligation upheld by custom, and
some spheres of conduct in which society intervenes to
punish transgressions by such collective force as it has at
its disposal. Yet in the main the prevalence of retaliation
and compensation indicates a mentality or outlook which
has not yet reached a notion of an impartial rule impartially
applied; and the mode and manner of retaliation and the
sphere of its application suggest that the notions of responsibility and purposiveness essential to the fully formed ethical
judgment are as yet but crudely apprehended. Further,
the sanctions lying behind custom, namely, taboos or other
magical terrors, and the fear of vindictive and resentful
spirits, often enough secondary incarnations of curses and
taboos, are essentially non-moral. The feeling of revulsion
which follows on the violation of a custom has in it potentialities of higher things, yet at this stage its expression is
prudential and egoistic.

A higher stage is reached with the development of impartially administered law by a recognised authority which
represses retaliation and enforces definite sets of rights and
duties. Yet at this stage too the sanctions remain non-moral,
and rest upon external and prudential considerations, such
as the fear of punishment either in this or another world,
but they are ethical in so far as they have an element of
generality and impartiality. Moreover, at this stage religious
ideas tend to take on a more ethical character, and there

arises a conception of a just deity who deals with acts according to their deserts and perhaps of a future life in which there is orderly retribution. This growing relation between morals and religion in the higher barbarism and the archaic civilisations is traced by Hobhouse in elaborate detail, and cannot here be followed. He shows very clearly that their moral codes are a blend of love and hate, of justice and aggression, of self-surrender and self-assertion, of the passion appropriate to the struggle for existence among ill-organised groups. In detail there are great variations, but all peoples in this stage, and in the previous stage, are characterised by a "group morality" which confines moral obligations to members of the group. As the group widens, distinctions within it arise. Class morality is added to group morality, and different loyalties on a basis of subordination replace the rudimentary equality of the earliest phases. There is in this common-sense morality no effort to think out the grounds of moral judgments or the basis of rights, which are thus upheld in crude and confused form by tradition and the extraneous sanctions of reward and punishment.

The group morality which goes well with the general level of culture in the earlier phases, and which in actual life persists even in the higher stages of civilisation, is in principle overcome by the higher religions and the philosophical reflections of the stage of conceptual reconstruction. The spiritual religions are universalist. In ideal they are for all humanity, and their ethical content is altered accordingly. They discredit vengeance and even warfare. They preach good will to all mankind, and notwithstanding their inconsistencies and limitations it remains true that they engendered a new species of ethical truth, the conception of a spiritual order based on self-sacrifice rising above the temporal order based on self-assertion. The supernatural itself is interpreted as the incarnation and expression of moral perfection. Yet they have their limitations; they do not rest upon clearly thought-out theories, and though lit up by wonderful inspiration and insight, they remain one-sided and partial. The notion of self-surrender is exaggerated at the cost of the claims of self-development, and the distinction between the spiritual and the material is drawn so sharply that it becomes impossible to see how the material could be moulded so as to become amenable to the influence of the spiritual. The result is a humanitarianism which yet paralyses human energy, and a universal benevolence which does not secure even the claims of justice. Its comparative failure in practice is, in Hobhouse's view (*Social Development*, p. 173) not to be attributed solely to the hard-heartedness of men but also to its inherent limitations.

The contribution of the Greek philosophers to ethical idealism lay in a more positive direction. In its earlier stage Greek ethics achieved two things: it overcame the antithesis between the individual and the social by the doctrine that the true well-being of the individual was to be found in his contribution to the civic life; and it made the harmonious fulfilment of functions rather than their suppression the end of conduct. In its later phase it provided a new basis for universalist ethics in the notion of a law of nature valid everywhere and applicable to man as man.

When the problem of rational ethics was taken up in modern times it was soon realised that a much more thoroughgoing reconstruction was required than that attained by the Greeks. The problem had been complicated, on the one hand, by the deeper conflicts opened by the larger religious experience which the world had gone through in the interval, and on the other by the increase in the complexity of social life, the multiplication of conflicting loyalties which made the ready identification of individual with social welfare preached by the Greeks inapplicable to modern conditions. The modern reconstruction is yet in the making. Its task is to reconcile the heightened claims of personality to a many-sided freedom,

with the claims of an infinitely complex social order to the
realisation of great ends common to the race. The key to
the solution to this problem, the modern mind—Hobhouse
thinks—has found in the notion of development. Thus the
relation of liberty to order, for example, takes on a different
form when viewed dynamically from the point of view of
an expanding spiritual development. For the fulfilment of
character cannot in the long run be achieved by coercion,
and spiritual growth can only flourish in an atmosphere
which encourages active self-expression. Further, liberty
can only be given a positive or social meaning in the light
of the conception of the ethical order as a realisable harmony
of a many-sided development. The furtherance of such
development is the ground of rights which thus become
integral conditions of the common good rather than its
limitations. Finally, the idea of development has in the
modern world enlarged and widened the scope of the
common good. Humanitarian ethics has touched every
department of practical morals—class and race divisions,
the position of women, the treatment of criminals, the
rights of association, religious equality—and has exerted an
influence far wider than that of all the schools which could
be called distinctively humanitarian. It is true that recent
history suggests the possibility that the humanitarian spirit
was but a temporary product of the eighteenth and nineteenth centuries. It may further be that its triumph is not
assured, but it remains that so far on a review of the stages
of ethical development universalist humanitarianism is the
highest yet achieved and the most distinctive of the modern
mind. In the course of the evolution here rapidly sketched,
four discoveries of capital importance have, in Hobhouse's
view, been made by mankind. "The first is the establishment of the impartial rule, the foundation of common-sense
morality. The second is the establishment of the principle
of universalism, the foundation of religious idealism. The
third is the social personality (if we may use a modern

phrase to express the real centre of the Greek doctrine) which governs the first stage of philosophic ethics. The fourth is the idea of freedom as the basis alike of personal development and social co-operation which emerges in the modern reconstruction of ethico-religious idealism" (*Development and Purpose*, p. 186). These achievements afford evidence of a real if not continuous enlargement of the idea of a spiritual order and its penetration into the sphere of moral experience.

Hobhouse does not appear to have made any extensive studies of the development of art. He suggests, however, that it exhibits phases closely linked with those traced in the advance of the intellect and of ethico-religious ideas. Thus the lowest grades of art reflect an incoherence of ideas. Its attempt at figure are childish,[1] and its stories are rambling and incoherent. The second stage is illustrated by early oriental art, and reflects the clear-cut concrete ideas of common sense. The third is the idealistic or romantic phase, the imaginative expression of conceptual reconstruction in which the mind moves in an order of its own creation. The fourth is the phase of realism, of which the wider developments are essentially modern, and which correspond to the stage of experiential reconstruction, which with a certain cool detachment and a critical attitude towards ideals yet conveys a longing for what is beyond experience and knowledge.

The series of movements which have here been briefly outlined may be conveniently brought together in the table shown opposite. The phases distinguished in the movement of human thought as reflected in the growth of science, in ethics and religion, in imaginative creation, and in the methods of industry, are not of course precisely parallel, nor is their rate of progress equal. Yet on the whole, making due

---

[1] Hobhouse, however, notes here a significant exception, namely, the animal drawings and carvings of Aurignacian and Magdalenian man and the art of the Bushmen.

SCHEME OF DEVELOPMENT

Stages of Mental Development.	Historical phases of Intellectual Development.	Stages in Control over Environment.	Stages in Religious Development.	Stages in Moral Development.	Stages in Artistic Development.
Emergence of General Ideas.	Prescientific (as actually known Lower Hunters to Agricultural III).	Semi-dependence on Nature.	Magico-animistic.	Customary Morality.	Incoherent.
Establishment of general ideas in concrete experience, "Common Sense".	Protoscience from invention of writing to beginnings of Reflection.	Empirical Arts and Use of overt Forces of Nature.	Anthropomorphic Gods.	Moral common sense of Impartial Rules.	Concrete.
Concepts defined and correlated.	Reflection.		Spiritual Religions.	Ethical Idealism.	Idealistic Romanticism.
Critical reconstruction: Analytic. Experimental. Evolutionary.	Greek Intellectual Synthesis. Modern Experimental Science.	Use of underlying Forces of Nature.	Critical Spiritualism.	Realistic Humanitarianism.	Realism.

allowance for differences in conditions and different periods of time and different parts of the world, they indicate a correlated net movement and afford some measure of mental development. Hobhouse next proceeds to argue that on the net result there is a broad correlation between mental advance and the growth of the social fabric. Reverting to the criteria of social development above explained, he shows that in the early phases of thought there is good evidence of the expansion of organisation in scale and efficiency, but at the cost of mutuality and freedom. The kinship society is small in scale, and though there is a certain mutuality and a rudimentary equality, the individual has little scope for development apart from the common life. In the authoritarian phase his life is determined by his status and he has no means of self-determination as against constituted authority. There is increase in scale and efficiency, but there is also increased subordination At the beginning of the stage of reflection and he growth of critical thought, forms of free government arise, and in theory, at any rate, there emerge ideals of a unitary spiritual order, but the embodiment of these ideals is exceedingly restricted in the ancient world. In the stage of experiential reconstruction there is not only an advance in scale and efficiency, but the elements of mutuality and freedom are beginning to receive concrete embodiment on a world scale, and we find attempts at a genuine synthesis of personal and political freedom with moral universalism. The rights of the individual underlie law, but also rest on law, and efficient social co-operation is increasingly harmonised with the claims of liberty. It is true that this wide synthesis is still unachieved, yet it is claimed that the advance towards it is substantial. A broad survey thus suggests that there has been correlated growth or development in the sense defined and the hypothesis is therefore urged that this expresses the growing power of mind.

To understand the nature of this correlated growth we

must recall Hobhouse's view of society. Societies or communities, he thinks, though not organisms, exhibit varying kinds and degrees of organic character. They are systems of interdependent parts, maintaining themselves as wholes by the mutual adaptation of the parts to the requirements of the whole. In so far as there is genuine organic harmony, in so far as communities rest upon free co-operation, their parts have both interdependence and self-determination Actual communities, of course, realise the principle of organic harmony only imperfectly, for in them the interdependence of the parts, if marred by much self-centred indifference and mutuality of service, is limited by inhibitions and suppressions. These limitations are deeply rooted, since they are due to the fact that human beings not only have need of one another, but also limit and obstruct one another. Individuals are mutually interdependent, yet each individual, and, which is perhaps more important, each group of individuals, is in varying degrees self-centred and even hostile to others. The result is that though somehow the community maintains itself as a whole, and the needs of the common life are somehow met, yet within wide limits individuals, in following out their own lives, impinge upon one another's activities, hinder and thwart one another, and this not only out of selfish individualism, but because genuine social needs come into conflict with one another, and no one can grasp the needs of the community in their entirety or is aware of the conditions requisite for their harmonious fulfilment. The problem of social development is, in fact, how to reconcile individuality and sociality, how to secure those conditions in which each individual in realising his own powers serves the social whole, and in which at the same time that social whole helps him and sustains him in the realisation of his faculties. Social development, Hobhouse argues, depends upon or expresses the growth of social mentality, that is, the progressive recognition by individuals of their mutual relations in the common good. By social mentality is not meant a unitary common self or mind, nor even an articulate system of ideas and purposes, but rather a mental condition widely dominating thought and action, a sum of habits, dispositions, ideas effective in a group of interacting minds. Such a group constitutes not a mind or will, but rather a network of minds, related to one another in a thousand different ways, each conscious of himself but only dimly aware of the nature of the interaction between himself and his fellows, and certainly not aware of the whole in all its complexity. The growth of the common mind and will in range, in impartiality and generality, is reflected in the advancing movement of civilisation. By this is not meant that there is necessarily a strict causal relation between them, but rather that there is a broad correlation between systems of institutions and the mentality behind them. The underlying force of historical evolution, Hobhouse claims, is to be found in the growing power of mind, and the essence of his thesis would seem to be that the work of the mind lies deeper than its conscious manifestations, that it is fundamentally an effort towards unity and integration. The sense of this unity is what constitutes the spirit of the social structure, and lies at the root of religion and morals. In the world of knowledge the rational impulse is seen in the effort towards articulate system, in the world of practice, in the striving towards a harmonious life. The work of mind is social, since it depends upon interaction between countless individuals, and operates through tradition, selection, and co-operation. Not being the expression of a unitary mind, social development is not continuous nor regular. "It does not move with the assured sweep of a planet in its orbit on a mechanically determined curve, nor does it resemble the inevitable unfolding of a germ through predetermined stages with harmonious correlation of parts to an assigned maturity of type. It more nearly resembles a series of efforts to grapple with an obstacle, the nature of which is only half understood, which in consequence, when forced to yield at one point returns to another." The method throughout is one of trial and error, yet gradually the growing knowledge of the conditions underlying development comes to be utilised for the further-ance of organic harmony. Social development goes on in many distinct centres, and reveals far-reaching divergencies, yet by ever widening syntheses higher levels are reached.

The development is not direct because it does not proceed from a unitary centre, nor is the convergence of different aspects of development complete. There is in particular a lag in the accommodation of social to ethical development. Yet so far as it goes, the convergence can be no accident. If society is not the expression of a purely spiritual unity, neither is it the playground of merely blind forces. Its suc-cesses and failures alike reflect the growing power of mind, gradually obtaining a firmer grasp over the conditions of its development, but as yet not completely in control over them. There are many evolutions of culture, and within each culture many strands of development, but gradually they are woven together and the process of unification is an integral part of the movement of progress. There is thus orthogenic evolution in the history of humanity, and the hypothesis is put forward that along this line, as in the field of comparative psychology, we are witnessing the increasing power of mind in evolution.

It remains to inquire more fully into the ethical value of the criteria so far employed in the study of development, and into the relation between the evolution sketched and progress. This necessitates a preliminary study of Hob-house's ethical theory and social philosophy.

M

CHAPTER IV

ETHICS AND SOCIAL PHILOSOPHY

Hobhouse's ethical work may be described as an attempt to trace the function of reason in the sphere of practical life. We have seen that on the cognitive side the rôle of reason is to correlate the elements of experience so as to lead up to a system of consilient judgments. When applied to the world of practice the work of correlation is directed towards linking up the elements of endeavour into a harmonious whole or synthesis of impulse-feelings. Hobhouse seeks to show that the world of conduct, of values, is amenable to rational tests, that there is a good, self-consistent and objective, in the sense of being based on universal principles inherent in the system of purposes taken as a whole. Put very shortly, his view is that the good generically is a harmony with some disposition of mind. The rational good is a harmony carried consistently through the world of mind and its experience, a harmony of mind with itself and its objects, a consilience of all living experience and endeavour in a comprehensive system of purposes. Such a rational good is obligatory or binding, Hobhouse argues in Kantian fashion, because it is rational; the constraint that it imposes on us is analogous to the constraint that reason imposes on us in the sphere of knowledge. This very general statement must now be explained in detail.

In our account of Hobhouse's psychology we have seen that the ultimate basis of action is to be found in what he calls the root interests or fundamental needs, which, in the lower levels, express themselves in impulse-feelings determined by heredity, and in the higher are made definite and articulate in conscious purposes and systems of purposes. If for a moment we confine ourselves to the lower levels, it will be recalled that, according to Hobhouse, effort is initiated very generally by felt impulse, but that it is also sustained by feeling in cases where there was no antecedent effort or overt appetition. In all cases, however, there is in accordance with the theory of root interests an underlying need, a susceptibility to stimulus, a dormant capacity seeking realisation. If this disposition, or susceptibility, finds the object appropriate to it there is fulfilment. This fulfilment results in what Hobhouse calls a harmony. By harmony he means a form of mutual support. In the case of an incipient conation finding satisfaction, the feeling of pleasure sustains the effort while the maintenance of the effort is the condition of full fruition. When there is no antecedent effort, for example, in passive states like the enjoyment of warmth or the contemplation of a beautiful view, the pleasurable state gives rise to the effort towards its continuance and the feeling thus prolongs the effort, and there is again an inner harmony. The judgment "this is good" asserts a harmony between an experience and a feeling. The experience may be conational or another feeling or cognitive. Strictly it is the total relationship of harmony that is good, though we speak of any term that enters into the relationship of harmony as good "by right of membership". The objects of impulse-feeling must not be taken as constituting a self-contained good, nor must the feelings be separated from the experiences which they tone or qualify. The good is an organic whole constituted by the terms experience and feeling in a relation of harmony. This harmony is felt as pleasure, or rather as happiness, but happiness must not be separated from the kind of life in which it is sought. The rational object of human action is a type of life and not a type of feeling.

The relation between feeling and harmony, and the judgment which "expresses" it, must now be explained. The judgment gives definiteness and explicitness to the practical attitude or disposition felt as favourable. It asserts that there is a harmony between an experience and a feeling, or perhaps better, that the susceptibility or disposition is receiving appropriate expression; and this would seem to imply that the object in which it seeks satisfaction is appropriate to its development (compare *The Rational Good*, p. 114, note). The judgment is true if there is such a harmony, and false if not. The question therefore arises how the judgment is to be tested, and this necessitates an inquiry into the nature of the rational as applied to conduct.

The judgment of value recognises and defines a relation of harmony. The problem whether the judgment is rational can be answered by applying the tests of rationality. Thus, in the first place, the purpose held good must be consistent with other purposes, and if there is conflict some means must be found of reconciling the opposition. In the second place, the judgment must have a ground or reason with which it is connected universally. It is not its own evidence, and in accordance with Hobhouse's theory of knowledge we must not expect to find principles as its ground ultimate in the sense of being self-evident or intuitively apprehended.

First principles here, as in all cognition, must depend for their validity upon consilience and mutual necessitation in a systematic whole. In other words, the general principles will be of the nature of interconnecting generalisations formulating comprehensive purposes in which concrete and specific ends can find their appropriate function. Finally, rationality implies that our judgment is based on objective grounds in the sense that it must not be influenced by peculiarities of feeling incompatible with universal relations. The reasonable system is one in which like things are treated alike, and different things differently. To be reasonable in practice is to connect or subordinate any partial good to the whole good, and the function of the practical reason is to discover the means and methods of effecting this correlation in a manner which shall do justice to all the claims of the component impulses or ends. Rational conduct should be consistent, coherent, and as far as possible harmonious in the sense that in cases of conflict it should proceed by mutual adaptation or modification of impulses rather than by the method of complete suppression or extinction.

To understand the nature of this harmonious correlation it is necessary to supplement our somewhat meagre account of the nature of the good. The good has been described as a harmony of experience with feeling, but so far only the isolated experience has been considered. We must now note firstly the effect of the repetition of acts and the reaction of the organised personality upon classes of similar acts, and secondly, the relation of different classes of acts to each other and to the ideal personality. As the self matures and achieves organisation, the harmony which constitutes the good is between the permanent organisation and the impulse or experience, and secondly, one of mutual adjustments between impulses to different objects. The line of rational behaviour seems to be one in which radical impulses are so adjusted, or their expression so modified, as to result in their harmonious fulfilment rather than in the excision or suppression of any of them. More correctly, no impulse should be suppressed merely for the sake of suppression. Modification or suppression is only justified by the requirements of the "organisation" as a whole. This leaves open the theoretical possibility of the existence of radically bad impulses which can only be dealt with by complete extinction, but experience does not seem to confirm this supposition, and in general impulses seem to admit of inclusion within a harmonious system by the adjustment of their objects or mode of expression. In any event, when the end can be equally achieved by the method of partial subordination or by suppression, the more rational procedure is clearly to choose the former. The teaching of psychology, moreover, suggests that in general repression involves inner disharmony and does not really achieve its object, while the method of reorientation or redirection, if more difficult, is also more likely to lead to healthier and more enduring results.

This account enables us to understand the distinction between subjective and objective, apparent and real, good. The subjective good is that which is based upon a momentarily felt harmony between a single susceptibility and an experience. The objective good is that which stands the tests of rationality by being brought into relation with other "goods" required for the progressive fulfilment of the whole personality.

So far we have been dealing with harmonious fulfilment of conation within the limits of a single personality, but such procedure is naturally highly abstract. We must now consider the individual's relations to others. This "trans-personal" reference has presented great difficulties to theorists. Hobhouse's method of dealing with it may be briefly put thus. There is an intimate relation between the growth of personality through the attainment of conational harmony and the development of society. The synthesis of elements within the individual is impossible without the "trans-personal" reference. What is even more fundamental, it is essentially the same effort after harmonious unity which inspires the growth of personality and binds men together in society. It follows that, rationally regarded, the end is harmonious development but not of the individual as such but of the widest possible group which can form stable and organic relationships. Self-realisation is good so far as it goes, just as the fulfilment of any impulse within the individual is so far good, but precisely as the fulfilment of partial impulses has to be remodelled in the light of the requirements of other impulses, so the good of each must be brought into harmony with the good of others, or rather the good of each cannot be definitely fixed till the whole is considered. The trans-personal reference is thus not based on the axiom that the good of others is equal to my own, but is an inference from the general principle that a partial good is rationally subordinate to a wider or total good and the minor premise that conative experiences exist in many centres of consciousness, and that there is, in fact, an inter-connection between them. In moral obligation we are dimly conscious of this growing unity and the development of morality reflects the endeavour of the practical reason to extend and perfect it. The function of the practical reason is closely analogous to that of rational thought. The impulse of reason in the theoretical sphere is to interpret experience and to embody fresh experiences in an ever-expanding system. The impulse of the practical reason is to develop harmony by securing unity of conation within the mind and by an extension of the control of mind over the conditions of its life. It is true that the conception of the harmonisation of conational experience is indefinite, since there are no assignable limits to conation as such. The harmony attained at any given stage, moreover, is incomplete and its rules are therefore liable to modification. Yet at any given moment and under any given conditions the injunction of the prac-tical reason is to hold that as good which on the most com-prehensive survey of all the elements affected is likely to lead to the greatest possible harmony under those condi-tions; while it holds itself ever ready to seek fresh experi-ence and to establish an ever-widening harmony and to revise its principles in the light of a more mature experience.

The conception of the good as developmental harmony has much in common with the principle of general happi-ness, especially as worked out by J. S. Mill. It differs, how-ever, from the latter profoundly in its psychology of the springs of action, in its view of the nature of obligation, of which nothing further will here be said, and more particu-larly in refusing to consider happiness in abstraction from the mode of life in which it is found. Every realisation of conation is a form of harmony felt as pleasure. Happiness is a deeper harmony resulting from the satisfaction or fulfil-ment of the more stable and organised parts of the personality as a whole. In so far as happiness is generically a subjective expression of harmonious development, the promotion of this development is also a promotion of general happiness. But happiness does not exist in the abstract; it is a feeling that we experience in relation to certain acts, and it requires to be defined in terms of those acts or experiences, just as much as in terms of the feeling which accompanies them. The feeling in abstraction cannot be taken as the basis or standard of action.

The relation of Hobhouse's view to that of Ethical Idealism, especially in the form given to it by T. H. Green, is even closer. The conception of developmental harmony is indeed only a fuller elaboration of the notion of self-realisation in relation to the common good. There are, however, significant points of divergence. One is that Hobhouse is anxious, as against Green, to retain what he considers to be an element of value in Utilitarianism, namely, the emphasis on happiness as a feeling attendant upon the successful realisation of the capabilities of human nature. Feeling is an integral element in the good, though it must not be severed from the objects with which it is connected in experience. Another point of difference is perhaps more fundamental. Green's view tends to exaggerate the unity of the good of the individual and the good of the whole. In an ideal society the development of each personality would be harmonised with the development of all, and social development might be correctly interpreted as the synthesis of the development of the component individuals. In actual conditions there is no such harmony, and the greater good of society may require the sacrifice of the partial good of the individual, and even of his life. It is idle to tell the individual in such circumstances that in serving the interests of others he is really serving his own. The line of solution is rather to urge that the rational good is not the good of the individual as such but the good of the whole of which he forms an integral part. Such greater good may, in certain circumstances, justify the sacrifice of the individual, but it is not good that such circumstances should be.

The view of the good as rational postulates in Hobhouse's view a moral order which is universal, independent of any particular social organisation, binding upon all rational beings that come into relation with one another. We must, however, refrain from personifying this moral unity, and especially from regarding it as something already achieved. It appears to be rather a principle of growth and development, a conational principle striving for harmony and ever extending its own field of application.

With the bearing of these implications on metaphysics we will deal in Chapter VI. It remains now to discuss Hobhouse's applications of his ethical theory to the problems of social organisation.

Social and Political Philosophy.—The theory of the good as harmonious fulfilment of capacity enables Hobhouse to avoid, on the one hand, the false separation between the individual and the social effected by the Individualists, and on the other, the tendency to merge finite individuality into a colourless absolute noticeable in so much of the social philosophy of the Idealists. It follows from our discussion that the common good of a group is not the sum of individual goods, for these cannot be independently ascertained, and involves a trans-personal reference, nor is the common good another good opposed to that of individuals. It is rather the harmony of which each individual good is a constituent. The function of social institutions is to provide the conditions necessary for the realisation of the common good thus conceived. From the rationality of the good it follows that rights and duties which are the conditions of its fulfilment are in essence universal, but groupings have their justification in so far as they represent a specific form of development, or render possible a more intimate kind of harmony than is attainable without them. At the same time, of course, groups have claims to special conditions only in

so far as they can be harmonised with the claims of out-
siders. Social institutions are thus a means to an end. In
working out his views, Hobhouse felt it necessary to examine
the arguments of those who, as it seemed to him, had a
radically different view of social organisation, a view which
he designates the metaphysical theory of the state. The
essence of this view is that it erects a state into super-
personal entity, absorbing the real living personality of men
and women, a being above moral criticism, an end in itself,
to which the lives of men and women are mere means.
Against this theory Hobhouse launched an attack written
with great force and clarity and even with passion (*The
Metaphysical Theory of the State*, 1918). I do not propose
here to follow his argument in detail, but rather to concen-
trate attention on the central issues so far as may be required
for an understanding of Hobhouse's own political views.

The position of the Idealists, in the form which is given
to it by Hegel and expounded by Bosanquet, against which
Hobhouse's attack is directed, may be summed up as follows: The essential problem of political theory is concerned
with the nature and basis of political obligation. Now a
moral imperative must be self-imposed; hence ultimately no
command of an authority can be binding unless it can be
shown to be so self-imposed. But governmental control is
prima facie something externally imposed; how then can it
be binding? This is the "paradox of self-government" and
in Bosanquet's view the problem thus raised is insoluble so
long as the antithesis between the self and others is insisted
on. It can only be solved by what is in essentials Rousseau's
theory of the Common Self and the General Will. Briefly
put, this theory amounts to this. Firstly, we must distinguish between our actual will, that is, our conscious will at
any moment, and our real will, which is our actual will
made coherent and consistent. True freedom lies in the
conformity of our actions to the real will. Secondly, the real
will is the general will. Thirdly, the general will is most

fully embodied in the state, and in obeying the command of the state we are therefore obeying our real selves and are free or self-governed. "The imperative claim of the will that wills itself is our inmost nature and we cannot throw it off. This is the ultimate root of political obligation" (Bosanquet, *The Philosophical Theory of the State*, p. 149).

Hobhouse will not admit the truth of any of these propositions. The argument raises fundamental issues in ethics and metaphysics, and a study of the controversies to which it has given rise shows that neither party can hope to convince the other without bringing about a radical change in metaphysical outlook. A full examination is here impossible. I shall restrict myself to the task of bringing out the essential points of divergence between Hobhouse and the Idealists.

(*a*) Hobhouse admits that in a certain sense we may rightly distinguish between the actual will, that is, the overt or conscious voluntary act, and the more enduring or permanent system of organised purposes which may be called perhaps the standing will. He refuses, however, to identify this standing will with the real will if by that is meant a rational system of purposes free from contradiction. Hobhouse indeed, as we have seen, holds that in essence the rational impulse is an impulse towards a harmonious system, and there is therefore something in every individual which answers to the conception of the good life. But the elements of disharmony are equally present and equally deeply rooted in the self and in society, and the contrast or conflict between them is only obscured if expressed in the terms real and unreal. If it be argued that the rational or real will is logically implied in the actual, as that which would complete or perfect it, Hobhouse replies that the individual cannot be said in any strict sense to will these implications until and unless he is "reborn" or becomes another man.

(*b*) If, for the sake of argument, we accept the real will, we may next inquire whether it is correctly identified with the general will. This identification, Hobhouse thinks, has its roots in several confusions. In the first place, it involves a confusion which, we shall see later, Hobhouse regards as in the long run underlying all Idealist metaphysics, the confusion, namely, between the act of experiencing and what is experienced. One reason for the identification is certainly that the system of purposes which constitutes the real will is identical for all rational beings and is therefore taken to constitute a universal will residing in each member of society and identical in all of them. Hobhouse argues that even if the objects of the real will were qualitatively identical, this would nevertheless not affect the privacy and distinctness of their acts of volition. While Bosanquet holds that individuality is "in substance, stuff, and content universal, communicable, expansive", Hobhouse urges that qualitative identity of content is not sufficient to prove numerical identity of existence. Secondly, Hobhouse argues that, apart from this confusion of experience and content, perhaps a deeper divergence arises from the radically opposed views held by him and Bosanquet regarding what has been called the "concrete universal". The mental elements operative in society might plausibly be regarded as a system; in other words, the standing will of each individual may be said to be related to the whole system of such wills as a component particular to a system. Now such articulate systems in the Hegelian metaphysics are described as universals, or rather as concrete universals, to distinguish them from the abstract universals which result from considering a general character in abstraction from the variations of its manifestations. The universal is held to unite the instances which fall under it into a self-sustaining system of which the particulars are regarded as phases of manifestation. Already in *The Theory of Knowledge*, in his discussion of identity, Hobhouse had pointed out the ambiguities which lie behind this identification of individuality with universality. He there distinguishes between complete resemblance, numerical identity, and continuity. Complete resemblance does not prove continuity, and continuity does not prove complete resemblance. "Two babies are more alike than either baby to his grown-up self, and dimness of resemblance does not interfere with completeness in continuity in development" (*Theory of Knowledge*, p. 121). There is indeed a certain resemblance between the concept of an individual and the concept of a universal. Both may be conceived as systems exhibiting a certain unity amid differences. Thus the individual is in a sense one and the same thing from birth to death; he is also different from moment to moment. He further combines many characteristics into a unity. Similarly the concept of a universal, for example, colour, may be regarded as a scheme or system of elements—that is, colours, related by resemblances and differences of tint, luminosity, and saturation, etc. Both are schemes which we construct by bringing numerous elements of experience under review, and both have a sort of unity amid difference. But the form of unity is very different in the two cases. In the concept of an individual the unity is one of physical continuity and persistence in time. In the concept of the universal the unity is the generic character of which we have now this and now that specific determination, a unity which does not imply any kind of substantial continuity. Individuals marked by common characters do not on that account form an identity in the sense in which that term may be asserted of an individual. In short, articulate complexes of quite different kinds are lumped together in the doctrine of the concrete universal.

It will be noted that we have incidentally used words which imply a distinction between the "concept" of a universal and the "universal", the former being a way in which the universal is conceived. This distinction will enable us to avoid another confusion which appears to be here involved. The concept as a thought is a unity, in other words, as a scheme it maintains its unity through all the differences of its realisation. But the objects to which the concept refers and which it binds together into a system may be scattered throughout the universe and not be possessed of the interconnecting thread which makes an individual whole. Identity of reference does not make the mass of facts referred to, an individual. Perhaps the point may be summed up by a quotation. Bosanquet says, "The ultimate principle is sameness in the other. Generality is sameness in spite of the other. Universality is sameness by means of the other" (*Principle of Individuality and Value*, p. 37). To this Hobhouse replies: "Generality implies a plurality of things similar but not necessarily connected in any other way. Individuality is a connection physical, psychical, or whatever it may be, running through many parts and constituting of them one whole" (*Metaphysical Theory of the State*, p. 69). There is thus a fundamental distinction between the individual and the universal, and it is the confusion between these two kinds of unity which, in Hobhouse's view, dominates the whole theory of the common self and the general will.

(*c*) We now come to the third proposition of the metaphysical theory of the state, namely, that the general will is embodied in the state. Strictly, if there is no such thing as a general will, this question does not arise. It may, however, be put in a different form—we may ask, namely, are the rational purposes of the individual in the fullest sense of the term particularly and peculiarly bound up with the state? Hobhouse's argument here is that Hegel's and Bosanquet's views confuse the state with society, and political with moral obligation. Bosanquet himself seems to have given somewhat different accounts of the way in which he conceives the relation between the state and society or community. Perhaps the clearest is that which is given in a paper on "The Function of the State in promoting the Unity of Mankind", which has in mind some of the criticisms that had been made against this position by several writers in a manner somewhat resembling those made by

Hobhouse. By the state, he says, "I understand the power which, as the organ of the community, has the function of maintaining the external conditions necessary to the best life". He explains further that when he speaks of the state as absolute he does not mean that it is the whole end of life or the only object of loyalty, but that it has the last word in dictating adjustments in matters of external action, and that the relation between the individual and the community at present exemplified by the nation state is unique because it alone represents "the special system of rights and sentiments, the complement of his own being, which the general will of his group has formed the state to maintain". Both these points are open to attack. Dealing with the second point first, it must be urged that it obscures the distinction between society or community and the state. For the state as a particular system of government is not an embodiment of the whole life of society. When Bosanquet says of the individual "that the nearer he approaches to being himself the more he approaches identification with the communal mind", would his view be at all plausible if, for the communal mind, we wrote "the mind of the government for the time being"? Yet this identification is implied in Bosanquet's attitude to the rights and duties of the individual towards the state. For if rights are correctly described as necessarily social relations, the term "social" must be taken as much wider than the term "political" in the strict sense. Accordingly, rights do not owe their validity to recognition by the state, but on the contrary the moral authority of the state rests upon the validity of the rights which it asserts. In a still more fundamental manner it must be urged that the obligations of man as a social being are not to any particular community but to community as such. When Bosanquet says that "Love and beauty and delight are at their best the possessions of particular communities", and it is therefore to them that we owe our duty and not to "the multitude of mankind", the question may be raised whether it is so certain that these perfections are best guarded and stimulated by particular states. In short, we must maintain that neither in its internal nor in its external relations can the state be identified with the entire organisation of life, still less does the state cover those more intimate and profound relations of life which escape formulation and organisation.

Coming now to the second point we referred to above, it will be noted that it involves a serious limitation to the omnipresence and omnicompetence of the state, for it confines the activities of the state to the field of external action, and even there, as Bosanquet explains, "to the hindering of hindrances". Here our criticism would be not that the state is given too much power but too little. It cannot directly promote freedom, and must intervene only when it is sure "that there is a better life struggling to utter itself and the dead lift of interference just removed an obstacle which bound it down" (*Philosophical Theory of the State*, p. 198). If now the claim that the relation between the individual and the state is unique be combined with the limitation of state activities to the removing of obstacles, the inevitable result is that we get, as Hobhouse puts it, the worst of both worlds: "On the one side a state which absorbs and cancels individual personality and knows little or no morality in its external relations; and on the other side the social morals of the Charity Organisation Society, a state which cannot actively promote the well-being of its members, but can only remove obstructions and leave to them a fair field in which to run the race" (*Metaphysical Theory of the State*, p. 78).

In sum, Hobhouse refuses to accept the claim that the relation between the individual and the state is so unique and inclusive as to entitle us to regard it as anything but a means to the realisation of the good life; and he declines either necessarily to confine the activities of the state to the hindering of hindrances, or to give it absolute authority even in matters of external action. Rather would he regard the authority of the state as secondary and derivative and its precise function as determinable by an investigation into the means which are at its disposal towards the realisation of the good life; and he would particularly urge that both the functions of the state and its appropriateness as an organ for their fulfilment are to be judged in their relation to the whole life of humanity and its common good.

We may now return to our discussion of Hobhouse's own theory. As we have seen, he takes as his starting-point here the notion of the good as harmonious fulfilment. Now the harmony at which it is reasonable to aim is as inclusive a harmony as possible. Indeed, the rational good may be said to postulate as its ideal expression a society coextensive with humanity. Such a society, it is not necessary to add, has never yet found organised expression, though it is on this view clearly the duty of statesmanship to work for its achievement. For the moment we must confine ourselves to a study of the principles of community, if we may so put it, which should govern all permanent or stable aggregates, and for this purpose we deal first with the internal relations of a community living under organised law. In such a community each personality being a centre of good and evil is contributory to the sum-total of the common good. Each man's good is an absolute good so far as it is compatible with the good of others, and thus deserves the fullest consideration compatible with the welfare of the whole. Morally, all are alike members of the community. The full development of every personality is good conditionally on its capability of harmonisation with the development of others. All that in each individual is so capable of being harmonised may be summed up in the phrase "social personality" and in ideal circumstances it would receive full expression. In actual circumstances curtailment and even sacrifice may be necessary on the ground of the requirements of the whole. In such circumstances there is a net loss both to the indivi-

N

dual and to society in the sense that under ideal conditions such curtailment ought not to be necessary. Rights and duties are based on the common good; rights are claims to the conditions requisite for the fulfilment of personality in harmony with the common good. Speaking generally, a right is a claim forming an integral part of a system of conduct the end of which is good, or which is good as a whole. In another way it is something due to (as a duty is due from) some element in the system or to the system as a whole from its elements. Thus the rights of the community are duties of individuals, and since the community not only recognises obligations binding on it as a whole towards its members, but also is an authority guaranteeing the rights of individuals against one another, we may say that the rights of the individuals represent duties of the community. Rights are thus integral elements of social welfare and are not to be conceived as prior to, or independent of, social relationships. This was, of course, recognised by Green, but the latter's metaphysics required him to say that anything which exists must be in somebody's mind, and that therefore "there is no right but thinking makes it so"; and his tendency to regard the good as ultimately the good will, led him to emphasise the consciousness of a common good as a prerequisite of rights. (For qualifications see, however, *Principles of Political Obligation*, Sections 140, 141, 143). In Hobhouse's view rights and duties are based on the conditions of harmony. Accordingly there are rights and duties wherever there are individuals in relation, and conditions requisite for their harmonious development. To avoid ambiguity we must distinguish between (1) cases in which there are social relations in the widest sense, that is, any human intercourse; (2) durable societies with a regular structure; and (3) politically organised societies or states. "There are rights and duties wherever there are social relations. There are recognised rights where there is a durable society, though there may be no political power to enforce them and possibly no recognised means of enforcement. There are crystallised and enforced rights when there is a political society with a developed judiciary and police. In every case the moral right is a claim which is a true element in the true common good of those affected" (*Elements of Social Justice*, p. 135). It follows that there can be no rights which conflict with the common good. But this does not mean that there are no rights against the community, for the community may misinterpret the common good, and there may be no social recognition of a particular mode of action as contributory to the common good, though in fact it may be so contributory. In such circumstances there is a right, though it is not recognised, and a claim ought to be made for it, though its validity may not be granted by anyone.

Rights and duties, on this conception, are not absolute. This limitation is due to the complexity of the relations that arise and their intermingling in actual life. A given right or duty expresses the requirements of distinct or specific elements of the common good. But in actual situations, various elements are involved, and the rights and duties to which they give rise may come into conflict. The task of practical statesmanship is to determine what is right or due in the given situation, and this may require a complicated and profound synthesis in which the substance of each claim is preserved while its spirit is transformed in relation to the common good. From the practical point of view, what is important is to remove causes of disharmony, and in doing so to give due weight to each valid claim, but to remember that what is "right" can only be determined when all the relevant conditions have been compared and that any violation of substantial claims will bring in its train consequences detrimental to the welfare of society.

The notion of harmony is further utilised by Hobhouse in his discussion of moral and social freedom. Freedom implies negatively the absence of constraint, and positively self-determination. The latter has often been interpreted in a narrower sense as meaning determination by law, though a law imposed by the individual upon himself. But this is an inadequate view. Much depends on the kind of law and its manner of realisation. The law or principle may be such as to put heavy constraint on part of our nature and may lead to the cramping or narrowing of character. (Cf. Appendix to *Metaphysical Theory of the State*, p. 138.) True freedom there is only when there is harmony, that is, when the impulses are adapted and shaped by the requirements of life as a whole, and when the active unity of the self finds expression in and through the harmonious co-operation of the impulses themselves. All harmony involves restraint. There is freedom when the restraint is in the interests of the total harmony of the self and not in the interests of some partial and overriding interest restrictive and repressive of the rest of the personality.

In his account of social freedom Hobhouse may be said to have supplied the philosophical principles of liberal or radical legislation. Fundamentally the theory of liberty rests on the spiritual conception of the social bond and is deducible from the notion of developmental harmony. If a man is compelled to his good, so far as the compulsion goes, he is not developed but only coerced, If he is persuaded or stimulated to it, he is developed. Similarly, if society is to be harmoniously developed, it must be through a forbearance which enables each to grow without impinging on the sphere of another. Spiritual development is a process in which the mind grows from within in unconstrained mutual relations with other minds. Such growth must depend on accord of feeling, on comprehension of meaning, on the assent of the will, and cannot be forced.

What, then, is the sphere of compulsion? Hobhouse has devoted a great deal of attention to this question, and the reader must be referred to his own works if he wishes to get a thorough understanding of Hobhouse's formulation of liberal philosophy. In what follows I will try to put what I conceive to be the spirit of his teaching in my own way, and as briefly as possible.

(i) In a sense liberty rests on restraint. The general liberty of an individual must be differentiated into "liberties", that is, rights, which define the powers he can enjoy and the claims he can make, and against interference with which he can expect society to protect him. Society, in other words, rightly uses compulsion in the guaranteeing of rights. Acts which invade rights are not free, and as Kant pointed out, interferences with them, being a hindering of the hindrance to freedom, are themselves in accordance with freedom.

(ii) Compulsion is rightly used not only in maintaining rights but in balancing them or in defining them for the sake of a greater or more real freedom. Thus, for example, the modern state has defined and limited the right of free contract in order to prevent individuals from putting undue constraint on one another. Where the powers of the contracting parties are unequal, freedom of contract may be merely nominal, and individuals may be forced into accepting conditions incompatible with the fulfilment of other rights, as, for example, in this case the right of a capable worker to the minimum conditions of a civilised existence. More generally, society rightly uses force to prevent individuals under the guise of freedom of contract from taking advantage of, or exercising undue influence on, people who for various reasons are acting under greater or lesser degree of constraint.

(iii) Society rightly uses compulsion in cases where universal conformity in outward act is necessary for the fulfilment of a specific purpose. In such cases the will of a recalcitrant minority, if allowed freedom, would succeed in coercing the majority; and if the purpose is sufficiently important, the community may rightly use force to prevent such coercion. An example of this is to be found in the compulsory early closing of shops, which partly also illustrates the second point.

(iv) In all cases we must consider whether in putting one restraint against another we are on the whole furthering true freedom, or, on the contrary, interfering with it. In many spheres compulsion is incapable of achieving its end, and in others the remedy may be worse than the disease. Broadly, in applying compulsion, we ought to ask ourselves the following questions: (*a*) Is the end intrinsically such that its attainment can be secured by compulsion? (*b*) Will the liberty furthered by restraint in any one sphere not affect other liberties equally or more important in other spheres? (*c*) Is the use of force necessary or can the end in question be attained by suasion, and again, can it be attained without securing universal conformity? The first point rules out from the sphere of compulsion all types of conduct or will or opinion which depend for their value upon inner growth and spontaneity. Thus we ought not to coerce a person for his own moral good, or seek to make him religious by force. Such objects can only be attained by appeal to reason and feeling and not by constraint. Indeed, the resort to coercion in such matters is not merely futile but harmful. It blocks the road towards genuine development by means of willing acceptance and mutual stimulus, while it pauperises the reason by requiring it to abdicate in favour of force. Matters of character and opinion only come within the sphere of compulsion when they result in acts interfering with the rights of others. In this respect the distinction between expression of opinion and action is important. Opportunities for free discussion and experiment in thought are necessary for rational development, and should be left free so long as they are not accompanied by acts preventing others from doing what they think necessary. In practice, of course, it is difficult occasionally to distinguish between expression of opinion and incitement to action, but this difficulty does not affect the principle itself. Similarly, religious worship is free so long as it invades no rights of others. The point of the second question formulated above may be illustrated by the case of the rules regulating the closing and opening of shops on a Saturday or Sunday, which affect religious denominations differently. Here it is true that in a sense the majority is entitled to be protected against coercion by a minority who, by standing out, might force the hands of others under conditions of free competition. But the liberty thus gained by the majority is here offset not merely by denial of a similar liberty of the minority but also of another kind of liberty, namely, that of religion or conscience, and in general this liberty may be far the more important of the two.

The third point raises the question of conscientious nonconformity on the part of a minority in cases where uniform action is believed to be necessary to the common welfare. Here, granted *bona fide* conscience on both sides, there are two points to be considered. Firstly, can the majority go on their way unimpeded despite the abstention of the minority? If so, they have no right of coercion. It is only when universal conformity is provedly necessary that compulsion is justified in overriding conscientious conviction. But, secondly, if the conscientious objection is really fatal to the collective efficiency, and measures of suasion or adjustment have been tried and found unavailing, then there is an essentially tragic situation in which the community must vindicate its right of action, while the recalcitrant individual must take the consequences of defiance. This is, of course, not a solution of the problem but a frank recognition of the realities of moral conflict in an imperfectly harmonised social order.

(v) With regard to the immature and those whose mental health is impaired society recognises a duty of protection. The principle of autonomy may indeed be said to demand as a right that the young should be trained to the point of self-determination. With regard to the others, tutelage should be directed towards bringing out such powers of self-determination as the individual is capable of, and should cease when there is evidence of powers of self-control. As a permanent condition, tutelage is applicable only to those who, by the criteria of the alienist, are incapable of appreciating the consequences of actions.

In general, then, liberty is defined by rights and restraints. The problem is not to be conceived necessarily or exclusively in terms of the opposition between personal liberty and state control. "There are other enemies of liberty than the state, and it is, in fact, by the state that we have fought them." On the other hand, the extension of state authority *may* be antagonistic to liberty. The problem is rather whether restraint is necessary in the interests of the common good, and its solution necessitates a definition of rights and of the methods by which they can be guaranteed or enforced. On the whole, social freedom may be measured by the degree in which appeal is made to intelligent will and loyalty rather than to fear or physical coercion, and in which co-operation is based not on submission and subordination but upon the harmonious interrelations resulting from mutual needs and sympathies and active interest in the common good.

From the fact that each man's good, so far as it harmonises with the good of others, is an absolute good, it follows that each man's needs deserve alike the fullest consideration which the circumstances within the community allow. This is the fundamental ethical principle of equality. Rights grounded on it are not primarily dependent on duties performed nor forfeited by duties unfulfilled, or by crimes committed. But men being of unequal capacity for development, their claims will differ. In respect of such differences, it follows from the principle of harmony that the claim each has upon the common good is proportionate to his own qualifications for sharing in it. The conditions of harmony constitute the only ground for differential treatment; in so far as needs are equal, claims are equal. From another point of view the life of the community may be regarded as the sum of functions performed by its members. These functions differ greatly in value and individuals differ greatly in their way of performing them. Good social organisation requires such an adjustment of the conditions of life as will maintain and stimulate to their highest degree of efficiency all the functions which contribute to the attainment of the common good. Reward should thus be in proportion to the requirements of the effective performance of function. It is clear that, on the one hand, the equal claim to equal needs is subject to the qualifications arising from the necessity of adjusting conditions of development to functions; while on the other hand, functions themselves have their various degrees of urgency and importance. These points are brought together in the definition of distributive justice as "equal satisfaction of equal needs, subject to the adequate maintenance of useful functions" (*Elements of Social Justice*, p. 111). For non-function and mis-function, curative and preventive treatment should be provided. From these general principles conclusions of great importance emerge. Firstly, the economic organisation must be such as to maintain the necessary economic functions, that is, the needs of the workers must be prescribed for in harmony with their functions. Secondly, there should be no functionless wealth; income should be the reward of social service and (cases of charity, of course, apart) of social service alone. Thirdly, there should be a minimum remuneration sufficient to maintain the least capable worker actually required by the industrial system in a condition of normal healthy development. Fourthly, beyond that minimum the adequate performance of function may justify differential reward proportioned to the value of the services rendered in a manner which can only be determined by experience. The analysis of property and of the individual and social factors determining value, which Hobhouse next undertakes, confirms the main results of his analysis of social justice. It leads him to the conclusion that forms and sources of wealth not dependent on the resources of specifiable living individuals should fall to the common stock. Accordingly, the community ought to be the owner of land, of all capital accumulated by past generations, while the individual should have as his own property his personal accumulations. The individual has a right to scope for initiative, choice of occupation, and opportunities of improving his own economic position by greater and better social service. He is accordingly not to be tied down to equality of income. There is no reason against the private organisation of industry provided that profits can only be made (*a*) by a man's own efforts and not by the use of unearned wealth, and (*b*) by a system of exchange in which precaution is taken against inequitable or otherwise unsound methods of gain. There remains the question of the direct organisation of industry. Hobhouse does not present a cut-and-dried scheme, but recommends considerable elasticity according to the nature and requirements of different industries. Though he looks forward to an extension both of public ownership and management in a variety of forms, he does not think it will ever cover the whole of industrial or professional life, and subject to control, there is indeed a case, according to him, for individual enterprise. The functions of the state, however, are wider than those of the direct management of industry. "In the first place, it is responsible for the general regulation of industrial conditions; in the second place, it is responsible for the provision of the fundamental conditions of healthy development for all its citizens; in the third place, it exerts the financial control through which it can make such provision and develop the common life itself to its highest power, and in the fourth place, it can exercise an ultimate control over the direction of industry without necessarily assuming managerial responsibility." The system that he finally recommends is one in which the universal and elementary conditions of work and remuneration would be laid down by law and adapted in detail to each industry by such bodies as the Trade Boards. Actual management would be in the hands of joint boards of consumers and producers, municipalities, co-operative associations, or private enterprise according to the requirements of particular industries. On the whole, the system advocated is more in harmony with social liberalism than with socialism proper. Whatever the means, the end is to transform industry from an unorganised chaos of competing interests to a co-operative service in the interests of the common good.

So far we have been dealing with rights and duties as exemplified in politically organised communities, that is, states. The principles involved, however, are of universal applicability, and in ethical truth there is only one ultimate community, which is the human race. It must not be assumed that the state as we know it is necessarily the most appropriate organ of final adjustment even in outward acts, either in relation to other states, or even in relation to its own constituents. The theory of independent sovereign states is not in strictness applicable to modern democracies either in fact or in ethical theory. Not in fact, because in truth there is no organ in the state which can unconditionally prescribe its will or get its will accepted. Not only is successful legislation dependent on public opinion, but it is often based on compromise with powerfully organised associations with whom the state is often forced to negotiate as equals. The powers prescribing the acts of the community are thus not capable of specific determination or localisation in all cases. Not ethically, because there are many relations which transcend political boundaries, and which either have or ought to have organs of expression entitled to just as much loyalty as are political governments.

The difficulties of modern democracies are perhaps to be brought under the following heads: Firstly, there are those which arise from gross economic inequalities; secondly, the anarchic relations due to the divisions of the political world into states claiming independent sovereignty, and their failure up to the present to institute an effective League of

Nations, and within many states to solve the problems of nationalities and dependencies. Thirdly, there is the exposure of the weaker or less organised peoples to exploitation. In dealing with these difficulties, Hobhouse envisages a political organisation somewhat on the following lines: (1) The state will remain the organ of internal adjustment between the various organisations and the community, subject, however, to certain supreme conditions laid down by the League of Nations. (2) There will be international functional organisations of various kinds cutting across state divisions such as guilds, churches, co-operative societies, and the like. (3) The mutual relations of these organisations and their several relations to the states would be under the control of the League, which perhaps should have representatives not only of states but also of international functions. (4) The League would further decide all interstate questions, limit armaments in all countries, guarantee elementary rights, and act as court of reference between any state and disaffected nationalities. The greatest danger threatening the world at present, Hobhouse saw in the widespread disbelief in reason, in the worship of force, the loss of grip on the hard-won conception of liberty, and the tendency to identify justice with weakness. He was convinced that it is only by a change of temper and belief that the civilised order can be saved. Given such a change, he was not without hope that solutions could be found both for the problems of economic inequality and international anarchy.

We must now, in concluding this section, bring together Hobhouse's conclusions in ethics and social philosophy with the main results of his sociological studies. It will be remembered that according to him the study of society may be conceived as a science of facts and as a philosophy of values, and that the link between them is to be found in the notion of development. He has shown that from the scientific point of view development may be measured by the criteria of scale, efficiency, mutuality, and freedom, and consists essentially in the extension of the organic principle. The most developed community would be one which has achieved the widest synthesis of human energies and capacities on a basis of free co-operation and harmonious integration. In the light of his ethical studies it will now be clear that development thus understood is in a direction which satisfies the requirement of the rational good. For the rational good is, as we have seen, a mode of life in which the whole body of impulse-feeling is linked up into a harmonious system, guided and sustained by all-embracing purposes, a harmony carried consistently through the world of mind and its experience. Such harmony can only be realised by the co-operation of all mankind, resting upon free and rational conviction, and aiming at the collective control of all the conditions of life, internal and external. Social and ethical development have thus a common end and can be measured by the same criteria. The coincidence is not a mere dialectical trick, but is rooted in the fact that the good is the principle of organic harmony, and to the extent to which social development embodies this principle it is good. Nevertheless, social development only coincides with ethical development "as a whole and in its completeness". In actual fact, development proceeds by a union of partial developments, and these may not be, and often are not, in conformity with ethical requirements. What is claimed is that on the whole a substantive advance has been made as judged by ethical standards. In the extension of organic harmony Hobhouse finds the reality of progress. This is essentially the work of rational mind working in individual centres, but expanding in scope and articulateness, linking up partial growths into wider and wider unities and having for its final purpose the harmonious fulfilment of human potentialities on a world scale. Progress is accordingly not automatic, but depends upon human thought and will. The belief in the reality of progress rests ultimately on the fundamental rationality of mind, on the possibility of forming an intelligible conception of a good common to humanity, and of securing an effective will directed to this good. Such a conception is not yet an effective force, and there is always the danger of disruptive agencies gaining the upper hand. Yet in the end "it will conquer all invalid ideas, because they will at some point contradict themselves, while that which is valid will appeal at an infinity of points, and all of them will be found at last to lead to the same centre. This is the final ground of the belief that in ethics good, as in science truth, will prevail."

CHAPTER V

THEORY OF KNOWLEDGE

WE have now completed our account of Hobhouse's study of mental evolution and of the development of the ethical order. Before dealing with the metaphysical implications of this extensive survey, it is necessary to inquire into the validity of the methods and principles employed in the processes of cognition and especially into the reliability of the processes of critical reconstruction which have been shown to be characteristic of the highest phase of mental development so far attained. Does the synthesis of experience give us knowledge of a real order, or does it merely put us into contact with a world of appearances or phenomena? Can the process of critical reconstruction perform its task adequately, or does it point beyond itself to some other form of apprehension, feeling, or intuition, to which alone perchance the deepest truths are capable of being revealed? These problems constitute the subject of Hobhouse's *Theory of Knowledge* and of the epistemological portions of his *Development and Purpose*, which may be briefly described as an inquiry into the logical foundations of a rational reconstruction of experience.

In approaching these problems Hobhouse felt that the difficulties in the theory of knowledge arose on the one hand from a false estimate of the nature and value of immediate perception and judgment, and on the other, from a separation of the conceptual order from the experience out of which it arises. Natural, or naïve, realism assumes the infallibility of the immediate deliverances of consciousness and thus falls an easy prey to its critics when it is faced with the difficulties of error and illusion. In another way the search for immediacy has led to the various forms of subjective idealism on the assumed ground that the only thing that is immediately known is the knowledge which actually

is the thing which it knows. The process of rational reconstruction, if it is to be successful, must therefore begin with
a critical analysis of what is given in immediate perception
and of its value in the system of thought. In this side of his
inquiries Hobhouse is an ardent critic of empiricism and of
phenomenalism. On the other hand, he is anxious to maintain and justify the claims of the empirical order. Ultimately
all claims to validity must be based on a synthesis of experience, and he devoted a great deal of his work to a refutation
of the charges of inherent contradiction which were alleged
to beset the empirical order. The general principle which
Hobhouse employs in his reconstruction of experience consists in the impartial application of the idea of consilience.
This involves a constant checking of what claims immediacy
in the light of other immediate judgments, and concepts
formed from them, and a reference back of concepts to
the experiences from which they were crystallised. The
function of rational thought is to establish interconnection
and not merely consistency. Its procedure is, so to speak,
not linear but systematic, and is directed at revealing
the pervading unity in a body of judgments in mutual
corroboration.

This organic view of rationality is combined by Hobhouse with an evolutionary account of the growth of the
mind. Human thought is regarded as an organic structure
held together by the mutual support of its parts, undergoing
correlated change as it develops, but maintaining its identity
through modification. The notion of development is thus
conceived as lying at the basis of validity itself. The entire
system of knowledge is in process of growth, utilising the
data of an ever-accumulating experience and undergoing
transformation as the result of criticism and reconstruction.
The wider and more articulate the system, the stronger are
its claims to represent reality. There is no finality but only
an increasing coherence, a deeper insight, a more articulate
expression.

It is essential to Hobhouse's point of view that the methods and tests employed in epistemological inquiries are strictly similar to those which thought employs in dealing with other data of experience. Our knowledge of knowledge is arrived at by the action of mental activities on given facts, in this case the processes of knowing. We must deal with them as with other facts—by way of analysis, comparison, and generalisation—and as in other cases again, we must appeal to the convergence and consilience of our judgments as our ultimate test (compare especially *Development and Purpose*, p. 307).

So far there is no essential difference between epistemological and other inquiries, yet there is one peculiarity in the system of cognitions which requires examination. Cognitions, including cognitions of cognitions, regarded as processes in living minds, refer to objects other than themselves; they have, as we say, objective reference. Can this claim to such reference be justified? And how exactly is it to be interpreted?

In dealing with this question Hobhouse seeks to be true to an implication of the organic view of knowledge which, in his opinion, was insufficiently grasped by the Idealists. If he agrees with them that truth is in the whole, he is more eager than they to maintain that the explanation of the whole is to be sought in the interrelation of the parts. In dealing with thought, over-emphasis of the whole leads to a view of knowledge as a closed circle with no reference beyond itself. Hobhouse seeks to show that each partial judgment refers beyond itself to an object, and that the body of judgments which constitutes the system of knowledge is an ordered and coherent reference to reality, the test of orderliness being mutual consistency. In working out his conception of objective reference Hobhouse may be regarded as one of the founders of modern realism, though he has no sympathy with some of the more recent forms of realism which tend to reduce the cognitive function to a minimum, or to regard it as merely a conational direction of the mind upon things.

In setting out his own realistic theory, Hobhouse seeks to refute the arguments of the opposed views and here, in the main, he turns the results of the Idealists against themselves. He shows that most forms of idealism, in fact, assume the position of Subjective Idealism while pretending to reject it. They all rest on the assumption that what is within the sphere of mind must be in the mind, or that what exists for knowledge exists only by our knowledge. He is concerned to maintain, on the contrary, that from the mere analysis of the nature of knowing nothing can be inferred restricting the sphere of what is known or knowable. What they are can only be learned from the reports of our immediate judgments in so far as they can be reduced to system. Three types of fallacy are shown by Hobhouse to underlie the Relativist or Subjectivist position. The first is that which is prominent in Berkeley, namely, that in perception it is the perception which is our object. This involves a confusion between the act of assertion or cognition and that which is asserted or cognised. Once this distinction is clearly apprehended, we can see that there is nothing in the cognitive act itself to show that what is cognised must itself be either mental or non-mental. The reference of objects to self or not-self is, in fact, something that cannot be determined by immediate apprehension, but is a problem to be examined by the methods of analysis and generalisation, and its validity depends on our success in applying these methods. The second type of argument is that which is based on Kant and is broadly that the order which is in the world is not found there by the mind but introduced by its fundamental forms or categories. This, Hobhouse regards as in the main disposed of by the work of the post-Kantian Idealists. The notion that order in nature is due to the apprehending mind was rendered necessary by the assumption that what was given in sense perception was a formless manifold. The critics of Kant had shown that such a chaotic manifold of sense was a figment due to false abstraction and an insufficient analysis of immediate apprehension. But in insisting that even in sense awareness relations were already involved, the Idealists have undermined their own position, for if the relationless sense datum was a figment there appears to be no reason for ascribing relations to the work of the mind, and the order of the world could accordingly be properly regarded not as an attribute of mental operations but as a characteristic discerned in real relations. There remains the more general argument that knowledge is relative because it involves a relation between subject and object. Hobhouse finds it sufficient to retort with Riehl, "Relativ ist nicht das Sein der Objekte, sondern ihr Objektsein". To know is to be in a relation, but it does not follow that the relation is the only thing known. "All that the argument legitimately proves is that B, to be known by A, comes into that relation to A which we call being known. From such a tautology no human skill can educe a substantial result either positive or negative" (*Development and Purpose*, p. 257).

We may now proceed to a more detailed account of the analysis that Hobhouse offers of knowledge. Cognition consists of two elements in a relation: (1) an act of mind aware of asserting, considering, suggesting (2) an object. The object (*a*) may or (*b*) may not be a constitutive part of the act of assertion itself. In either case (3) the content of the asserting act is what it asserts. In the case (*a*) the object and the content are one. The asserting act then asserts that its content *is*. In the case (*b*) content and object are two, but the content involves, or rather is, a reference to an object other than itself. The content is a constituent part of the assertion, but it is not the content which is asserted, but the object. True assertion is the assertion of an object which exists, and the relation may be named one of correspondence between assertion and object. If the assertion is false the asserted object does not exist. If the question be raised—How reference can be made to an object which does not exist, the answer is to be found in a revised definition of the reference in the content. Instead of saying that the content involves a reference to an object beyond itself, we should say that it refers to a body or system of objects which collectively we may call reality, of which it is one, though, of course, a microscopic part. What is asserted then is that reality contains a certain object, or a certain object as entering into, constituting a part of, reality, the part of reality and the relation of the object to other elements of reality being more or less defined according to the particular nature of the assertion. If the assertion is true, reality does contain the object as asserted. If false, it does not. In the latter case it is true to say that the precise object asserted does not exist. Neither is there reference to it in the content. The reference is to reality as a whole. What we are saying in denial is, in fact, that there is no object corresponding to the assertion, or (compare Stout) that the reality referred to does not correspond to the assertion which refers to it.

We may now deal with the case (a) where the assertion is taken as asserting only its own content. It may be questioned whether this is ever a true analysis of assertion, though admitted *prima facie* as a possible case. If the assertion is referent to a system of reality, then even if it asserts its own content it places the content in reality. It may thus be the case that the distinction between object and content falls to one of aspects. As having a place in reality, that which is asserted is object. As constituting a part of the element of reality which is the act asserting it, it is content. It is, however, perhaps more conducive to clearness to suggest that the supposed case is to be regarded as one in which a state of the asserting consciousness is the true object of the assertion. If we take this view, we may describe assertion generally as an act or state having a definite character called its content which is referent to a system of reality (within which it is an element) and with which it corresponds if the assertion is true, and does not correspond if it is false. This is, of course, not a definition, for assertion is indefinable. It is merely a description of the relation of act, content and object, and reality, in assertion. The act asserts reality to contain a certain element. Reality so characterised is said to be its object. If reality does contain the element, the object asserted exists, and the assertion is said to correspond with reality and to be true. If not, no object exists in correspondence with the assertion. Reality, as actually characterised, does not correspond with it, and it is false. True or false, the assertion has a character belonging to it as an existent; this is its content. The content consists of the asserted reference to reality as constituted in a definite manner. It corresponds with the object of the assertion if true. If false it does not correspond, but still exists as characterising the assertion. In either event it may be the object of another act of assertion, but as content it is not the object of the assertion which contains it. The content is asserted in the sense that it is constitutive of the asserting act. The object is asserted in a sense that is indefinable but which involves reference to a reality transcending the asserting act. Assertion is of an object; the specific character (as distinct from the general assertiveness) of the assertion is its content. Whether what is given in apprehension is the kind of content which exists merely as a qualification of the asserting act, or whether it exists independently and transcends the act, cannot be determined by immediate intuition. It was the mistake of naïve realism to start with the assumption that the independence of the percept is immediately given; while subjective idealism assumed that the object is first given as inward. In Hobhouse's view it is not in fact given as either, and the determination of its nature in this respect involves judgment and inference, resting on a study of the behaviour and relations of the object in question.

The Forms of Assertion.—Hobhouse distinguishes four

forms of assertion—simple apprehension, analytic attention, memory, construction.

Apprehension may be described as immediate consciousness. By saying that it is immediate we mean that the entertainment of the content *eo ipso* involves the assertion. In
mediate assertions the content may be entertained without
being asserted; the assertion requires something more than
the content to determine it, and by this something it is said
to be mediated. Apprehension is an assertion or cognition
of the present. There is probably no way of defining the
presence of an object to the mind except by giving the time
reference and the sense reference. What Hobhouse calls
apprehension seems to be equivalent to what some writers
have called knowledge by acquaintance. It should be noted,
however, that he does not assert that such knowledge ever
exists by itself in the sense of forming the whole state of
consciousness for the time being, but merely that such an
activity is found by analysis in many of our mental states
which as concrete entities may be very complex and contain
much more besides apprehension. It is definitely to be distinguished from judgment, which involves reference to what
is not present, and characterisation in general terms. Apprehension as such is not the assertion of general attributes.
This does not prevent what is apprehended as present being
in fact, and capable of being later known as, the correlate of
countless other terms. The fact *is* a centre of relations, but
this we do not know in simple apprehension. Hobhouse is
anxious to maintain that the contents of immediate consciousness are not necessarily simple units between which
relations are only established as a result of thought; on the
contrary, the contents of apprehension are concrete and
continuous wholes within which elementary relations, including time and space relations, are directly apprehended
exactly as are elementary qualities.

Relations as well as qualities may thus be given in concrete wholes, but as given or presented, they are not singled

out or distinguished. In analytic attention we become aware
of any element of the given as a part of a whole distinct from
other parts. Analytic attention does not necessarily advance
beyond the present; it is rather a movement of attention
within the sphere of the given. Through it we are aware of
a whole, but also of points or parts or aspects within it. The
process of analysis facilitates the formation of general ideas,
and is facilitated by them, but as such it is not the formation
of general ideas since it need not go beyond the present, nor
is it a subsumption under a general idea.

Memory is used in two senses: (1) the power of asserting
anything that has once become known, (2) the power of
asserting that something has been presented to the self.
Memory is not to be explained as an identity of past and
present, or as a continued presence of the actual past fact.
The remembered fact is not present to the mind like the
apprehended fact; it is asserted and asserted as past, as
having been presented, but as being presented no longer.
How it is to be explained, Hobhouse does not consider, but
he insists that, however explained, it is an ultimate postulate
of knowledge and cannot be resolved into any sort of inference from premises not themselves involving it.

The fourth factor in knowledge is construction. This
appears in many forms. Generically it is the assertion of a
content never apprehended as a whole, but composed of
elements every one of which has been apprehended, or
otherwise arrived at, before its work begins. A simple illustration may be taken from the comparative judgment, when
one element is given as present and the other remembered.
In such a case we put together or construct, say, A and B,
and detect the resemblance as a part of the whole A–B by
analysis; or, again, in watching a long process we are not
aware of the whole as a present fact, but can assert the whole
only as a result of a memory synthesis constructing or
bringing together all the contents given into the compass of
a single assertion. In actual fact analysis, memory, and con-

struction are not normally isolated, but work together on what is given. We analyse what we construct and the elements of our construction are arrived at by analysis. Apprehension and memory are relatively constant factors in the growth of knowledge. The varying complex forms of judgment and thought result from the repetition and combination of acts of construction and analysis.

Construction operating on the contents supplied by simple apprehension, analytic attention, and memory, produces many forms of assertion; for example, synthetic memory, comparison indefinite and definite, and general ideas. Comparison, it should be noted, is not a distinct faculty; it is the apprehension of given relations of resemblances and differences. In the simpler forms it is nothing but the analysis of the given directed to these relations. In the more complex forms the detection of the resemblances or differences presupposes an act of construction; for example, a combination of memory with present perception. Analytic comparison varies in definiteness. We may know vaguely that A resembles B, or we may ascertain that A is like B because they are identical in the point P. Repetition of such acts of analytic comparison will eventually give rise to the converse judgment. P is identical in A and B. We then come to have a content occurring in more than one fact. If P is often repeated, A and B are lost sight of in memory, and we get the notion of P as qualifying several apprehended facts, that is, as a general content. The generality of a content means that that is suggested of it which has been found in other cases by comparison. It implies similarity of content qualifying facts differing numerically or otherwise. Some plurality is essential though the number is indefinite. A general idea may thus be described as "A content suggested as qualifying reality at many points constituting a resemblance between those parts of reality which contain it" (*Theory of Knowledge*, p. 98).

Abstract and Concrete.—Reality is extended in space and

time. The total that fills a part of space during a part of time is concrete existence. A concrete has characters, and each character may be an object of thought. The character is real in the sense that it is an element in reality, but it is not real except as an element in the total to which it belongs. The relation of any character to the united total is called the relation of attribute to the whole. Concrete existence is thus unitary; it is also both continuous and discrete. A character is continuous throughout a region of space or time which extends through the region without break or change; thus continuity rests ultimately on identity of character. When, in such an extension, there is a change in point of the character considered, there is in that respect discreteness. If beyond this point of change there is an object indistinguishable in point of the character considered, then we have two instances of the character. The two character elements of reality are discrete. When characters are united in some specific mode, and when the total thus formed extends over a certain space-time, we have continuity of concrete existence. If this form of union persists to a point and then a change occurs, the point is the limit of the concrete existence, which then may be called one individual. Beyond the point is another individual discrete from the first.

Now characters are related by resemblances and differences revealed by analytic attention, and giving rise, as we have seen, to the general content. The universal is a system or scheme of affinities among individuals. Thus, for example, green includes all the greens in a relation of affinity. It is not merely the relation of affinity but the terms in the relation, or the system of affine elements. All greens are not identical; they may differ from one another in saturation or intensity or in actual greenness. When I say the sea is green I assert that the colour of the sea falls within the range of greens without assigning it a more definite place within the system. With this view may be contrasted that of Professor Stout. He says: "When I assert that the sense datum is red

I mean just that particular red with which I am immediately acquainted. I cannot mean any other because there is no other belonging to this particular datum" (*Arist. Proc.*, 1914–15, p. 348). Hobhouse, I think, would have said that in using the general term "red" I am placing the datum in the range or system of reds indefinitely while distinguishing it from other colours. I am regarding it, in fact, as an instance of red. The essence of generality is not to be found in a mode of existence which is not individual. Individuality and generality are not mutually exclusive. The general terms employed in describing an individual bring out the points in which it resembles other things, but a thing does not lose individuality by entering into relations to other things. Hence it is misleading to assert, as is often done, that of the individual nothing can be known but what is general (compare Hobhouse "Some Problems of Conception", *Mind*, N.S., vol. vi, No. 22, p. 12). The term universal stands for a system of affinity; it is ambiguously used of any element in such a system: this should be called a character. A character exists as something real and is universal only in the sense that it is an instance or realisation of a system of affines. To predicate a universal is to assign a subject to the system, that is, to correlate it with all its affinities.

Judgment.—The special function of the judgment is to characterise what is given in terms of ideal contents, that is, contents which have become definite and constant objects of reference, and therefore nameable. Hobhouse here in the main follows Bradley and Bosanquet, but he is anxious to point out that when a judgment is described as qualifying reality by ideal content, it is not implied that the judgment institutes the reference to reality, but only that it asserts it. The reference to reality is already contained in the idea, but there only as a suggestion. The judgment asserts it. What the judgment asserts is that the total S in which, say, M has been singled out is also P, or has P as an element in it. Four forms of judgment are distinguished—the qualitative, the comparative, the relative, and the descriptive. In (a) the qualitative judgment we analyse an apprehended fact and assert a resemblance of the element analysed to elements in other wholes. We regard it as a case of a general content, that is, as a centre or nucleus of resemblance to an indefinite mass of facts. The explicitness of the generality of the idea varies from case to case. In (b) the comparative judgment we assert resemblances of two or more facts in point of a known general quality, or, put in another way, we assert a general quality to exist in two or more facts. For example, these colours are alike in tint or in intensity or in saturation; these notes are of one pitch, of different timbre. Such a judgment involves a repeated construction of the relations of the two qualities to one another, and of the conformity of both to the general quality contained in the idea. The qualitative judgment results from a combination of idea with analytic attention; the comparative judgment asserts the relation between some of the individuals to which the idea applies.

(c) The relative judgment: A relation is a distinctive character of a whole constituted by two or more terms. The relation is something asserted of the two terms together, a characteristic, therefore, of the whole. Thus in A is before B we have the whole—A–B, two distinguishable parts, and the relation between them. Since each of the three words used is of a general character, we thus have as our content two given qualities as cases of two general qualities in a relation which is a case of a general relation.[1]

---

[1] It may be remarked in passing that in his account of relations, Hobhouse supplies an answer to the well-known difficulty of the infinite regress raised by Bradley, in a manner essentially similar to that subsequently made by Stout, James, and others. The point may be put briefly thus: relations between terms are not related to the terms; that they appear to do so is due to the fact that relations are ordinarily based on some analysis of terms. Thus ARB means that A as a RB as b. The uniting relation here is not ARB but aRb. Now aRb may be regarded as an attribute of ARB and therefore as related to it, but R is not related to aRb. R is non-existent apart from ab and the relation aRb is not related to ab, is not an attribute of the whole ab but is the whole. a or b may exist apart but ab is aRb and R is ab and aRb is ab.

(d) *The Descriptive Judgment.*—The qualitative judgment concentrates on one element singled out by analytic attention and relates it to a general content. It does not describe the fact as a whole. The relative judgment puts different elements together, but tends to lose sight of the whole to which they belong. The descriptive judgment, exemplified in the description of a person or landscape, keeps the whole in view by detailing the parts. It thus implies a repetition of the act of analysis, and in the complete form would exhaust the whole nature of the given by enumerating all its aspects and parts, and relating them to general contents. It is, in fact, nothing but an elaboration of the judgment of quality and relation.

We come now to the general character of judgment in so far as it may be regarded as the attribution of a predicate to a subject, and we may say that, broadly, judgments can be reduced to two types. In the first, we start with a whole, S, in which we single out, say, M and then find that what is M is also P. The reason for using the terms S and M to indicate the subject of the proposition is to bring out what Hobhouse terms "the ambiguity of the subject" which has given rise to many puzzles about predication. Thus, for example, Bradley has argued: "If you predicate what is different, you ascribe to the subject what it is not; and if you predicate what is not different you say nothing at all." Hobhouse's answer is that "We predicate that which the subject really is but is not apart from the predication known to be". Thus, for example, looking at a stone I may first see its size and colour and then, say, its roughness. What I assert then is that that which is big and greyish has also a rough surface. Of course, the colour is not the size, but in S what has colour M has also size. The whole complex has P as an element in it. In the second type of judgment—the relative judgment—for example, A is like B or before B, our subject is really the two terms A and B, and the relation is asserted as holding of them, or characterising them as taken together. Thus we may again regard the predication as the qualification of a whole by a character. The judgment either starts with a relatively indefinite whole, distinguishes parts, and interrelates them, or it may start with parts distinct and then bring them together. The taking together, or the distinguishing, is the work of the judgment, and the total content of the judgment is always more than that of any of its terms.

The types of judgment so far described would enable a mind to deal with facts so as to arrange them in a spatio-temporal order, and to classify them according to resemblances and differences. They have, however, been treated as confined in the main to what is or has been matter of apprehension. We must now consider the further development of thought which enables it to transcend the given.

Forms of Inference.—Inference is a process of construction proceeding from a datum to a conclusion in which the datum is the ground or condition from which the conclusion follows as a necessary consequence. Broadly, the problem is to show by what methods thought can move from a partial experience to a knowledge which extends indefinitely beyond it. The answer is that it proceeds essentially (*a*) by analysis and synthesis, leading to the formation of wholes, not necessarily found as wholes in the empirical order, and possessed of characters not necessarily present in any of its original constituents. (*b*) By generalising the relations so found. (*c*) By systematisation of the results so established, and their mutual correction or corroboration.

The function of reason is essentially to interconnect, and this consists in the discovery of grounds for the existence of anything in any given relation, and, in drawing out the consequences, of truths already established. The media of interconnection we find in the sensible continuity of experience, and in the resemblances between things which enable us to discover characters common to the different objects of experience. In naïve thought we argue from resemblance and continuity, but later we learn to criticise our procedure, and an analysis of the grounds of our criticism shows that there are certain assumptions which underlie all reasoning. Confining ourselves, for the moment, to generalisation, it can be shown that we argue from observed uniformity, and when we inquire what is implied in any generalisation, we find that it implies what Hobhouse calls the Principle of the Ground or the Inductive Principle. Every datum of experience has a ground with which it is connected universally, or as such. A ground generically is such that if a judgment asserting it is true, then another judgment asserting something else called a consequent is true. It is assumed in reasoning that if an element in reality has another element as its consequent, a precisely similar element will always have a precisely similar consequent. The consequent is said to be true of the ground "as such", and this means true of it in its general character, that is, the character of the object as distinguished from all its surroundings, its location in space and time. What is true of the object as such is true of it whenever and wherever it exists. On the basis of this assumption we conclude that in any observed relation G–F, F is either the consequent of G or of some other term which is not a consequent of G. Hence, further, if G_1, G_2 are data precisely similar in respect of G, then if G_1 is related to F_1, given G_2, F_2 will be similarly related to it unless there is a difference in the circumstances (c) which has a difference in F as its consequent. In other words, any observed relation is universal unless there are facts related to it a change in which has a change in the relation as its consequent. It follows that if we observe any relation and can deny that it is consequent of any other fact, we can generalise it. There are thus two evidential factors in generalisation; the first is the observation G–F; the second is evidence of whatever nature bearing on the existence of other facts which are the grounds of one of its terms. Put in another way, given G–F, we assume the relation to be general. If we find G2 without F, we inquire into the ground of the difference and we find this ground either by showing that (1) G2 is not really precisely similar to G1 or (2) there is a difference in the circumstances outside G. We think, in short, that one difference implies another. It is clear that this implies that F has a ground, for else a change in the relation G–F would not disturb us. Inductive procedure seeks to disentangle what is uniform in different complexes and to eliminate possible concomitant circumstances which may account for one of the terms in the relation. The problem of induction is to eliminate or rebut such external grounds, and so to establish the observed relation as universal.

It must be added that there is a similar implication in the application of a general principle deductively to a given case. If the result expected does not follow, we try to explain the deviation by the presence of concomitant modifying circumstances involving the operation of another principle modifying the action of the first. The principle of the ground thus underlies induction and the use of deduction in the unravelling of phenomena. It is thus fundamental in any interpretation of experience that goes beyond the given.

The principle of the ground, when applied to objects in space and time, gives rise to the principle of continuity (Substance and Causality). Consider first a persistent identity A, and take a series of points or sections of the identity—A1, A2, A3. By the principle of the ground A1–A2 is either universal so that we have A–A, or the consequent of some other ground. In the former case since A2 is in character A, we have A2–A3, etc., that is, a self-determining persistence or substance. In the latter event we shall have persistence unless a change occurs elsewhere in reality which has a change in A for its consequent. Contrast with this the relation A–B, A and B being events, and A not being B or a process which being continued becomes B. Then by the principle of the ground, since A does not give rise to B in this case, it will not do so in any other case. Thus, given A, there must be a change such as produces B. A as such does not produce B. Let C act on A. Then either we have A–C unchanging. This will not yield B without a further cause, and so *ad infinitum*; or A–C is a process of change. Let this change be from A–C to D. Then if D continues it will not yield B without external grounds, and similarly, if D yields E. But if E in continuing becomes B, then A–C may become B without external condition. Hence A can only give rise to B by becoming B immediately or mediately. The point may perhaps be put somewhat more briefly thus: If B is not immediately preceded by A, then it is not produced by A as such. Hence B will not in any case be produced by A unless there is a circumstance C which in conjunction with A is universally followed by B. There must be continuity in transition.

In inductive inquiries we look for self-determining persistences and changes; that is, persistences and changes which are independent of their settings or environment. In general, an inductive argument is a synthesis of two sets of considerations. One of these consists in the observation and analysis of the relation in question and the other of the observation and analysis of concomitants. Positive evidence alone gives no ground of probability, but with the negation of negative evidence does so. If specific negative evidence is negated, there is ordinary practical certainty with a reserve of the general possibility of unobserved concomitants. Negation of evidence is of two kinds. We may show by a negative instance that a given concomitant R is not a ground of C, but that it is not a factor in the ground, replaced in another instance by a given factor S, is not capable of direct inductive disproof. On the other hand, we have just as much difficulty in proving C–B as A–B. The elimination of the doubt, or its measurement, is the problem of induction.

Into the detail of the methods employed by scientific induction it is impossible to enter here. A lucid account of them will be found in the *Theory of Knowledge*, chapters xiii–xv. Here only the general character of inductive procedure can be indicated. The main points appear to be these. The inductive principle tells us that a given or observed relation of elements is either universal or follows universally from some other element. The other element must not be one from which either of the terms of the given relation follows. Otherwise the relation would still be universal. Such an element may be called a concomitant. A given relation then is either universal or the universal consequent of a concomitant. This assumption is really the same as the assumption that everything has a ground applied to a world of intermixed concomitants. If everything has a ground, the relation A–B either has its ground in A, so that given A there will always be B in that relation to it, or the relation A–B has its ground in something else, and if this something else varies in relation to A, then the relation A–B varies. Our object in inductive procedure is to eliminate the concomitants. The ground for asserting the relation A–B is ultimately observation of the relation. If the observation is not uniformly confirmed there is so far reason for doubt, but given no exception in our observation, suggestions of specific external grounds as possible conditions may still be made on the ground of cognate experiences. These possible grounds we seek to remove by the inductive methods, and it must be admitted that owing to possibly inadequate analysis and the difficulty of isolating cause factors, there remains in such procedure an element of doubt. In regard to such doubt it must be remembered, however, that doubt itself should be grounded, and in respect of such grounds the same difficulties will arise as in the proof of the relation under consideration. There is, secondly, a more important resource. We may appeal to the convergence of independently arrived at probable generalisations. There are several varieties of such methods of corroboration; thus, for example, the causes under investigation may be examined in different degrees and quantities, or again in composition with one another. If there is no reason to believe in the likelihood of precisely the same errors affecting the different investigations, the induction is so far strengthened. Again, inductions separately arrived at may support one another, or may form parts, each with a probability of its own, of a whole or a larger induction also independently arrived at with a probability of *its* own. In short, induction as it is practised in the sciences appears as a growing body of judgments mutually supporting one another, in which the dependence of the several component inductions becomes gradually clearer, so strengthening their own probability and concurrently the probability of the system as a whole. There are no fixed truths serving as ultimate starting-points, but a mass of judgments in process of attaining certainty, gathering clearness, connection, and vigour as it grows.[1]

We may now turn from generalisation in which we arrive at a universal, asserting an indefinite number of facts that are not given on the strength of certain facts that are given, to the methods whereby universals are interconnected, or, more generally, to the way in which concepts are applied to one another or to percepts. Essentially the process is one of analysis and synthesis, or, better, of analytic construction. Two main types may be distinguished: (*a*) subsumptive reasoning, typified in the syllogism; (*b*) other forms of construction, for example, in mathematics, in which two or more relations are combined and the resultant relation asserted.

In subsumption, for example, in the syllogism, we construct a whole out of the elements which are given in the premises and then detect by analysis a feature or relation within the whole (compare Bradley). The major really states a universal, that is, a connection of content, A as such

---

[1] *Cf.* especially Induction and Probability, *Development and Purpose*, Pt. II, ch. iv.

is B, and the minor applies this to a particular. So again, if we infer this is A because it is B, we raise the question—Do you mean that all A is B, or if not, what makes the difference in this case? If you infer, there must be something from which you infer as such, and so universally. Without this assumption there would be only syllogisms with collective major premises. Underlying syllogistic arguments there is thus a general axiom which may be called the Axiom of Analytic Construction. Postulating that we can combine elements into a whole, and conversely, analyse wholes into parts, the axiom asserts that the related elements are the sole and sufficient ground of the wholes which they form, and of any subordinate or emergent characters that we can discern within the whole. Thus in syllogistic reasoning, if we omit any elements that really enter into the whole, or if the character does not really follow from the whole alone, we fall into fallacy.

In non-syllogistic construction a similar axiom may be seen to be involved. Consider $A = B$, $B = C$, therefore $A = C$. Here the first two propositions are constructed into a whole $A = B = C$. Examining this whole, we find it contains the element $A = C_1$. That is $A = B$ and $B = C$ are brought into synthesis and in the whole thus formed $A = C$ is recognised as a constituent fact. Similarly in geometrical constructions. They are only sound if we are assured that in the process of analysis and construction, nothing has been surreptitiously introduced or unconsciously omitted. Results so arrived at can be safely generalised. If we know that in the case before us the elements in combination are the sole ground of the whole and of any subordinate characters distinguished within the whole, we can, by the inductive principle, infer that the relation will hold in all cases. The difficulty here, as in all inductive reasoning, is the difficulty of making sure that no concomitant conditions are present which have escaped our attention, and our generalisations are therefore regarded as holding subject to correction in the light of subtler analysis and corroboration by consilient generalisations. Mathematical generalisations thus rest essentially on the inductive principle combined with the postulate involved in all judgment and construction, namely, that the data used in analysis and construction are the sufficient grounds of the wholes which they form and the results detected in them. The analytical generalisations which lie at the basis of mathematics would appear on this view ultimately to imply the same principles as those of the physical sciences.

The view of the nature of knowledge here briefly sketched implies that methodological and epistemological principles are obtained by a systematic study of the judgments forming the body of knowledge, in other words, by generalisations, which link the thought processes into a consilient whole. Knowledge is truly organic, and there is a mutual connection between all its parts. First principles are neither deductively proved nor intuitively based, but, like all other elements of knowledge, depend for their ultimate validity upon mutual consilience and mutual necessitation in a systematic whole growing in coherence and comprehensiveness. They must not be regarded as *a priori* truths or as assumptions which miraculously turn out to be consistent with experience, but rather as formulations of what is implied in the process of thought so far as it is consistent with itself. The general conclusion with regard to the nature of scientific knowledge that emerges from these considerations is that science is not a purely deductive system, that is, a body of judgments rigidly deducible from first principles supposed to be intuitively given and above criticism, or, as more recent upholders of the deductive view of science would say, hypothetically assumed. Such a view, Hobhouse argues, makes it impossible to bring the body of science conceived as a self-consistent system of truths into relation with truth regarded as a correspondence of judgment with reality. It further tends to blur the distinction between hypotheses which arise as tentative generalisations from observed facts, and others which, owing their origin to the inventive imagination, are but slightly grounded on fact, and are continuously forced to have recourse to a growing series of subsidiary hypotheses in order to be made to fit the facts. But if science is not purely deductive neither is it, in Hobhouse's view, merely descriptive, that is, confined to the analysis and synthesis of observations. Rather is it a growing body of tentative generalisations going beyond actual observation, tested by their coherence and consilience, and moving towards ever greater systematisation, whereby the probability of all the connected elements, as modified by their interconnection, is progressively increased without reaching final certainty.

CHAPTER VI

THEORY OF REALITY

THE general trend of Hobhouse's epistemological inquiries is to validate the processes employed in experiential reconstruction and to justify us in regarding them as likely to lead to an increasingly coherent and reliable account of reality. We turn now to his metaphysical constructions. These are based partly upon arguments derived from his survey of mental evolution and partly upon considerations based on the logical requirements of systematic explanation. He seeks to show that both lines of thought lead us to conceive of the world process as a growth or development of organic harmony effected through the increasing power of mind, working under mechanical conditions which it gradually comes to master or control.

We may first consider what he describes as the "historical" or "empirical" arguments. His survey of orthogenic evolution in the various forms of organic life and in human societies leads in his view to the conclusion that at any rate within the field studied development consists in an extension of harmony, and that the method it employs is that of correlation or the bringing together of elements into relation with one another so as to form a whole. A study of the stages of correlation, whether in the organisation of behaviour in individual organisms or in the formation of societies, suggests that the agent of correlation is mind gradually extending its scope of operation, and arriving at ever-widening syntheses by the discovery of factors of unity in elements apparently unrelated or in conflict. Mind has been shown to be a real agent, operating even below the level of consciousness, but gaining in strength and coherence as it reaches the stage of conscious and articulate purpose and becomes capable of controlling the conditions of its own development. As a measure of the growth of mind, he takes the expansion of the sphere of conscious control of racial life, and his survey shows that there has been such an extension which, if not continuous and direct, is yet of such vast import as to justify the hypothesis that the conditions which make it possible must be permanent or at least of very wide reach. The emergence of so much life and consciousness, the growth of the mind in ever-widening spheres, can hardly be a casual result of a rare concatenation of circumstances, but justifies us, on the contrary, in regarding it as the central fact of the story of evolution. Physical science, moreover, has extended the conception of evolution to the inanimate, and although there are still gaps in the scheme, there seems to be no good ground for doubting the validity of the notion of development connecting the lowest with the highest orders of being. A synthesis of experience shows then that nature is a system which maintains itself amidst the innumerable changes of its parts, and this implies a continuous interrelation of functions. Evolutionary science adds that there is continuous development in the sense that in the processes of change finer and more articulate structural wholes appear. This is taken as evidence of an underlying correlating activity operating continuously with cumulative effect. This correlating activity is of the nature of a nisus or effort, a conational force acting under conditions which limit it, but gradually attaining an increasing mastery over them.

These considerations are supplemented by broader metaphysical arguments, which in Hobhouse's opinion justify us in extending the notion of development, as an extension of harmony due to the efforts of a spiritual principle working under limiting conditions, to the wider whole of reality. His starting-point here is what in the *Theory of Knowledge* he calls the Principle of the Ground, that is, the assumption fundamental in all reasoning, that everything that exists must have a ground in reality. This leads, as we have seen, to the conception of the rational ideal as a system of interconnected judgments asserting a reality of interconnected parts. Each part must have its ground within the whole, but if everything has a ground there can be no unconditioned datum. It follows that the system must consist of elements in a relation of mutual conditioning; in other words, reality is a whole of elements each conditioning and conditioned by the others. The problem is then as to the nature of this interrelation within the whole.

Hobhouse has approached this problem in a variety of ways. He proceeds partly by an examination of the kinds of wholes or species of correlation which we find in experience, and an inquiry into their reducibility and applicability to the world whole; partly by an examination of what is logically involved in the application of the notion of a system of mutually conditioned parts to an order in which there is process and development. The result of the former procedure is to show that of the three types of system revealed in experience—the mechanical, the organic, and the teleological—the mechanical and the teleological are distinct, while the organic is not *sui generis* but may be explained in terms of mechanism qualified by teleological factors. In other words, the various forms of organic life may be interpreted as variations in the interplay between the principle of purposive mutuality and relative indifference or independence of parts, which is identified with the mechanical. When applied to the world whole, the notions of mechanism and organism are shown to be inapplicable, and it is claimed that the facts of development are explicable in terms of a conditioned teleology in which the mechanical and the teleological principles are interwoven. The results of the epistemological analysis is to confirm this conclusion and is directed at showing that the notion of system applied to a developing order involves a conational or teleological element operating on other elements otherwise mutually indifferent.

In following this argument we must first inquire into the

meaning that Hobhouse ascribes to the terms—mechanical, teleological, and organic wholes or systems. Put in the briefest form we may say that, according to him, a whole acts mechanically when its parts act uniformly as a result of forces immediately impinging on each of them, and in a manner which is in principle indifferent to the results of their action or to the state of other parts. A whole acts organically when the operation of the parts is varied in accordance with the requirements of the whole as a self-determining structure. A whole acts teleologically when its acts are determined by their own tendency to produce results affecting the whole. In mechanical wholes, Hobhouse argues, the action of part on part is in principle indifferent to concomitants, and to results or values. This point may be illustrated from man-made machines which though, of course, obviously purposive, yet clearly exhibit the characteristics of mechanism. "In a machine, though all the parts are so compacted as normally to act in relation with one another so as to produce a certain joint result, yet each several part acts uniformly without relation to the rest in response to the forces operating upon it, whatever they may be. The chain of the bicycle is pulled by the teeth of one wheel and pulls the teeth of the other wheel. Normally, in its complete fitting, this serves to propel the bicycle, but if either wheel is in some way out of gear it makes no difference to the chain. Pull it by hand, and the pull will be propagated along its links in just the same way, and will move the wheel into which it fits in just the same way. The action of the part does not depend on the action of any other part as such, but only on the pull or push affecting it, whatever the source of that pull or push may be. Similarly, the action of the part does not depend on any result accruing from the action. Given the pull or push, the action is just the same, whether the result is the normal one of propelling the bicycle, or is simply to whirl the hind-wheel round in the air, or to create a jam and a wreck. In a mechanical whole, then, each part acts uniformly in response to a given force independently of the condition of other parts, and independently of the results of its action" (*Arist. Proc.*, 1917–18, p. 469).

Hobhouse, of course, does not deny that in physical structures the system does in a sense determine the action of each part in such a manner as to maintain itself in the absence of disruptive external forces. But he points out that in all such cases the systems are derived from antecedent collocations and the behaviour of the parts is not determined by the requirements of the whole, but follows at any moment from pre-existent factors or collocations of factors without exhibiting any inner principle of configuration, or self-direction. In organisms, on the other hand, growth, structural and functional modifications, exhibit mutual interdependence of parts relative to the whole. The parts though distinct act so as to maintain the whole, and are dependent on their position in the whole. In other words, the action of the parts is so shaped as to meet their mutual requirements and so to maintain the whole as a whole. In contrast with the mechanical, the parts of an organic system are affected by the combinations in which they enter and assume characteristics specific to the combination. Teleological systems may be best understood by comparison with the mechanical and the organic. They differ sharply from the mechanical in that the acts which enter into the whole are varied, discarded, pushed forward, combined, and in general, so related as to produce a result, while mechanical acts do not vary in accordance with the results that emerge from them. The teleological has more in common with the organic as defined above, for if the end of the series be included within the series we may regard means and ends as mutually necessitating one another, and so to stand in organic relation. Yet in definition, the teleological differs from the organic. The differentia of the latter is mutual conditioning; of the former, determination by relation to ends. The phrase "determination by relation to ends" is not to be interpreted even in the higher forms of purposive endeavour as meaning determination by intended results, for these may not, in fact, be realised. It means, rather, determination by an effort referent to the outcome as it emerges from the given situation and the effort whatever it may be. The reference is explicit in conscious purpose, but below there are, as we have seen, several grades of conational adjustment implying sustained and varied effort and explicable only in terms of a felt want or disturbance of varying explicitness directing action until relief is attained.

Are these conceptions reducible, and how far are they applicable to the types of structure which we find in our experience? Hobhouse thinks, as we have seen, that the mechanical and the teleological differ fundamentally. The mechanical system is determined in its action by the resultant of the forces then and there existing, each having its uniform effect unaffected by the relation of its behaviour to any later stage including the ultimate effect. In the conational system, though the action is determined from moment to moment by the situation at that moment, yet the bearing of the action on the effect is directly or indirectly the determining element in the situation. In the conational system the constituent details are determined by their place in the whole, while the details of the mechanical system are not so determined. In this sense the conational system is determined by its tendency to promote the effect, and this differentiates it from the mechanical system. On the other hand, the organic appears capable of being interpreted in terms either of mechanical or teleological causation, while in its fullest development it involves both. These conclusions are based partly on an analysis of the concepts involved, partly on a consideration of the ways in which they may be fruitfully applied in the interpretation of experience. A survey of living organisms reveals varying degrees of organ-

icity in the sense used above, that is, varying degrees of
mutual dependence and adaptation to the requirements of
the whole as a self-maintaining structure. The problem is to
determine in what way the "requirements" of the whole are
served. The term "requirement" is clearly ambiguous. It may
mean no more than a physical condition falling short of the
normal, or exceeding it, which acts as a stimulus leading to
certain types of action. Thus, for example, if the blood is
insufficiently oxidised, the lack of oxidation may act as a
stimulus on a certain tissue, such as the respiratory centre,
exciting it to an enhanced activity; this would be a mechanical explanation. On the other hand, the term "requirement"
may be teleologically interpreted as implying an effort
determined by a tendency to produce a result. Hobhouse
is not inclined to dogmatise about the extent to which
mechanical explanations may be legitimately applied in the
interpretation of organic activity, but he suggests that the
complexity of the adaptation of part to part, and especially
the power of dealing with novel situations which organisms
possess, make it extremely improbable that they will ever
be reduced to combinations of mechanisms. That a structure
should be transmitted by heredity, and so formed as to
respond appropriately to infinitely varying stimuli and not
merely to type situations, is wildly improbable except on the
assumption, as Hobhouse puts it, of a Calvinistic deity and
a detailed predestination—a view which, apart from other
difficulties, does not get rid of teleology.

The interpretation of the notion of "requirements" in
terms of internal purpose, however, comes up against the
difficulty of imputing ideal direction to lowly forms of life.
This difficulty Hobhouse endeavours to meet by drawing
attention to the more elementary forms of conation. We have
seen that conation may be traced to the simplest organisms
and possibly may be attributed to the cells of the metazoon.
If so, it may be that life itself depends on conation in its
simplest form, and that the mutual adjustments of its parts

are governed by persistent effort at self-maintenance. The
process is conational in the sense that it exhibits persistence
in direction with variation in detail in a manner which suggests a persistent trend or striving. There is presumably no
awareness of the results of the tendency or trend such as
belongs to true purposive or sensori-motor action, but only
continuous effort to maintain balance or equilibrium, every
departure from which stimulates compensatory or supplementary action generally on the lines laid down in the
hereditary system, but occasionally also on novel or experimental lines.

The point may be made clearer, perhaps, by considering
more in detail what is meant by saying that a response is
conditioned by its tendencies. The tendency of a conation
may mean several things. It may be (*a*) a phase of a process
which, as it continues, becomes the end. In a sure and successful purpose we may say that each element of the means
adopted is adopted because of the causal relation in which it
does, in fact, stand to the end, which is, in fact, about to be
produced, while the guiding idea is intrinsically a reference
to the end. It may be (*b*) an element in such a process, a
factor or condition needing other conditions to complete
it. In this case, though the end may not, in fact, be realised
owing to the non-fulfilment of other conditions, yet the
tendency of the step actually taken to promote the end is a
definite character of that step, which really belongs to it,
and it is taken because of that character. It may be (*c*) a
step taken because it is believed to promote the end, though
in fact it does not. Here the position is more ambiguous, but
if we assume, as experience justifies us in doing, that conation is so far successful on the whole, that its ends will much
more often be secured by it than without it, then we may
say that it is the general tendency of the class of act in question to contribute to the class of end in question that determines its adoption in the particular case. Briefly, in the third
case conative action is determined by its generic tendency

to produce the end. (*d*) In the lower forms of conation the end is not defined by anticipation in idea. The conation appears in the form of a continuous, or frequently repeated, series of changes, or departures from every state except the end. This formula applies *pro tanto* to all conations, even clear purpose, for every stage in such purpose is incomplete and stimulates the system to pass beyond it until the end is reached. Experience shows that even the lowest forms of conation, which merely exhibit unrest and random activity in all unsatisfying phases, do on the whole succeed in achieving the satisfying result in large numbers of instances. We may therefore regard such change as an instance of determination by the generic tendency to the production of the end.

On this view the organism would be regarded as a psycho-physical whole in which mechanical modes of action are qualified by teleological ones. Whenever we observe action which varies in accordance with its tendency to produce a result, and with no other observable condition, we are entitled on ordinary inductive principles to impute conation. Investigation shows that psycho-physical organisms differ enormously in their capacity for differential response and the power of correlating and co-ordinating experiences relevantly to wants or ends, and this is, in fact, our ground for assigning them to various grades of mental development. The relation between mind and body is not to be interpreted as one between two substances. The mechanical and the teleological are modes of action or behaviour of the concrete whole, the psycho-physical organism, but these modes of action must not be hypostatised and regarded as substances, nor must the one be regarded as the substance of which the other is the quality. Both qualify the total reality, which may include also other elements which as yet elude our observation and powers of inference. Hobhouse's psychology and biology have thus many affinities with what is called the Hormic point of view. He avoids, however, the animistic tinge sometimes given to this type of theory, since for him the element of teleology is not regarded as constituting a substance but rather as a mode of activity.

We must now consider the applicability of these categories to the whole of reality. The notion of mechanism in the sense used by Hobhouse may be rapidly dismissed. In a mechanical whole the elements are, as such, indifferent, and have in them no principle of union to account for the combinations in which they enter. Any particular combination can only be explained by reference to an anterior combination and so *ad infinitum*. It is clear that such a mode of explanation cannot apply to the whole of reality, for this includes variable combinations or collocations for which only an endless series of external grounds can be found without ever reaching an explanation of collocation as such.

The conception of an organism does offer a ground for combinations. In an organic whole the parts are in a relation of mutual connection and depend on the function which they fulfil in the whole. But taken by itself, Hobhouse argues, the organic principle is inapplicable to reality as a whole. For if the requirements of the whole were the governing condition of the action of each part, there would be complete mutual support or harmony, and the world would not exhibit the phenomena of disruption, dissolution, and conflict. The world is, in a sense, a unity. It has also an element of conflict or antagonism, and at lowest, of indifference. The organising principle cannot be such as completely to determine the relations of the parts that enter into the system of reality; and if the organic conception is to be used at all in reference to the world whole, it is only on the understanding that the elements which make up the whole condition and limit the whole as much as the whole limits the parts. The conception of organic union, moreover, suffers from the same defect as that of mechanism in that it fails to account for variable collocations (cf. *Development and Purpose*, p. 437). It would seem that reality is made up of elements which are partly self-determining and "mutually indifferent" yet also correlated and brought into a condition of systematic interdependence, and this is not in accord either with the conception of complete mechanism or complete organism.

We may now inquire whether the conception of teleology is better adapted to express the nature of reality as a system, and in what way the relation between the teleological and the organic principle is to be conceived. We have seen that the law of the ground applied to reality as a self-contained whole implies that reality is a system of mutually connected parts in which each is conditioned by, and conditions, the remainder. Now, Hobhouse argues, if this notion of a system of reciprocally determining parts is applied to an order in which there is development, we obtain a continuum in which conditioning is not unilateral; in which, therefore, any point that we start from as the cause of what follows must be also conditioned by what follows, so that any phase in the process not only determines, but is determined by, successive phases. Now a process which at once determines and is determined by its own outcome, or by a tendency referent to the outcome, is teleological or conational, and the world development therefore falls under this category.[1] It remains to inquire into the relation between the element of purpose and the other elements of the real. Purpose cannot be completely organic with the rest, that is, it cannot arise from their requirements of the elements as such, nor can it completely mould them or determine their nature. Such a conception is incompatible with the facts of conflict and disruption. We must conceive of the conational or teleological element as conditioning the relations between the elements of the real, and so systematising them, but as also conditioned by them, and as itself undergoing change in the process of development. In short, it would seem that there are two principles which have to be recognised in a theory

---

[1] See *Development and Purpose*, p. 425, note, for a modified form of this argument which avoids the reference to temporal distinctions.

of the universe. There is, first, the principle of mechanism, according to which the elements of the real are indifferent to one another. There is, second, the principle of organicity according to which they form a correlated whole. To overcome the contradiction, we must conceive of the correlating principle as not arising out of the elements but as a mind striving towards unity and harmony, operating on elements which, apart from its activity, are indifferent and uncoordinated. In the course of development they are so ordered and reorganised that instead of being checks and hindrances to one another, they are translated on to paths along which they can move freely in adequate co-operation. The argument may perhaps be resumed briefly thus. Reality reveals indifference and conflict, but also an increasing trend towards unity. The unity cannot be that of a mechanical system, for then we should be unable to account for the emergence of varying unitary systems in which the elements appear in varying collocations. Nor can the system be completely organic, in which case the same difficulty would apply, and we should further be unable to account for the element of indifference. We need a system of elements to some extent self-determining, and thus so far in principle indifferent to the action of other elements, but also containing something in them that makes for mutual determination and growing correlation. The correlating factor is conational. It may be supposed to operate through trial and error, and later through conscious purpose. It proceeds by a series of syntheses from that which is manifested in the emergence of the structured wholes of the physical world to that of living organisms and societies of organisms. The process is, however, neither unitary nor direct. It involves continual disturbance of equilibria, and is thus a potential source of conflict. In the higher phases the process comes to some extent to be consciously directed, yet even then its problems are not thereby necessarily simplified. The power behind development, or the correlating agency, Hobhouse

calls Mind. This, though coeval with reality, is not all
reality, but only an element within it, and like other elements
determining and determined. The system is thus to a certain
extent pluralistic, since it supposes elements indefinitely
numerous, each in a measure self-determining; yet the system is organic, for the self-assertiveness of the parts also
constitutes their contribution to the whole by which they
are conditioned. The principle of unity does not generate
the parts, nor does it absorb them; it merely conditions them
as it is conditioned by them. We thus have strictly neither a
monism nor a pluralism, but a system of elements, distinct
yet mutually conditioned.

The conception of the evolutionary order that emerges
from the preceding considerations may be pictured somewhat as follows. We may assume as the limit of the undeveloped a mass of elements each with its own energy and
power of self-assertion, but unco-ordinated and therefore
thwarted or inhibited. These original elements are not to be
identified with matter. Matter is itself a compound and its
constituents are not necessarily themselves material. Development begins by a rearrangement of the forces and
their liberation, with the result that they come to work
in definite relations to one another and so to build up
enduring structures. In what we call material or physical
structures the original non-material elements are linked
together in a peculiar way so as to form wholes of various
types, but such that the mode of action of each part persists
in whatever combinations it may enter. Living structures
are not to be conceived as having originated from dead
matter, but rather from the original pre-material elements
out of which the inanimate is also formed but on a more
intimate principle of union. On this view the living substance, though possessed of ascertainable physical and
chemical properties, has yet as a whole a specific kind of
activity distinct from that of formed matter. Living organisms, since they consist of a fusion of the mechanical and

conational principles, retain an element of "indifference" to others and therefore of potential antagonism; hence the clash of forces and the struggle for existence. Further advance is achieved through the growing power of correlating experiences acquired by individual minds as we ascend the scale of animal evolution, and by the gradual supersession of the principle of struggle by that of co-operation, mutual aid, and the growth of sociality. How changes of type come about is, of course, still a matter of dispute. Hobhouse points out that, in any event, such change involves a new synthesis, for though the innovation may be traceable to variation or mutation in a single factor, yet for the variation to succeed it must be harmonised and co-ordinated with the other factors so as to form a new whole. In what way these changes are connected with conational effort is difficult to say in the present stage of our knowledge, but Hobhouse suggests that the method is one of trial and error, that is, indirectly by acting on the environment the mind improves the chances of survival on the part of variations which are in harmony with the requirements of the racial life at a given stage of development (cf. *Contemporary British Philosophy*, vol. i, p. 181). The growth of sociality has already been discussed, and need not here be further elaborated. Thus the correlating factor is conceived as making its way gradually through differential forms of grouping and by ever-widening syntheses extending its scope of operations, and becoming at last conscious of its efforts in the growth of humanity. The process of development, it will be seen, is made up of a great number of partial developments, that is, the emergence of innumerable structures and organisms, though in the higher phases it tends to become unified and purposive. It is argued, however, that in a sense the partial developments are applications of a principle working on a cosmic scale, and the expression of an underlying unity and interconnection. The comprehensive purpose is not to be conceived as emerging by chance from the clash of separate forces. Throughout, the element of mutuality is operative, and as this is conational in character it does not passively accept the results of contending forces, but tries, throws out efforts, and seeks to dominate them. Development consists in the gain of the correlating element over that of mechanical indifference. But, since it first expresses itself in partial centres, each with a life and mind of its own, the process gives rise to continual disturbance of equilibria, which in turn leads to further efforts at harmonisation by new methods of liberation and co-ordination. The development does not result in the creation of new energy, but rather in the release of energies already present, but so locked as to inhibit one another; and it proceeds throughout on principles of interconnection which pervade the universe and are coeval with it.[1]

How is this correlating agency to be conceived? Hobhouse, as we have seen, speaks of it as Mind, or as the Central Mind, and he insists that it is neither the whole of things nor the omnipotent creator of things, but only a factor within the whole conditioned in its operations by, though subduing as it advances, the equally real and significant element of disharmony. A study of his various expositions will enable us to amplify somewhat this very general statement. Firstly, it is not to be identified with the Mind-Stuff of certain recent theorists, for the Central Mind does not exist in scattered atoms, but is a principle of unity inherent in all process. Secondly, it is not to be conceived on the analogy either of the individual mind or personality or of that of the union of personalities effected in social groupings. Individual minds perhaps are among its constituents, but they contain within themselves elements of assertiveness and particularism, and to that extent are expressions of the opposing element of mechanism or indif-

[1] For a discussion of the difficulties arising out of applying notions implying time to the whole of reality, reference may be made to *Development and Purpose*, p. 271, seq. and the essay in *Contemporary British Philosophy*, vol. i.

ference. So, too, the social group has in it elements of contingency which differentiate it sharply from the kind of unity of which we are in search. In any event, the Central Mind must be conceived as operating long before organic life, and accordingly individual minds, appear. They are, therefore, in a sense its products. The permanent Central Mind is, rather, a common factor in the growth and being of minds as we know them in individuals or groups. Their growth and evolution, in other words, depends on deeper conditions of unity and principles of interrelation which they do not invent but find. It is the systematising agency which is the ground of these conditions to which Hobhouse, with full consciousness of its inadequacy, gives the name of the Central Mind.

In essence the conception rests upon two facts. Firstly, that reality is a system of elements exhibiting growing correlation, and secondly, that the correlation is not derived from the elements as such or necessitated by them. There must, therefore, be a ground behind the indifference of the elements working for unity. This ground of correlation is in a sense another element or factor, that, namely, which systematises the rest. Its mode of operation has the generic character of conation, and, in the higher phases, of purpose. This is what is meant by calling it a Mind, but it is a process or activity rather than a substance, and it is interfused, though in varying degrees, with the physical and the organic throughout reality (cf. Important Note in *Contemporary British Philosophy*, p. 177). We may perhaps put the point in Hobhouse's own words. "It is itself an aspect of, or element in, reality—just that aspect in which all elements are correlated. It is, in fact, the principle of interconnection among elements, each with tendencies of its own, by which it is strictly conditioned. Abstract this relation and we have the reverse aspect, under which each element acts in indifference to the remainder. In the concrete both aspects, the Teleological and Mechanical, are presented and their interweaving is the fundamental characteristic of Reality" (*ibid.*, p. 182).

This general position, Hobhouse thinks, is supported both by an empirical study of mental evolution and by an analysis of the logical presuppositions of knowledge, and he claims that its peculiar strength lies in that both types of argument lead, in the main, to the same conclusion. But above all, it is strengthened by certain deep-rooted convictions which, in his view, must form the fixed points of any rational philosophy and which rest, not so much on argument, as on simple, direct, and deeply felt experiences. Of these experiences we had better let him speak for himself. "The First is the conviction of goodness—goodness neither laid up in heaven nor moving as a metaphysical principle upon earth, but warm and real in the hearts of living men and women. There are those whose faith is founded on inner certainty of the Divine. There are others of us who have seen something of the qualities we call divine in man, sometimes doubtless sadly broken and mingled with a different clay, yet bearing to any understanding mind the ineffaceable stamp. And there are those more greatly privileged who have learnt to know some nature crystal-clear, compact of mother-love, with thoughts by instinct bent on others' needs, sensitively tender, yet of indomitable spirit, fearless, and believing no evil, through very selflessness enjoying and reflecting the charm of life. This, the sceptic may say, is to describe a woman as a man sees her in the hour of romance. It may be so, and it may be that in that hour some real things flash out which are afterwards obscured. Be that as it may, there are not wanting those who have put the vision to the test of lifelong companionship only to find it gaining in clearness and truth. No other relation of life can yield such intimacy of understanding, yet comradeship in great causes does not fail to reveal men of noble thought and faithful heart, men who sink themselves in their mission, but do not let their friends sink, men whose staunchness stands the test of long years. The being of such men and women is not a matter of faith but of experience, though an experience which like every other requires the eye that can see. But what general conclusions can philosophy draw from it? you ask. If there are the noble and the good, are there not also the mean-spirited and the knaves? Why should the one be more significant than the other? To this question the theory of development supplies a ready answer. The failures are the undeveloped, and if you would know what development can do you must look at the successes. More precisely we conceive the elements of things acting severally each on its own lines, and yet drawn together in a relation which at its height becomes Love. Whatever is repellent, fearful, suspicious, unimaginative, brutal has remained, relatively speaking, self-centred. All that love touches has the nobler quality. But of this we may be sure. No man or woman such as I have ventured to speak of, nor yet any such quality as theirs, though less developed and marred with imperfections, ever came out of the clay, unless the clay itself has mind. No rational observer (if we may revert to that fancy) from another universe would admit such a hypothesis. With the utmost allowance for what development could do he would demand some continuity, and if he was assured that their origin was from matter he could only infer that matter was alive and instinct with some very wonderful imaginations. As the geologist is sure that the isolated boulder does not spring out of the alluvial on which it rests, but is a detached fragment of the mother rock, so with even stronger logic would he refer the radiant soul to its matrix of spiritual being. Every detailed hypothesis of origin that we may construct may be faulty. The immanent spirit may be no nearer the truth than the transcendent Creator. The idea of development may pass away like that of special creation. One truth will stand firm. The world which has engendered such beings as we have known, is no mean world. It is a world worth living and fighting for, the world which they have trodden. It is the dwelling of a spiritual power, be it what it may, which will some day come into its own, be that how it may. Of the how and the why our philosophies give what account they can, but behind them lies something surer than faith, firmer than abstract reasoning, those most intimate and sure experiences which reveal the true capabilities of the human soul" (*Contemporary British Philosophy*, vol. i, pp. 187–8).

CHAPTER VII

CONCLUSION

WE have now surveyed Hobhouse's chief contributions to social science, psychology, and philosophy. It may be well, in conclusion, to bring out the guiding ideas which inspired all his work, and to indicate his position in the general history of thought. It will, I think, be found that two closely interwoven conceptions lay at the root of all his work, undergoing modification as it grew and as he came to apply them to ever-widening fields of experience, but preserving a recognisable unity throughout. These were the conceptions of rationality as organic, and as intelligible only in the light of a theory of development. Both these conceptions are fundamental also in the Idealist philosophers, but Hobhouse's use of them is characterised by a robust realism and respect for experience, and by an interpretation of development which, unlike that of the Idealist systems, rests upon the results of modern evolutionary science. He seeks to avoid the vagueness which so often attaches to notions like "organic whole", "system", and constantly insists upon the importance of remembering that if the parts of an organic whole are only intelligible in the light of the whole, the whole in turn can only be understood in terms of the parts in interrelation. He seeks to maintain a just balance between the claims of analysis and synthesis, parts and whole, mechanism and spirit.

These points may be illustrated from the whole range of Hobhouse's inquiries. Firstly, in the theory of knowledge he emphasises the conception of knowledge as an organised system. The grounds of rational belief lie in the interconnection or mutual support of judgments each having a measure of inward probability, but also corroborated by, and corroborating, other judgments so as to form a coherent whole. It is essential to his view that there are no fixed starting-points in knowledge immune from all change, and above all doubt. On the contrary, since all experience is interwoven, the growth of knowledge involves a progressive modification of all its elements, and rational thought can claim superiority only on the ground that on the whole it gives an increasingly coherent and comprehensive account of reality. It is equally essential to his view that it is only through an interrelation of partial experiences that our knowledge of the whole grows. In an instructive note in *The Theory of Knowledge* (p. 413), Hobhouse explains that here is to be found the root of his difference from the Idealist logicians. It is, he says, mainly from Bosanquet that he learned the value of the notion of systematic connection in the interpretation of thought. But he complains that throughout Bosanquet's great work he is "haunted by a system which is always operating in a powerful and effective manner, while its origin and validity are wrapt in what is to me total obscurity". In another place he argues that Bosanquet's denial of any certain generalisation except by "determination" makes it impossible to understand how the "system" is ever arrived at (p. 419). Hobhouse's interpretation of the organic view of rationality may be described as an endeavour to derive the principles of interconnection themselves, upon which all reasoning rests, from our partial experiences, and to insist that these partial experiences need no "merging" in a higher unity, though they are liable to continuous modification in the light of a more extended experience.

From this point of view it was incumbent upon Hobhouse to inquire into the charges made against conceptual knowledge and the categories of science by such thinkers as Hegel and Bradley and, in another way, by Bergson. He showed that the contradictions which were alleged to beset conceptual thought were not inherent in articulate thought as such, but resulted from a tendency to regard concepts as independently real and unitary entities while, in fact, they were derived from partial characters of experience never given except as intertwined with other partial characters. Thus he argues, for example, that the antinomies arising in connection with the categories of substance and cause are due to the tendency to take what are aspects of concrete experience for self-sufficient entities, and are resolved when it is realised that they are expressions, on the one hand, for the element of continuity, and on the other for that of correlated changes of character, which are both features of concrete existence (cf. *Development and Purpose*, p. 263). Further, Hobhouse protests against the view which excludes any knowledge of individuality from the sphere of the intellect on the ground that analysis, which is its instrument, kills the living whole and breaks it up into parts to which nothing corresponds in the real world. Of the misuses of analysis and the pitfalls of abstract reasoning, he is sufficiently aware, but he insists that errors thus arising must be corrected by processes of articulate thought and by nothing else. "To say that life and soul and all that has individuality are known by instinct is to deny that they are known at all, for instinct is not knowledge but a predisposition charged with feeling towards action. To attribute them to intuition is pointless, for all judgment is primarily intuitive in that it is the deliverance of the mind, or physically and metaphorically 'looking at' something, and the question about all intuitions is whether they cohere or contradict each other, that is to say, the question of their truth is a question for the rational intelligence" (*Theory of Knowledge*, p. xiii). He shows that analysis is not destined to reduce everything to terms that can be mathematically handled, but may lead to the detection of elements not further analysable in mathematical manner yet sufficiently clearly presented to the mind to be of value for scientific thought. "It is probable", he says, "that the attack on rational method confuses the defective analysis of our actual thinking with the limits that there may be to analysis in the nature of things, and so imputes the fallacies into which we may be betrayed by reasoning from insufficient data to inherent defects of the rational method itself" (*Development and Purpose*, p. 282). The remedy is not to be sought in a revresion to dogmatism and an appeal to the feelings, but in a closer criticism of the assumptions of articulate thought and an inquiry into its relation to the vaguer mental elements operating unconsciously and underlying the whole process of mental development.

Hobhouse's theory of knowledge may be described as a critical realism, but it has little in common with the forms of realism that have been worked out in England and America since the first edition of *The Theory of Knowledge*. In his view these schools of thought, in their eagerness to show that the mind does not in any sense "make" the object it asserts, have ended by reducing the cognitive act to a mode of the object and so have come by another route to an identification of knowledge with its object. Such "ultra realism" must eventually fall back into absolute idealism or helpless scepticism. In contrast, Hobhouse's own epistemology is directed at vindicating the reality of the self as well as of the not-self, and showing that the conception of the self is experientially sound, being built up by the same processes which go to the making of any other valid conception.

The conception of the rational as harmonious integration of experience also underlies Hobhouse's treatment of comparative and social psychology. Broadly, as we have seen, he seeks to show that the essential function of the mind is the correlation of experience, and that mental development is a process whereby (*a*) the factors correlated are increasingly brought to consciousness, and (*b*) the scope of correlation widens. On this view each stage of development may be regarded as bringing to light factors which before were working in the dark, or as a fresh synthesis of elements present throughout though previously held in check or abeyance. Guided by this conception, Hobhouse is able to do justice to the claims of the unconscious elements of the mind and of impulse and feeling, while avoiding the exaggerations of those who claim supremacy for these mental elements over intellect and reason. "The mind at any stage", he says, "is more than reason, yet reason is not a separate faculty dominating one compartment and legitimately excluded from another on which it wrongfully encroaches, nor does it aim at an aggression which is to dominate or destroy. The weakness or defect of reason is equally the weakness or defect of the non-rational elements. Its extension to them, their inclusion within its sphere, is their redemption. Its legitimate empire is coextensive with mind, for every feeling, impulse, and even fancy has its legitimate meaning and true development within the harmonious whole through which its moves" (*Development and Purpose*, p. 288). That this is not grandiose rhetoric but a claim fully justified by detailed and painstaking observation and analysis will be clear to anyone who has followed Hobhouse's account of instinct and impulse in their relation to will, of sense and thought, of the interplay between the conscious and the unconscious, and of the part played by these elements of the mind in the development alike of the individual and society.

Hobhouse's ethics and social philosophy are also, as has been shown above, applications of the idea of the organic. Here again he seeks to do justice to the parts as well as to the whole which they constitute The organic is here used as an ideal conception to which actual societies approximate in varying degrees, and by which their development is measured. But if he regards societies as a form of mental union, he strenuously avoids the notion of a common self or super-personality; and if he insists on the trans-personal reference of the good and uses the notion of the common good as the basis of his theory of justice, he is equally careful to maintain that the good of society must not be opposed to that of its component members, but must consist of a harmonious interrelation of these component goods.

In Hobhouse's metaphysical work the notion of the organic receives the fullest analysis and is brought into relation, as we have seen, with the categories of purpose and mechanism. Already in *The Theory of Knowledge* he saw clearly that whatever view was to be formed of reality as a whole, it would have to be such as to allow of the element of variability as a permanent fact not capable of resolution into mechanical combinations of uniform sequences, and that the variability was determined by the necessities of the system as a whole. But at that time the organic, which seemed likely to afford an interpretation along these lines, appeared to him to be distinct both from the teleological and mechanical, and he felt that in any case further positive investigation of the working of these principles was needed if light were to be thrown on their relations. He turned to the empirical study of the working of mind in the animal world and in human societies and came to the conclusion that mental evolution required for its interpretation the conception of a progressive realisation of a conditioned purpose. Epistemological analysis, which he later resumed, enabled him to find in this notion of a conditioned teleology a fresh mode of interpreting the principle of organic connection. For though the central mind is conceived as operating on elements which are as such indifferent or mechanically related, yet a measure of reciprocal connection remains in virtue of which dualism is overcome and the whole is seen to be in a sense organic, since the elements are as necessary to mind as mind to them (cf. *Development and Purpose*, p. 446).

Hobhouse himself recognised that his conception of the rational brought him back in the end into unexpected contact with Idealism, and in describing the unity of the world whole he occasionally uses language which is reminiscent of that system. "The unity of mind", he says, "is not created but discovered in the development of individual minds. As a reality it is that which determines development

from the beginning" (*Development and Purpose*, p. 476).
Yet the divergence is no less clear, for, in his view, mind is
not the whole of things but only a factor within it whose
purpose is conditioned by other elements equally real
though unorganised. The teleological principle, in other
words, is only one part of the explanation of the world order
requiring to be supplemented by the mechanical principle,
and it is only in the interweaving of the two that he finds an
explanation of the process of development.[1]

A word may perhaps be said here of the relation of Hobhouse's position to some recent views of the evolutionary
process which also stress the organic interpretation. Lloyd
Morgan's "levels of emergence", Smuts's "wholes", closely
resemble Hobhouse's notion of the stages of correlation
through which mind passes in the course of development.
But while Lloyd Morgan excludes all problems of agency
and direction from the sphere of science, relegating them to
what he calls theory of reality, Hobhouse attempts a synthesis of the two and claims to show that the *nisus* towards
higher levels of emergence is due to a correlating factor,
which operates with cumulative effect in all elements of the
real, though it is also conditioned by them. For Smuts, the
holistic principle, though described as an organising, order-

---

[1] The question may be raised how far Hobhouse's argument would be affected
by the possible existence of wholes other than mechanical, teleological, or organic.
His attitude may be indicated by an extract from a letter to me dated January 8,
1929. "On your philosophical point, I should like to hear your view developed.
I don't think that the existence of a 'variety of genuine wholes' could affect my
argument, because the wholes would then become the elements, and my point
would be that there must be a system connecting them, however much each of
them follows Spinoza's law *in suo esse perseverare*.   What would affect my
argument would be such a collapse of mechanistic explanation as appears in
Whitehead, for example. But, if you will consider it, you will see that even if
Whitehead's organic theory is correct—which I very much doubt—it would only
affect the form of my argument. He is a more thoroughgoing exponent of the
organic than I am. The collapse is really much more complete in Eddington's
book, but I believe that on consideration the materialistic philosophers will find
that his version really amounts to an overthrow of the relativity theory as an
interpretation of reality rather than of mechanism. In fact, though my whole drift
is anti-mechanical, I cannot think that mechanism counts for so little as its recent
exponents are telling us."

ing, and relating activity, is not to be identified with mind, which in his view is an organ only of one form of wholeness, and that a comparatively recent one in the evolutionary order. Hobhouse, on the other hand, regards the existence of structured wholes as evidence for the operation of a central mind which is the organ of correlation and whose final end is harmony. All, however, use the conception of a *nisus* towards wholeness, and it is arguable that Hobhouse has faced more frankly than the others the teleological implications of this conception.

In attempting now an estimate of Hobhouse's contributions, it will be convenient to consider, first, his more specialised researches, and then his comprehensive metaphysical synthesis. He was a pioneer in many fields, and several branches of inquiry which were in their initial stages when he began his work have since definitely entered the rank of the sciences. This is certainly the case in comparative psychology and comparative ethics; less clearly perhaps in social psychology and sociology regarded as a synthesis of the social sciences. It is thus possible to some extent to weigh his achievements in the light of these later developments. In comparative psychology it is, I think, fair to say that in the main its general tendency has been to confirm Hobhouse's principal conclusions both in respect of the lower and higher organisms. In comparative ethics the encyclopædic researches of Hobhouse's colleague at the London School of Economics—Professor Edward Westermarck—are also, I think, in so far as they cover the same ground, generally in harmony with his results in spite of fundamental divergence in ethical theory. In social psychology Hobhouse's work is not so well known as that in animal psychology and comparative morals. Yet in the end it will, I venture to say, be found among his most important contributions to social science. He has done more than any other recent writer to correct the current tendency to emphasise the element of impulse, of instinct, of the unconscious, in the mass movements of mankind, and it is not too much to say that he has given us the most penetrating and powerful restatement of modern Rationalism. Of his achievements in sociology as a synthetic science it is more difficult to speak in general terms. Many will doubt the possibility of establishing such generalisations as those attempted by Hobhouse on the evidence at present available. But all must be impressed with the vastness of the material that he has gathered, and with the fruitfulness of the methods which he has devised for dealing with it. In stressing the synthetic point of view, in his clear demarcation of the relation between the philosophical and the scientific approach to the study of society, in insisting on the importance of painstaking detailed studies as well as of comparative investigations, above all, in elaborating a method for the study of the interrelations between institutions, he has laid down the general lines which sociologists will for long have to follow if sociology is to be placed firmly "on the secure path of science".

His achievements in sociology are still more impressive when they are considered in conjunction with his work in ethics and social philosophy. He provides both a scientific social morphology and criteria for the evaluation of the forms distinguished and the evolution they undergo; and while careful not to confuse questions of fact with questions of value, yet seeks to bring together the results of his inquiries in a synthesis culminating in a theory of the nature and possibility of social progress. Viewed as a whole, his work must assuredly come to be recognised as the most comprehensive and successful attempt made in recent times, whether in England or abroad, towards a systematic sociology.

The theory of knowledge is, as we have seen, in a sense the basis of all Hobhouse's work. Here his faith in reason receives its theoretical justification. He sets out to reconcile empiricism with rationalism in the light of a critical reconstruction of experience. His work is thoroughly in line with the great tradition of the English empiricists but invigo-

R

rated, both by what he accepts and what he rejects of the teaching of the Idealist critics. The student now reading Hobhouse's *Theory of Knowledge*, especially if he compares it with the relevant sections of *Development and Purpose*, will be struck by the extraordinary vitality and freshness of Hobhouse's work and will find in it ample equipment for dealing with current controversies as to the nature of science and knowledge generally. His contributions to epistemology are certainly not as widely recognised as they deserve to be, yet there have been few treatises written from the realistic point of view so exhaustive and systematic as his, or supported by so much exact analysis of the body of actual experience.

It is this respect for experience that also characterises Hobhouse's metaphysical constructions. He explains that he could never attach more than a speculative importance to generalisations as to the nature of reality unless they were corroborated by a synthetic survey of experience; and, as we have seen, in his *Development and Purpose*, he seeks to supplement the arguments based on the logical requirements of systematic explanation by "empirical" or "historical" arguments on a big scale, and he attaches great importance to the fact that these two lines of investigation lead in the main to the same conclusions. Whether his view of "conditioned teleology" as the fundamental principle of reality will gain wide support it is difficult to say. By many his conclusions will be found attractive even though they may think the reasoning which he adduces in their support unconvincing and his empirical survey, however extensive it may be, as yet an inadequate basis for a theory of reality as a whole. Hobhouse's own attitude to his final position may be seen from a passage in a letter written by him to Miss Margaret Llewellyn Davies in 1927, when he was correcting the proofs of the revised edition of *Development and Purpose*, a passage which incidentally also brings out the rare and refreshing candour of his mind.

"I am getting proofs of my book now and simply hate

them. I have arrived at an unusual condition about that work. My mind is in three layers. The top layer accepts it as it stands and recognises that at any rate I have done my best and put the argument as well as I could, and am prepared to defend it. The second layer is sceptical. It says 'Your argument was based on a belief in modern civilisation, but in fact modern civilisation is going to pot. It is all going to be more and more machinery, more ugliness, more freedom for the motorist till there is none for the pedestrian, some form of class war to end in the triumph of Fascism, and probably an international war which will destroy urban life. At the very best you can no longer think of any humanitarianism as the soul of social development, and so the linch-pin is out of your argument.' When this stage is reached I begin to think of cancelling the book and paying Macmillan's expenses. But there is a third layer which is less articulate, but says something to this effect: 'Your arguments are all pretty poor, but your meaning's right. It is absolutely true that the world is neither mechanism nor spirit, but a spiritual struggle for wholeness or harmony in discordant parts, and the struggle makes evolution because it has a drive behind it which the inert mechanical parts have not. You'd betray your ideas if you gave up, because though a poor thing it is the best you can do. You don't express them well, but nobody else expresses them at all.' So it will go on—and there is a candid exposition of the writer's frame of mind. But it is a bore to feel a doubleness of this kind and to feel in fact quite deeply and keenly in opposite ways."

It may be of interest to indicate briefly the effect on Hobhouse's thought of the recent developments in the physical sciences. He devoted a good deal of his time to their study in the years before his death and intended to deal with them more fully on his retirement from the Chair of Sociology in the University of London.

As far as I can see, he was of the opinion that his main

conclusions remained unaffected by the new views. He thought, however, that they had already exercised a liberating influence on the general mind which was likely to result in a more vigorous and independent study of aspects of reality other than the physical, and thus to prepare the ground for a wider and more comprehensive synthesis of experience. This liberating influence was due to two things. Firstly, the newer views destroyed the belief in materialism proper, that is, the belief that matter is the only real and self-subsistent entity or substance, and tended to support the view that what we call matter was rather a way of describing certain modes of behaviour or process verifiable in the real world. Secondly, the recent changes seemed to Hobhouse to have a bearing on the epistemological character of the physical sciences, of importance for philosophical theory. They tended to show, namely, that striking successes in measurement might be achieved on hypotheses which are eventually discarded, and, what is perhaps more important, that in questions of underlying theory, physical science is capable of changes of front quite comparable with those for which philosophy has often been derided. The rigidity and primacy of the physical sciences appear thus to have been shaken. Yet Hobhouse was not inclined to find in these developments arguments for subjectivism or vague mysticism. His view is rather that, on the whole, thought is able to correct the errors that arise from the necessary abstractness of its method and by degrees to advance to a more concrete view. To the growth of such a concrete view, however, the rigid mechanistic views which prevailed in the last century presented a grave obstacle, and its removal must tend to widen the field of study and in particular to secure autonomy for the sciences dealing with the world of mind, of conduct, of society, of art. These extensions of the field of independent investigation are bound in the end to facilitate the task of the philosopher—which is to formulate a consistent system of all forms of experience.

SELECTED ARTICLES AND ESSAYS

WITH AN EDITORIAL NOTE BY

J. A. HOBSON

EDITORIAL NOTE

THE first and longest of the articles which follow was written as the introductory chapter to a volume of essays on what may be termed the new social-reformist policy, planned by Hobhouse and a group of his friends and colleagues in a private gathering at the School of Economics. The intention was to discuss the various aspects of the social-economic situation of this country in the new world order and disorder, and to endeavour to formulate the lines of an integral policy in accordance with agreed principles of economic equity, recognising the larger part which the State must take in the government of Industry, and the measures necessary to reconcile the larger share which the workers should have in the conduct and the fruits of industry with the maintenance and stimulation of personal incentives to efficient service. After the death of Hobhouse the project was dropped. But his statement of the Problem is so lucid in form and so convincing in its reasoning, as to make it an admirable illustration of his ability as a thinker in the realm of practical policy.

The shorter essays which follow are taken in nearly every instance from the "back-pagers" or leading articles contributed by him to the *Manchester Guardian* during the years of the War. His emotional and intellectual powers were during these momentous years keyed to their highest pitch, and his writing displayed powers of vision and a nobility of utterance previously known only to his closer personal friends. Some of these articles are attached to special aspects of war policy. Others deal with the profoundly important moral issues evoked by the irrational conduct of the belligerent peoples and their Governments.

I have added one or two articles written in lighter vein, illustrative of the rich enjoyment which he found in the quiet forms of literary humour.

THE PROBLEM

In the belligerent countries of Europe with few exceptions the war produced, or brought to a head, something of the nature of a social revolution. In specific character and degree the nature of the revolution varied with the circumstances of each country, and in some of them it has been followed by a counter-revolution, the fortunes of which have also varied. But the general effect was an upheaval in which, for a time, the mass of the workers came to the top and the propertied classes, so secure before 1914, were either ruined or very seriously shaken. In Russia, where the Government was exceptionally obstructive and corrupt and the governing classes feeble, political power was seized by the representatives of the urban artisans who were the only remaining organised bodies. The reaction, discredited by its acceptance of foreign assistance, failed completely and a stable and, by the accounts of visitors of all parties, relatively efficient Government has established itself on the ruins of the old system. But in Russia, as throughout Eastern Europe, the peasantry has proved the predominating partner, the dual need of man power and food working in unison. In France, where the peasantry was already well established, the fabric of society has undergone the smallest changes. In the industrial countries the effect has been varied. At the outset, towards the close of the war and in the early days of the peace, the working classes had the ball at their feet, but they did not know where to drive it and reaction took place. In Germany the middle classes were ruined, to the gain, it would seem, of few except the great industrialists, who were enabled to cancel their borrowed capital. In Italy a seemingly successful revolution led to a violent counter-revolution, which, though obviously insecure, is at present unshaken. In England hyper-excited nationalism engendered political cross-currents which, on the whole, have given political power to the reactionary elements and have left the trade unions as the one real organ of the workers, while they in turn were half paralysed by the commercial crash induced largely by the bad peace settlement. The propertied classes, however, were affected much as in other countries. The professional men, land owners, and rentiers, though not ruined, found their standard of living seriously lowered. Estates changed hands and the new rich, war profiteers and tradesmen, fat with the advantages sucked from food control and currency changes, rushed in to fill the void left by the decay of the older wealth. The working classes had a glimpse of real economic equality, which passed away, but not without leaving a permanent effect on the imagination.

The resulting position is highly unstable. The political machine, dominated by the possessing classes, and animated more by the aggressive activity of the new rich than by the untroubled self-satisfaction of the old, is used for obstructing anything of the nature of economic democracy, and only yields in jerks under pressure. Among the majority of the people, who, when it comes to voting, give the machine its power and keep it in being, there is a mass of discontent with their present status and of bewildered disappointment at the frustration of their hopes. The trade union organisation, the only effective organ of expression for this discontent, is essentially sectional in its structure and has all the blindness and collective selfishness characteristic of sectionalism. Strikes are ill considered, vastly damaging to all parties and as blindly resisted as initiated. The fighting spirits are in varying degrees influenced by Russian Communism, and the influence is carefully fostered and exaggerated by the commercialised Press, which knows well that (far from being seriously formidable) it is of the greatest value as a bogey which will rally the timorous voter of all classes to the side of security. In the background, if the bogey should unexpectedly put on the reality of flesh and blood, there is always the possibility of an imitation Fascism, which in this country would have a very large class of athletic, well-fed, and not well-employed young men to drill in its support. Outside there is the irresponsible influence of the Soviet Union, deeply resentful of England's action, fearful of England as the leading capitalist country of Europe, feeding its own doubters with the wild anti-Communism of the British Press, seeking every opportunity of making its power felt, but having not the most rudimentary understanding of our social life to direct its efforts.

But this is only one instance out of many in which world-wide relations affect our internal problems. The new spirit which consists in taking seriously the ideas of freedom and equality, personal and national, has spread to the Eastern peoples and confronts us, as in China, with a threat to our commerce and in India with a challenge to commercial and political ascendancy alike. Now the modern economic development of England rests on oversea trade. This result is the obverse of the destruction of our peasantry in the centuries between the first rise of the woollen industry and the consummation of the enclosures. We gave ourselves over little by little to dependence on oversea trade consisting in the exchange of manufactures and transport and financial services for food, raw materials, and luxuries. The balance was first seriously shaken by the rise of industrial competitors such as Germany, Belgium, and the United States. It is more critically affected by the rise of competition in the East, particularly when its edge is sharpened by political and racial antagonism. For any believer in the ideal of equal liberty there is a brighter sky behind the heavily moving clouds, for the world outlook is infinitely better if we can conceive it as a voluntary co-operation of free peoples than if our best hopes are for the more or less benevolent domination of one race holding others in subservience. There are many elements in the English mind which respond to this ideal, but as a nation we move slowly and our acceptances are apt to come too late, and to yield to-day that which would have satisfied our claimants yesterday. In our dealings with Africa we have even retrograded, for the government of Kenya would hardly have passed with such scant criticism in the much decried Gladstonian epoch, and, though we have washed our hands of the affairs of the Dominions, the reactionary measures against the Bantu peoples in the South African Union must affect those remaining under our control, besides redounding to the general discredit of the British Empire which led the older movement for the liberation of coloured peoples. The day when the civilised peoples of the East could be held in bondage is passed, but the danger of a systematic exploitation of the African is still with us, and is more urgent than it was a quarter of a century ago. At the same time, ideas of emancipation have begun to shadow themselves forth within the African mind, and we have on hand the germinal possibilities of as ugly a racial conflict as history has seen.

The post-war world, then, is a dangerous, but not an unhopeful, world. Tempers are ragged and the possibilities of international conflict, class conflict, race conflict are still numerous, but the conditions are better than those of such a peace of death as fell on Ireland after the Treaty of Limerick, or on all Europe for a while after the Congress of Vienna. The problem is not at bottom that of maintaining order against turbulence, nor the more difficult one of awakening hope in a cowed and crushed population. It is rather that of finding consistent direction for a mass of alert and indignant energies, untrained by experience and impatient of criticism, bent on freedom without appreciation of its conditions. There are here the materials of a better order than the past could show, for a system of free co-operation commending itself to the intelligence and the heart alike will compare favourably with the most efficient order imposed by the will of a superior. Politically it will be at once more stable as commanding the energetic support of the plain man and more elastic as responsive to divergences of local, racial, and even individual requirement. Economically it will be more productive, first, in that it will call on the mental as well as the physical energies of the average worker and enlist his good will as much as his personal desires; secondly, in that its fruits enure to the advancement of health and vigour, not merely among the specially capable or fortunate, but in the generality; and lastly, in that it saves the friction of competition and concentrates effort on the support of the common rather than the pursuit of the personal. Morally its superiority is that it calls on the energetic service of the individual and appeals to his social conscience, asks for his resourcefulness and tolerates his vagaries, repressing only what it holds definitely unsocial. Something like this has been the ideal of all aristocracies—for their own members—for aristocracies at their best have rested the common effort on the free initiative, the personal pride and the ready devotion of their members. The difference introduced by the democratic ideal is the difference between some and all. The democratic theory is that all normal men are in their degree capable of participation in such mutual service, that while there are considerable differences of character and capacity among men, there are in a people of homogeneous tradition differences of individuals rather than of class or genealogy, and that as between peoples of very different cultures their importance is really unknown until the experiment of self-government is tried, but that on the fairest interpretation of the available evidence the identities of human nature strike deeper than the differences. Furthermore, what is less controversial, in substituting "all" for "some" the democratic theory conceives the common good in the literal sense of common, i.e. as effectively shared by all members of the society to which we attribute it, as something entering into and enriching their personal lives.

What democratic theory has further to add is that, while

the world-wide extension of its ideal may or may not prove impossible, every failure of the ideal is a danger to such success as it has won. If we cannot succeed in dealing with the Indian people on terms of equal freedom, that is definitely a blow to the prestige of those ideals among ourselves. It will point the arguments of their critics, reinforce the self-confidence of bureaucracy, justify maxims of autocracy, lead us to tolerate reasons of State in justification of what we should otherwise denounce as an atrocity, prove itself, in short, a stone of stumbling and a rock of offence wherever the democratic principle is in controversy. Political principles, like other things, succeed by success and fail by failure. The triumphs of Bolshevism and Fascism are alike infectious, and those who justify the indiscriminate shooting of an Indian mob have at the back of their minds the Freudian wish that they might see the same treatment meted out to Welsh miners. Conversely, the success of responsible government in South Africa conduced to the settlement of the Irish Free State.

The problem of the present day, then, is a world problem, and, if in this volume we deal principally with its domestic aspects, that arises from the necessities of concentration. No solution, political or economic, of our difficulties is possible which does not on the whole tend to the elimination of world unrest and to just relations with the Orient and with the less fortunate races of the British Commonwealth. The principles of free co-operation which we lay down for ourselves are such as we would fain see others too adopting. Their application must be suited to the circumstances of each people, and it is of the circumstances of our own people that we, of course, are best able to speak. But there is at bottom a common cause. The spirit that confiscates the land of the Kenyan native and compels him by taxation to labour for the alien immigrant is the same spirit which lengthens the British miner's day or stops the extension of Trade Boards. The social forces are the same, the prejudices are

the same. In large proportions you will find the same men
in support of such policies in the Press and in Parliament
and the same men in opposition. Thus the principles of
which we shall speak are of world application, though no
two parts of the world may embody them in precisely the
same institutions, nor have reached the same point in the
struggle for their assertion.

The Liberalism of Cobden's time solved the problem of
economic freedom in very simple fashion. Destroy every
monopoly, break down all barriers to trade, do away with
restrictions of all kinds, cultivate peace, and lower taxation
to the bedrock minimum. There remain the spontaneous
energies of free and equal human beings, each seeking his
own, but constrained by intelligent self-interest to mutual
service. Cobden qualified this creed not illogically by advo-
cating national education both to supply the elements of
skill and intelligence and secure equality of opportunity.
Nor was he illogical in proposing to exclude children under
thirteen from the factory because the child was not in a position to effect the free and equal contract which was the pivot
of his system. But was the adult male worker in such a
position? One would have thought the answer clearly in the
negative, since there can be no freedom of contract where
there is gross inequality of conditions, but Cobden, too
much influenced perhaps by the conditions of Lancashire
commerce, considered that any man of known probity and
energy could get sufficient credit to start him on his own
account. Industrial conditions, in spite of the growth of the
factory system, were still sufficiently individualistic to make
this rejoinder to critics seem less absurd than it would do
at the present day. Business was still in the main organised
in undertakings small in comparison with the scale which is
now familiar. Cobden thought that the utmost possible
freedom in the life of these multitudinous little concerns
would prevent the growth of any overpowering monopoly
and enure to the most effective division of labour and the

best possible service to the community. A little later on
Karl Marx was putting forward a very different view of the
future. He saw competition destroying itself by overstrain.
Its day-to-day pressure would cause producers to sell at
prices which cut profits finer and finer till often they would
disappear and leave ruin behind. Producers would recognise
the danger and see the only safety in combination. Rings,
cartels, trusts, amalgamations would spring up out of the
little individualist undertakings. Competition contradict-
ing itself would relapse into monopoly, and then the proletariat, learning the lesson, would, in its turn, combine and,
taking over the highly organised machine of industry, turn
it to its own service.

Now Marx's economic theory may be as defective on one
side as Cobden's was on the other, but, if his vision was
limited, he had a keen eye for certain practical tendencies,
and the course of events has followed more nearly on his
lines than on those of Cobden. Perhaps neither of them
could, in the circumstances of their time, take sufficient
account of the wave of militant nationalism and imperialism
which was to cut across industrial development, adverse to
both of them alike in the new extension which it gave to the
scope and power of *de facto* Governments and in the renewed
national restrictions as against the cosmopolitanism which
both of them foresaw and desired for industry. This was the
rock which few, if any, before 1870 had reckoned with in
the chart of the future. We have seen how in the end it
proved fatal to the Governments which could not stand the
shock of war and defeat, and how in the weakest of these it
brought the urban proletariat into power with the paradoxical result for the true Marxian that the social revolution succeeded, not in the most, but in the least,
industrialised of the European nations. But for the moment
we are not concerned with the question whether the course
of events makes ducks with one form of political prophecy
or drakes with another. We have to observe that the actual

course of economic and political development has carried all nations farther away from the system of free competitive capitalism, which was Cobden's ideal, and has substituted combination in many shapes and forms, but always tending to grow in extent and power. Simultaneously, the advance of democracy and social and economic criticism has compelled the extension of legislative regulation and administrative control, together with fiscal measures adapted on the one side to the imperialistic and nationalistic spirit, on the other to the mitigation of the grosser inequalities of wealth and power which were the natural consequences of the movements of concentration. Competition failed and we live among its debris with no established freedom of social co-operation to take its place, but with the struggles of organised capital and labour confronting us, and that in a world seething with racial and national passions and bristling with international dangers.

On what lines are we to deal with the situation? Are we to go forward to a more complete control of the production and distribution of wealth in the interests of the common good, or back to the ideals of free enterprise in such form as modern developments will admit, or are we to search for some line of advance which shall combine the advantages of co-operation and freedom? In general terms probably few detached thinkers would deny that the third course is the best, if only we could find it. But as to this possibility they are sceptical, and, when they come to closer contact with particulars, the opposition between liberty and control breaks out among them again. On the one hand, those bred in the classical economic tradition would maintain that the conditions of free industrial enterprise impose a voluntary or involuntary co-operation, that the more we have of industrial freedom, the more men find that, to make their own living, they must serve others, and that the less restricted the range of choice the more accurate is the adjustment of supply to maximum demand. On the other hand, the

socialist would rejoin that the desired freedom of enterprise
is in fact the monopoly of the few, that for the many the
alleged freedom is at best a choice between one or two
equally undesirable conditions of toil, that much of wealth
is accumulated by no social service, but by hard driving,
sharp bargaining or simple speculation, and much, being
inherited, involves no sacrifice whatever in return for its
enjoyment. Such charges are, on the facts, difficult to meet,
but our detached thinker may still be sceptical about the
remedy when presented to him in the form of full-blown
State organisation of the entire industrial system. But this
is a false alternative. The direct management of producton
is only one of several methods by which the subordination
of industry to the common good may be accomplished and
it is not the most important. There is undoubtedly a sphere
for public services, national and municipal, and experience
has justified its extension in recent years, but the State has
much wider functions than those of the direct management
of industry. In the first place, it is responsible for the general
regulation of industrial conditions. In the second place, it is
responsible for the provision of the fundamental conditions
of healthy development for all its citizens. In the third place,
it exerts the financial control through which it can make
such provision and develop the common life itself to its
higher power, and in the fourth place, it can exercise an
ultimate control over the direction of industry without
necessarily assuming managerial responsibility.

The first pair of these functions developed historically in
close relation, for it was concern for the prime needs of the
worker which first led the State to resume the functions of
industrial regulation which it had abandoned in its old form
during the eighteenth and earlier years of the nineteenth
century. The State began, in fact, by refusing to let children
be overworked. It went on to protect women and "young
persons" in the same way and to make general provision
for safety and health in factories. It found that directly or

indirectly it was limiting men's hours by legislating for women, and, taking courage, it proceeded to deal with the male labourer directly. Finally, it began in the present century to deal with the wages contract itself by securing a minimum of remuneration. In all this current of legislation it was the human needs of the worker that supplied the driving force. As against the contention that the worker would always make the best economic bargain for himself, experience showed that he was often in too weak a position to make any effective bargain at all. He just had to take what he was offered, and the result was to beat down the less skilled or less fortunate to a point at which health suffered, hope vanished, and energy with it, while industry, adapting itself to these conditions and coming to rely on ill-paid labour, was not easily to be lifted out of the rut, although better payment with better organisation would, in the long run, have given better returns. Industrial regulation then sprang up first to meet the human needs of the worker in response to a larger conception of common responsibility, but at the present time the demand has gone farther than this and is urging the need of the community in general for co-operation and good will in the industrial system. The worker generally, skilled or unskilled, ceasing to be a mere pawn in the game, demands some voice in the playing of it. The demand may mean several things: a share in management, a share in profits, a continuity of employment, protection against arbitrary dismissal. Some of these demands raise very difficult questions. But there is one thing common to them to which we shall confine attention here, and that is the provision of conditions of payment and hours of work "fair" to each grade of worker. Now the question what is "fair" to different grades of labour opens up greater difficulties of principle than any with which industrial legislation has grappled hitherto. The conception of human needs reveals difficulties enough when we come to grips with it, but at least it is a principle of general application. It is founded, on familiar requirements of common human nature, as for food, clothing, shelter, for nurture in childhood, for the elements of education, for provision against accident, sickness, and old age. It has not proved impossible to make rough calculations of the money cost of providing for such needs, and, though there is a margin of error in all such calculations, those which have been most carefully made have not been without their practical utility. At any rate, the principle is intelligible and any gross violation of it can be exposed and suppressed. But when more than such a minimum is claimed, when effort, exposure, training, skill put in their claims, how are we to weigh one against another? Who is to compare the arduous and dangerous toil of the coal-hewer, the skill and responsibility of the express engine-driver, the manual dexterity of the cotton-spinner, the methodical accuracy of the accountant, and assess them against one another in terms of remuneration? Most people are inclined to reply simply "No one. It is a question for the higgling of the market. The State or the common sense of the community may determine a general minimum based on human needs, but everything above this must be left to settle itself." The more powerful Trade Unions are not ill disposed to this view, for it means that they will get what they can, and they think that they can get a good deal. But from the social point of view it is a counsel of despair. It holds the door permanently open to a quarrel whenever a change of conditions occurs, or whenever a combination of employers or employed sees a favourable opportunity for a move, and it leaves each quarrel to be determined by the strength of the parties at the moment, without reference to the permanent needs of industry. In fact, under post-war conditions, the economic strength of the workers in certain industries has been temporarily raised and that of the workers in other industries much depressed by the international situation, and there has been a lowering of standards in engineering, for example, which may well have enduring effects of a disastrous kind upon British industry. Meanwhile it is a commonplace that the perpetuation of industrial warfare is threatening our whole position as a commercial nation.

1. We are forced, then, to ask whether methods of peaceful adjustment are really beyond the wit of man to devise. Grant that any permanent peace must rest on conditions that all parties will regard as "fair", grant that we have no sufficiently clear principle to determine what is "fair" in terms of universal application. Is it or is it not still possible that, if we have suitable organs impartially constituted for dealing with concrete cases, they may by experience and through trial and error hammer out solutions which, going from precedent to precedent, would come to command general acceptance as the best obtainable results? As a fact, it is not especially difficult to grade rates within any one industry. Naturally controversies arise, but in a representative body of employers and workers the circumstances which have led to the existing grading are pretty well known, and it is generally held that graded rates should be of uniform application, while if there are reasons for any local exception or if there are arguments for a change, they are well within the powers of the technical men to appreciate. Both Trade Boards and Whitley Councils, as well as conciliation committees, deal with such rates, and the first thing to do is to strengthen such methods of determination, for example, by giving the Whitley Councils powers of enforcement. Workers and employers alike would thus become better accustomed to the principle of an impartial adjustment. There would follow the more difficult problem of adjustment as between trade and trade. This undoubtedly requires some organ for the comparison of different industries. A first step would be within the Trade Board system, to establish a central board to determine appeals referred to it by the Ministry from the existing Boards. Such a body, constituted like any Trade Board of employers, workers, and

an impartial element, would in any case hear the objections urged that a rate was unduly high or that it was low in comparison with those obtaining in other trades, that it was "more than the trade could bear", or, reversely, that it was so low as to discourage training and the adequate supply of skilled workers. It would feel after some level of adjustment, and, if it applied the measure of common sense for which we generally credit representative bodies in this country, it would at least hammer out something more equable than the settlement of industrial war. The Whitley Councils, revived and reinforced by the acquisition of compulsory powers, would require a similar central body, and between the Councils and the Trade Boards a large field of industry would be covered, so large that the pressure of opinion would be exercised upon the rest to come into a similar system. It is not possible to impose compulsory arbitration as a universal law on unwilling parties, but it is not impossible to build up modes of impartial settlement by common sense which shall eventually get themselves generally accepted by proving their superiority to the method of hard bargaining. At any rate, the renewal of willing co-operation is the condition of survival for British industry, and this is not attainable without provision for the agreed as against the competitive settlement of industrial conditions.

2. Salaries and wages on any scale that we can imagine becoming general will not meet all personal, still less all family, needs. Minimum rates have to be adapted to the minimum capacity that can find a useful place in industry and to the differences of circumstances under which different undertakings are carried on. In raising a minimum there is always a risk of contracting employment and, though the more normal effect may be rather to transfer employment from a less to a more efficient form of organisation, there will under any conditions be differential advantages remaining, so that, given a common rate of wages, some firms will show good profit, while others will barely

keep their heads above water. Such differences are not in essence removed by co-operative, municipal, or national organisation. In a municipal tramway system, given uniform charges and uniform running costs per mile, some routes will pay handsomely, while others, maintained for the benefit of the passengers, barely meet their costs. Such differential advantages are inherent in the nature of production, and they put a limit on the possibility of raising general minimum rates. On the other hand, all healthy industry provides surpluses, and, while the competitive principle holds that these are the appropriate reward and stimulus of the undertakers of the enterprise, the co-operative principle regards them as the appropriate share of the community, as that which remains when all engaged in production have received such reward as suffices to encourage and maintain their exertions at their best. One thing that the community can do with this surplus is to provide against the common risks of life and the requirements of childhood. This conception underlies the public insurance systems, which are gradually being extended to the whole of such risks. It is true that, if one could suppose a sufficiently high universal standard of wages, they might be met by self-insurance, but, on the one hand, such insurance would have to be compulsory, since otherwise the improvident—as we could not let them starve—would have it both ways; and on the other hand, there is the practical difficulty of establishing sufficiently high rates without dislocating production. It is better, in view of the differential advantages inherent in production, to adjust the minimum to the needs of the ordinary worker in work and to meet the risks and the extras out of surplus. How much the State should do outright and how far it should call on the individual for contributions are questions which have not yet been settled on any clear principle. A minimum old age pension was given without contribution, while health insurance was from the first contributory. The contribution of the em-

ployer seems to be based on administrative convenience
and does not, apart from industrial accidents and sickness,
rest on any general economic or social principle. In any
case, as the system advances a more generous provision
will be made by the State, but there are some good reasons
for combining with it a direct call on the individual. On the
one side, he should take his share in the responsibility for
his own life; on the other, he should have the indefeasible
title of a covenant and further than this he should have the
opportunity of adding to the minimum which the State
system will guarantee him. There is in this plan a true partnership of the State and the individual which marks the
dividing line between the competitive and the co-operative
system of industry. From the days of the Elizabethan Poor
Law the community recognised a common responsibility
for the destitute. The principle was applied grudgingly and
often so harshly as to have destroyed the once beautiful
name of Charity because the no less admirable ideal of personal responsibility was exaggerated, and many excellent
men believed that the right course was to make each man
responsible for himself and reduce help to the bare minimum
necessitated by sheer destitution. Such an ideal might have
been applicable to a different structure of society from that
which was growing up under the influence of competitive
industrialism. But in our industrial society it became progressively clearer that large numbers, perhaps one quarter
to one-third, of the population must live, in their best working time, on earnings affording insufficient opportunities
for provision against the many rainy days which industrial
vicissitudes as well as personal misfortune bring about. In
these circumstances, and on the stimulus of socialistic criticism, a new social ideal arose, or, perhaps more accurately,
an old ideal took shape. It was frankly recognised that the
elementary human needs are a matter of common concern,
that mutual aid is a better ideal than individual self-suffi-
ciency, and public service a better motive than personal

profit. That, if the community cannot make its members happy or moral or wise, it can provide the conditions under which they may cultivate their own faculties and sweeten the lives of their own circle, and feel that even in the monotony of industrial toil they are contributors to a wealth which is equitably shared and which in the bulk enures to the satisfaction of the common needs which they understand and share and to the advancement of the common objects of education, discovery, amenity, and wealth.

3. How is it possible to carry through such an ideal without injustice to individuals and such injustice as will sap the motives of production? This is the common form of criticism and touches partly the finance of social idealism and partly its conception of industrial organisation. On both points it is urged that the increased wealth of industrial societies has rested on free contract, the security of property, the stimulus of profit and the competition therefor, and the right of bequest. But there is another side of the matter to be considered before the importance of these factors can be fairly weighed. Larger causes than the desire of able men for wealth have conditioned industrial development—better government, improved social order, diffused education, public hygiene, increased population—all the factors which together make up a larger and more effective social life. If it comes to individuals, perhaps a few able Civil servants and medical officers of health have done as much for the foundation of the wealth of Lancashire and London as any manufacturer or banker. Such men were not paid by results. Of all individuals responsible for industrial development, inventors and the scientific theorists who made the inventions possible should be credited with the largest share. The former have occasionally made a commercial success, but in general are regarded as an exploited class, and for the latter payment by results has no application. We are likely to live more and more on the products of the labours of Volta, Gauss, Faraday, Clerk-Maxwell, but their

descendants will take no royalties. Great industrial organ-
isers have their reward, and often enough, no doubt, they
earn it well—that is to say, that even when they have drawn
very large profits, society is the richer for their work. But
profits as great and greater may be made by speculation or
skimmed off a booming industry by astute methods of
finance which create nothing but sweep accrued values into
private pockets. They also come about by incalculable
changes in a world market, or, as in our own time, by currency changes in which clever dealers managed to pouch
the balance of value. It is rejoined that these things balance
one another and that exceptional profit must be put against
exceptional loss. So it might be if both fell on the same individual. But what happens is that, while one set are ruined,
others with better luck, aided perhaps by more foresight,
perhaps by an additional dash of unscrupulousness, land
themselves once for all on the firm ground of established
fortune and draw tithes on the products of industry in per-
petuity. We would not overstate the case. The working of
competition is haphazard; the sun of its good fortune
shines both upon the just and the unjust. Its payments may
be won by useful service and by selfish aggrandisement,
and it is the function of good social regulation to minimise
the opportunities of the latter method. Lastly, the unregu-
lated rights of inheritance and bequest produce a form of
wealth which may in itself originally have been earned by
useful industry, but in its continuance goes to support a
class without economic functions, violating every one of
those maxims of responsibility, public duty, individual self-
reliance, and the rest which form the individualist armoury
of criticism upon the most modest provision for the needy.

Thus, without undue disparagement of industrial enterprise, we must maintain, first, that the winnings of competition do not coincide with the rewards of social service;
secondly, that the accumulation of wealth is due to diffused
social factors as much as to the energies of the individuals

who have made their own fortunes; and thirdly, that, by
the operation of inheritance, the fortune of the founders
becomes the basis of a permanent toll on subsequent generations. Without questioning that private property, free contract, reward of service, and even some right of bequest have
their permanent value in the social order, we have to insist
that all these rights have to be judged in the long run in
relation to the common good. Valid rights are true conditions of the social welfare, and, if we have reason to think
that any claim is in the long run and all things considered
incompatible with the general welfare, we must deny that it
is a right. Rights make their appeal to the plain man in
simple cases. What more obvious, for example, than that A
and B should be free to make what bargains they please as
long as they do no injury to C? But suppose they are not
equally free, suppose that one has the advantage of knowledge or position over the other, has he an unqualified right
to use such advantages? Confronted with cases of hardship,
the plain man soon begins to halt in his confidence about
simple principles and will be disposed to admit that free
contract is a right only under conditions which guarantee it
to be not only free but "fair", and what is "fair" will be
found on similar analysis to be definable only on principles
which we can conceive as a sound and self-consistent basis
of a desirable common life.

It is much the same with property. It is easy to see that
man can do nothing consecutive and purposeful without
the undisturbed use of material things. Security in this
respect is the germinal idea of property, but a germ which
all too easily matures into a full-blooded defence of the
absoluteness of proprietary rights and the virtues of economic individualism. Yet it should be recognised that in
some of its developments private property may mean liberty
for A at the expense of dependence for B, and that, if the
autonomy of the individual is the touchstone and if autonomy is based on private property alone, the State would

have to aim at such a diffusion of property as would put economic independence within the reach of all its members. This is not merely a doctrine of very revolutionary implications which would be shocking to the respectable men who urge its premises upon us, but is further a conception which, whatever application it might find in a land of peasant proprietors, is without meaning for advanced industrialism. As the scale of production extends, it is less and less possible for men in general to own the means of making their own livelihood. A man may own a share in the railway on which he works, but the share does not affect his title to his particular job on the line. In industrial society economic freedom must be sought on other lines, on lines which will be found to involve limits to the rights of private property. For property over things is the basis of power over any others who need those things, and absolute rights of disposal over things may be pushed to the point at which they give an extensive power of social control. This is easily recognised in the case of any monopoly which never is or can be tolerated beyond a certain point, but it has not been so fully recognised that all great aggregations of property are also aggregations of power over the lives of many, and it is with such aggregations that industrial society is faced. Economic freedom lies, not through the partition of property, but through the control of power, and, for the purposes of such control, the community is right in exercising its supreme authority in accordance with the best of its lights.

But there is another side to the question of property. Ultimately the validity of a right lies in the social functions which it serves. The feudal conception of property recognised this relation in making the tenure of land conditional upon certain services. In the overthrow of feudalism this relation was destroyed and proprietary rights came to be conceived as absolute and unconditioned. Indeed, a great deal of property, the property of the average investor at the present time, may be regarded as functionless—it carries no obligations. The debenture holder is just the creditor of a company. The shareholder has rights of criticism on the management which he exercises effectively once in a blue moon. We have, in the mass of rentiers as a whole, a vast body of wealth without specific functions seriously attached to it. But the function of this wealth, say its apologists, is retrospective. Property is the reward of effort; men work and take risks and long views in order that they may subsequently enjoy. Remove the security and you cut the sinews of production. The argument would be more plausible if there were no such thing as inheritance. The man who inherits property which enables him to live in idleness need have performed no function at all in respect of it. The argument has then to maintain that men would not save or accumulate but for their heirs. It is clear that this is only true in part. For, even if his rights were to cease at death, a man would still have his own life and in particular his old age to consider. But it is no doubt true that sufficiently drastic limitations of inheritance and bequest would check accumulation in private hands. This check might indeed be balanced by public saving and public accumulation. Still a wise and considerate statesmanship would respect the strong natural feeling which claims the right to provide for children. On the other hand, it would be within its rights in balancing against that claim such perpetuation of hereditary wealth as constitutes an irremovable burden on production. It is principally a question of amount. A desire to give a child the best possible start is altogether praiseworthy, but to make the able-bodied child independent of any energies of its own is recognised by sensible parents themselves as a much more doubtful aim, and to found a family is rather a motive of vanity than of parental love. Steep graduation of death duties has become an accepted principle of British finance, and it might be supplemented in accordance with Rignano's proposal by extra taxation upon each passage of property by inheritance. Inherited wealth would then be always a dwindling asset and the balance would go to the community. Nations generally have dealt pretty freely with bequests, particularly in respect of landed property, and it is in general clear that posthumous rights do not stand on the same footing as living rights, for the simple reason that the owner can no longer perform functions or exercise judgment in respect of them.

The conception of property as the stimulus and reward of work opens the whole question of the finance of social co-operation. It is argued that our objects may be intrinsically desirable, but, in applying the fruits of industry to general needs, the State is robbing their owners and thereby drying up the springs of initiative, enterprise, accumulation, and industry. The opposite view is that, in piling up wealth, the successful individual is robbing the workers of a part of their product, or the community of wealth due to the general progress of civilisation. Words like robbery are missiles that come easily to hand on either side. What is justified in the lawful and constitutional regulation of industry and pro-perty is that it will fit together in a permanent working plan of common well-being. If we do in fact so treat producers of any type in such fashion that we lose their services, and if those services are in fact desirable, we act inconsequently and also unjustly, for we are penalising good service. But, if it is also true that the community is, on its side, a great con-tributor to wealth, great evil may accrue if it obtains no proportionate share in the product. To take a familiar example. An industry, thriving through those general causes indicated above, brings together a large population in a great town. The owners of the land take toll on the population without needing to do anything for its industrial prosperity, and the town in consequence finds itself with a housing problem on its hands. If we could go right back on our land policy to the beginning of urban development, we should never contemplate a system which would leave urban

land in private hands. We should make it the developing
estate of the community, bringing in the financial returns
necessary to meet the cost of its growth. But, as urged
above, the social contribution to wealth is more pervasive
and many-sided than this example might suggest. As a
whole, it is not so much a definite portion which the community contributes to increasing wealth, it is rather a condition on which the successes of individuals depend. What
the permanent interests of the common welfare demand in
such a case is that the State on the one hand and individuals
on the other should, in the partition of products, receive that
which enables and encourages both to perform their functions. If taxation is such as to crush industry, the State
suffers with the industrialists. If a certain type of ability is
genuinely useful and will only exercise itself in the hope of
large rewards, it can command those rewards. There are
probably industrial magnates with five-figure incomes who
earn those incomes in the social sense, i.e. the community is
richer for these workers. We may think such riches wasteful
since they can certainly add little to the happiness of their
possessor, yet, if their owners pay their way in the sense
defined, we can have no serious cause of complaint against
them. It is all a question of the real value of the services.
The State should deal freely with unsocial, *a fortiori* anti-
social, methods of gaining wealth, but carefully with all that
encourages foresight, long training, ability, responsibility,
initiative. It can deal freely with unearned wealth, natural
or inherited, with speculative gains, monopoly privileges,
luxurious expenditure. In all such matters its problem is
merely that of finding the right technique. The general
principle of graduation on which it has mainly relied does
not satisfy all these criteria. It does probably hit most mono-
polistic advantages of any magnitude. But its main justification, practically and theoretically, is that it inflicts no
more real sacrifice on the large than on the smaller tax-
payer. Indeed, unless it should become much steeper than

anything yet known, it imposes less. The man with £10,000
a year can pay out £3,000 with much less impairment of
his real wealth than is inflicted on a man with £1,000 by a
charge of £300. The limit of graduation is, in fact, simply
productivity. If we graduate taxation to a point at which
highly paid men decline the effort of earning, we defeat the
object of the State, and that is the point at which we may
fairly be charged with doing them an injustice.

The financial basis of the social State, then, must be such
as to secure adequate rewards to all forms of social service
which are desired and to open avenues to initiative, ability,
and enterprise, but to call freely on all forms of wealth that
go beyond or are irrelevant to these requirements. Mistakes
may be made in the technique for applying such principles,
but in the principles themselves there is no conflict between
the personal claims of recognised service and the needs of
the community. On the contrary, there is explicit recognition that such needs can only be met by the willing service
of individuals according to their capacity.

4. There remains the question of the direct organisation
of industry. If we believe that the common service is preferable to competition for personal profit, it is natural to
proceed to the inference that the community should undertake the organisation of industry in general to supply the
common needs, but when fairly confronted by this conclusion most of us flinch before its complexity, its novelty, and
its uncertainties. Yet there are some common objections to
State control which are overdrawn. The commonest of them
is the alleged incapability of a Government department to
conduct the business. As to this, it is true that the ordinary
Government department has grown up, not for the purposes
of carrying on business, but for executing laws, and its
structure and traditions are such as to suit this function.
They enforce caution, responsibility, strict legality upon
every official, and they do not encourage risk-taking, enterprise, and experiment. Nevertheless, the Post Office does in

fact conduct a gigantic business, and on the whole, with all due allowance for the national habit of grumbling, conducts it well. We need not, however, enter into the question of the possible efficiency of Government departments because, if we desire the national management of any industry, we are by no means limited to this type of authority. We should presumably constitute a special Board, like the Port of London Authority, or the Broadcasting Committee, or the Electric Supply Committee, which would have their special composition, devised *ad hoc*, starting with men already expert in the trade on the one side and picked representatives of consumers on the other. On any view of the industrial situation there is a future for control of this type. Whether we welcome it as a road to Socialism or regard it as a departure from individualism, practical needs will induce the adoption of such devices on an increasing scale. There are besides measures of partial control which practical advantages will recommend. The State ought certainly to own the minerals of the country, and, as owners, might exercise an overriding control of great value, as is ably set forth by the authors of *Coal and Power*, even if it left direct management in the main to private firms. Lastly, private concerns, when they reach a certain scale, approximate in method to national enterprises. It has been argued that not much essential change of system would be involved in the nationalisation of the four great railway groups or the handful of bank amalgamations, and it is probable that the approximation to monopoly will itself eventually call for a formal subordination in such cases to an ultimate authority acting for the nation. Such changes are deprived of their sting if they do not involve confiscation, and confiscation will be avoided, not only because it is unjust to ruin particular classes of investors, but because it would involve a form of civil war, with a very doubtful possibility of victory for the national principle. The final ownership of capital must be dealt with as a question of inheritance and as a part of the general problem of national finance on the principles already indicated. If national and public management of industry are to advance with any success, there must be the greatest elasticity of method, varying from the control of monopolies, or semi-monopolies, to the ultimate ownership of the land and the materials of production, and from land-lordship to the direct executive functions of specially constituted authorities. Within such control there will still be much scope for individual enterprise, and in many forms of industry it is probable that the small man, setting up on his own, will always hold a place. Notwithstanding the great stores and the multiple shops, the little shop in the village or the by-street still has its place. The local garage, the cycle repair shed, and the cobbler's shop go on, and there is no reason why nationalism should lay hands on them any more than capitalism. What will be demanded of them is that they should foot the social bill of health by maintaining good conditions for employees. There is no reason for forcing everybody to become a public servant whether his services are wanted or not. In particular there are departments of life in which a good public service is desirable, but an exclusive State system would be very dangerous to progress. Medicine, education, and the law are examples. It is very desirable that there should be a first-rate public health and medical service, but, in the present state of medical knowledge, it would be a disaster if private practice were so curtailed that men with ideas and methods of their own could not get any chance of experimenting with them until they could persuade the General Medical Council of their superiority. The State may aid the finance of high-grade schools and universities and may set standards of competence and accessibility as a condition, but ought not to decide what they are to teach or what research they should encourage. If a point comes at which the conflict between educational and financial control is to be decided, the universities at least ought to refuse financial aid and prefer

T

liberty with a restricted range to extension, wealth, and intellectual servitude. The question of the spiritual and temporal power may have to be fought out again on this issue. On the other hand, there are things which only common action can secure. The prosperous individual may find a healthy and convenient home for himself, but even for health he will be largely dependent on the main drainage system, and for amenity of situation, efficient transport, and, in particular, security on the roads, he is dependent on others. As urban life extends, amenity, health, communication, and housing are more and more public matters in which control in the common interest can do for all what private effort can only achieve with great expense and imperfectly for a few. The well-to-do do not escape epidemics. Only the very rich can so surround themselves with beauty as to shut off the hideosity of industrial towns. Fifty per cent. increase of wages would not give the average workman a good house in a garden suburb. But by collective action such things are feasible, and the town planning which might in a generation restore the beauty of old days is not primarily, the experts tell us, a matter of expense, but of expert organisation with the right end in view. It is true that so long as the financial returns of such improvements fall to ground landlords, the common authority is ham-strung. But finance apart, we have here a great department where organised action by the community is the only method of securing a common end. The physical environment of happiness is a co-operative product, and it is in great measure the lack of it that drives men to the accumulation of the private wealth which may purchase an oasis in the modern wilderness.

We look, then, for an extension of public ownership and management in a variety of forms and degrees, and in some directions we regard it as essential to any social improvement. But we do not anticipate that it will cover the whole of industrial and professional life. At present it is in an early experimental stage, and experiment must decide how far and on what lines it will proceed. We regard it as a contributory part of a wider ideal of transforming industry from an unorganised mass of competing individuals finding their living as best they can and often working against, as well as with, one another, often making the greatest profits out of another's loss, and, as producers, regardless of the permanent social value of their work, to a system conceived as the co-operative service of the common good in which the human needs of all members of the community are the governing inspiration, in which industrial processes, hours, and wages are determined by the common sense of experienced and impartial bodies, in which it will be open to men to prosper and make careers for themselves by social service, but not by any kind of gambling or monopoly or beating down their rivals, in which functionless wealth will dwindle to the vanishing-point and the community will enjoy the elements of wealth which are due to its own expansion. We think of the individual not merely as a servant, but as a partner of the community. His well-being is not a means to an end; it is a part of the end. And the industrial system must not only reward his services, but find place for his energy and initiative. We seek no iron system manufactured to a perfect pattern on *a priori* principles, but a growing life, plastic, creative, modifying and adapting itself to new circumstances and in particular to the changes which its own growth brings about. We think of industry, in fine, as the service of the common good, and the common good, not as an abstraction floating above individual men and women, but as a life effectually shared by all, not repressive of personality, but opening for it a door to fuller and more harmonious development.

ABOUT HAPPINESS

"Man does not need happiness—only an Englishman desires it", is one of Nietzsche's bitterest gibes. When Hegel wishes to explain the futility of material aims he has to introduce the English word "comfortable", for which, apparently, he cannot find a satisfactory German equivalent. To Treitschke it is a sign of our decadence that we are very rich and that we have abolished duelling. We are enjoying while others are still toiling upwards, and there seems for him to be an antithesis between enjoyment and character. Altogether it seems to be a part of the case of the anti-English school of Germans that we have altogether too good a time. We have made the best of this world. We are rather easygoing, content to live and let live rather than impose our "culture" on other folks. We like to be happy, and do not want to make anyone else miserable. Therefore we must be decrepit. At any rate, if we are not we ought to be, and there is no justice in the scheme of things. Now it is always rather dangerous to call nations decrepit. It is not so very long since it was the fashionable and "patriotic" thing in this country to maintain that all the Latin peoples were "dying nations", and Treitschke himself has an occasional doubt whether if England's trade were threatened she might not "once again astonish the world by some act of resolute daring". But what interests me for the moment is not so much the question of national character as the contempt which I find uniting writers so opposed in most respects as Nietzsche and Treitschke for the notion of human happiness, and the tacit assumption that it is to be set against manliness. What is still more remarkable is that in this particular they agree with the ordinary moralist—a result from which Nietzsche at least might be expected to recoil with horror. A just contempt for human happiness is one of the established commonplaces of the moral pulpit.

But it is not usually found that those who most disparage doctors are less ready than others to run to them in illness. Nor are those who are most superior to happiness in general less concerned than other people for the actual element of their personal well-being. But it is characteristic of human nature to be most attracted in idea by what is hardest and even most repellent in experience, and the writers that command our allegiance are those that set us something difficult and even something unlovely to do. The hold that a man like Treitschke obtained was due to the fact that he preached a kind of national asceticism. The picture of the world as he would make it is one of the harshest, crudest, most unredeemed by any touches of suavity, humour, or the milk of human kindness that can be pictured. But it acquires, as one reads on, something of the fascination of ascetic rigour. The ascetic life in the end seems purposeless and dull. One would not like to have lived as an ascetic, but one would like to be able to do so at need. Few of us want actually to be martyrs at the stake, but we should like to be quite sure of our ability to burn without flinching or recanting. Of all things that capture the mind, strength of will and self-control are the most powerful. We can never withhold our tribute. It is paid with the willing recognition of an equal by the strong man himself, and with a sneaking reluctance by the weak. Talk about happiness, and you either tell men what they know already or forecast to them that to which they are but too much inclined. Tell them of hardship, effort, battle, endurance, and victory, and they listen and follow.

So the moralists, and the immoralists agree, and when Carlyle, the greatest of the earlier representatives of the German teaching in England, condemned the pig philosophy of Bentham all the circles of virtue applauded. But Carlyle himself makes in the end a notable admission. Man can do without happiness, he says, and instead thereof find blessedness. Is blessedness, then, not a form of happiness, and does not the whole question resolve itself in the end into the kind of life in which men believe happiness to be found? The much despised Bentham, who is once more duly bespattered with ignominious epithets in that excellent little volume *The War and Democracy*, devoted the whole of a long life with exceptional consistency and singleness of aim to the work of promoting the happiness of mankind as he understood it. "Happiness" was certainly his object, but it was the happiness of all men, or as he himself used to say, "of the greatest possible number". I cannot think ignoble a life of very strenuous intellectual activity devoted to every cause tending to the assuagement of human misery, and the opening out of those channels of freedom and opportunity by which human faculty develops and mankind attains such happiness as the gods allow. When I contrast such a life with that of a Bismarck, a Von Moltke, or a Treitschke, I, for one, do not hesitate to prefer the model set by my own fellow-countryman. When the English thinker invited men to aim at the general happiness, what he urged in effect was (1) that they should think and act socially, and (2) that they should think in terms of real values. By (1) I mean that he bade men put the well-being of self and other, and also of king and peasant, on the same level. "Every man to count for one, and nobody for more than one." I prefer this to Treitschke, with his radical necessity that the millions should plough and forge and weave in order that the thousands may paint and write and learn. I prefer it still more to his theory of the State as power, which makes it the German mission to dominate Europe, the Prussian's to dominate Germany, the Junker's to dominate Prussia, the Kaiser's to dominate the Junker, and every man's to dominate his wife. I react from all this pride of power, however ascetically miserable it may make the world, to that liberty and equality which may elude definition, but which break in on all this gloomy arrogance and ice-bound pride of race and sex like light and warmth.

And I contend (2) that when Nietzsche, for example, tells us that the "will to power" is the ultimate reality of the world, his world is founded on a phantom. Power is not one of the real values except as a means. Those who make it an end have lost the clue of life, which is love, and have caught self instead. Such men cannot believe in happiness, for all their interest is in striving, in surpassing, in destroying, in all that exalts themselves and debases others. By happiness the English philosophers meant something which was not always beyond and therefore always illusory, an object of interest only while unattained, but something which, like a good woman's love, would stand the test of possession and experience. The creed of social happiness means that there are such things in the life of man. It means that there are ends that men may pursue which will not mock them when attained. It means that life can be worth having, if men will seek its best gifts in common, as partners, not as lord and serf. It means that half the misery in life is inflicted by man on man through the pursuit of false aims, and that the radical test of false aims is that they divide, that they set race above and therefore against race, nation above and therefore against nation, class above and therefore against class, sex above and therefore against sex, self above and therefore against others. When the English thinkers called men away from those phantoms that arise out of instincts which man shares with the animals, they were not seeking to degrade. The social life which they propounded could not be lived by brutes. The rational control which they required could not be exercised without discipline and even austerity. They had their own notion of heroism, but it was that of the saviour of life, not of the destroyer. In many ways their statement of theory was weak and insufficient, but as against all the mazes of German mysticism, militarism, and megalomania, it was profoundly right and the true starting-point of humane feeling and rational thinking.

REPRISALS

In rude states of society security depends largely on the principles of retaliation. Kinsfolk, clans, or entire tribes are organised on a basis of mutual protection against their neighbours. There is no common authority to keep them all in awe, no court to which any injured persons can go with the certainty of obtaining redress. Instead of this, if a member of a clan is injured, if his wife or daughter has been carried off, or his son killed, or his cattle driven away, he summons his kith and kin, appeals to the clan, and organises a foray upon the wrongdoers. He may or may not light upon the actual offender, but he will be satisfied if he does as much injury to the aggressor's clan as he has suffered, if he takes as many lives, drives off as many cattle, carries away as many women as he and his friends have lost. This is the simple justice of the blood feud, which takes no account of the due punishment of the really guilty, but merely seeks to deal blow for blow. Courts of justice suppress this rude vengeance, and in its place award a determinate punishment falling on the wrongdoer himself, and not on any of his kindred who happen to come handy for the purpose. But among civilised nations when war breaks out there are no courts to secure and enforce justice. There are agreements which these nations have made, partly written agreements, partly long-standing assumptions, prohibiting certain methods of war, and in particular protecting non-combatants from ill-usage and their property from uncompensated destruction. These methods as summed up in the Hague Conventions provide an admirable paper code for the regulation of the methods of warfare by as large a measure of humanity as is consistent with the fundamental fact that war sets out to destroy. But what is to happen if one side or other violates these rules? If only two combatants are at war there is the opinion of the neutral world to appeal to, and in such a case that opinion might be a very important factor. In the present war nearly the whole world is engaged, and the combatants have no longer much to gain or lose from the opinion of the few small Powers that remain neutral. There is no legal sanction, and there is no longer any effective moral sanction, of the recognised rules.

In such circumstances the customs of war have always recognised an ultimate resource which, like war itself, is simply a return to the methods of the ruder societies. It is the method of reprisal. It is impossible to bring the actual wrongdoer to trial and punishment, so a compensating evil is inflicted on the enemy, involving some fresh departure from the admitted rules. If prisoners are killed on one side, then prisoners to the same number are killed on the other. The prisoners are themselves guiltless. The act is a reprisal justified in the minds of those who order it by the faint hope that it may deter the enemy from further outrages. The danger of such a retaliation is perfectly clear. The enemy probably considers that he has a case for his original outrage, and treats the act of retaliation as justifying him in a further excess. This is again the subject of retaliation, and so it goes on from worse to worse. All the time there is no impartial judge to decide who is really in the wrong, to limit the due amount of retaliation, and tell the combatants where to stop. Every time the reprisals fall on people who as individuals had nothing to do with the offence.

The problem has often been acute in this war, for Germany's methods have not been scrupulous. We, of course, are interested parties, not judges. But if we make the utmost discount from all stories of atrocities, the catalogue of the officially admitted acts of Germany makes a terrible list. When the sinking of a hospital ship is officially recorded as such there is no excuse or palliation to be made. It is a crime which violates no mere convention of war, but whatever of chivalry or of humanity has grown up to soften and mitigate the horror of the struggle. The agents

in this crime are beyond our reach. The captain and crew of
the submarine are merged among the rest, taking their
chance of war with others, never perhaps to be identified.
The real offenders, the Government of Germany, are
beyond our power while war lasts. We can inflict no punishment on the doers of the deed. An intense and just resentment then seeks expression. What can we do to satisfy it?
The Government considers the matter, and finally decides
to drop bombs in an old town of the relatively unwarlike
Southern Germany, with results apparently very comparable
to those of the air raids on unarmed places with which we
are too familiar, and which have bred in us a deep resentment
against the German methods of war. There are two ways of
looking at this reprisal. We may think of it as a satisfaction
of our feelings of resentment. Such a satisfaction seems to
be possible only on condition of our abandoning ourselves
to very confused and muddy thinking. What sort of satisfaction is given to our just indignation against a submarine
commander by blowing a woman to bits in Freiburg? How
do we punish the German Admiralty by destroying a child
in the Black Forest? We add woe to woe, but not to those
who brought woe to us, but only to others for whom they
care a little. The child who beats the chair that bruised it is
more rational, for at least he beats the same chair. On these
lines there is no justification whatever for reprisals.

There is, however, another way of regarding reprisals.
They may be justified as the only method of preventing
the continuance or repetition of the offence, or possibly
as the only means of defence against attack. When the
Germans used poisoned gas they violated an old principle
of war for which there was a sound basis in considerations
of humanity. But they also obtained for themselves what
threatened to be a very serious military advantage. When
we retaliated in kind we were forced, it is true, to accept
a lower standard of warfare, but we had a right to protect
our men. To refuse the retaliatory use of barbarous weapons

might be simply to give the victory, and therewith the future control of the world, to the more barbarous and unscrupulous side. That we are using such weapons in self-defence does not lighten the charge against the Germans of increasing the horrors of war by introducing them. Retaliation is justified when it means simply the adoption of the enemy's methods for purposes of self-protection. But reprisals raise a wider question. Do we protect hospital ships by bombing German towns? Presumably the Governments think we do, or at least that there is a possibility that we may do so. In view of the German attitude to the life of the individual and its little account compared with the victory of the State, this opinion seems very doubtful. Shall we stop the destruction of French villages by threatening to destroy as many German villages? The Germans will probably reply that we have still a long way to go before we reach any German villages. Should we be justified in taking ship for ship? Eminently so, for here no inhumanity is involved; but we have first to win the war, and the ship-for-ship policy will by no means deter the Germans from the pursuit of the one method to which they pin their hopes of preventing us from winning. The effectiveness of reprisals in dealing with a Power like Germany is most doubtful, and its dangers are not obscure. Germany has paid heavily for her misdeeds in the redoubled energy which her victims have put into the war, in the stifling of the thoughts of peace which would otherwise have been rising in many minds; above all, in the bringing in of great neutral forces on our side. In the clean game we can win. In a competition of horrors Germany will beat us every time.

STATESMANSHIP IN WAR

LORD LANSDOWNE was doubtless well prepared for the storm of execration that burst upon him yesterday[1] in a section of the Press. Profitable patriotism finds its easiest line in war-time playing up to the emotions of hatred and vindictiveness. Fortunately there is a saner mind which considers coolly the relations of means and ends. It is all very well to shout on the platform or in large headlines for the knock-out blow and to denounce a calm invitation to consider the actual position as a stab in the back. But Lord Lansdowne will be perfectly aware of the great body of less vocal but more weighty opinion which welcomes a considered attempt to remedy those very grave defects of statesmanship to which the misfortunes of the Allies are largely traceable. Nor will he be in the least surprised that the Government formally repudiate all previous knowledge of his deliverance or complicity in it. It is quite right that this should be stated, though in this country no one could suppose Lord Lansdowne to have acted as the spokesman of the Government. But they do not repudiate his views, though they do all responsibility for them. It would be difficult for them to do so, since in large part they are merely a recapitulation of views quite recently expressed by some of their leading members. Mr. Bonar Law, indeed, went a good deal beyond this in his speech at a private meeting of his party yesterday, of which an authorised report is published. But that speech appears to have been based upon a total misapprehension of the purport of Lord Lansdowne's letter. He treated it as a plea for an immediate peace. There could be no more complete misrepresentation. It was a plea for a clearer and more definite statement of war aims, the effect of which would inevitably be to weaken the war spirit of our enemies, while it ought no less to fortify the spirit and resolution of our own people by

* November 31, 1917.

bringing policy to the aid of arms. There appears to be an extraordinary inability in certain minds to discriminate between a demand for clearness in our war aims and a demand to abandon the war. The two are not merely the same; they are the antitheses of each other. If we wish to determine more exactly what are the objects to be attained by the war, it is primarily in order that we may wage it more effectively because with a clearer aim and a better heart, and if we should lose the war it would be largely because we have too long refused to face these essential issues. Mr. Bonar Law really knows better than this. In a remarkable passage of his speech he himself declared: "It is not only by decisive military results that the war may be ended. Let the Germans realise that we can go on longer than they, and the change of feeling in Germany, of which we hear so much, will grow every day, and will itself, perhaps, bring results which we all long to see." It seems, then, that moral considerations do count, and that the state of mind of the German people is really an important element making for success or failure in the war. That is precisely Lord Lansdowne's case. He says: "You have too long allowed the German people to be the victims of the extravagant misrepresentations of their Government as to the purposes of their enemies. Let them know clearly and on authority how different they really are, and a great step will have been taken towards making an honourable and successful peace possible—a peace which will give us all for which we are fighting and shall fight." Is that wise, or is it foolish? There must be a good many men even amongst Mr. Bonar Law's immediate associates who, if they put the case fairly to themselves, will have to admit that there is wisdom here.

For what is the situation which Lord Lansdowne desires to meet? It has been described in this column before, but the case is so little generally appreciated that it must be summarily stated again. It is that Allied statesmanship by its declarations of policy, and in particular by its failure to recognise new facts, has consolidated our enemies, weakened our friends, and in some degree threatened the unanimity of our people. It has consolidated our enemies first by threats which have led the German people to believe that we menaced their national existence. When the Reichstag passed a resolution against annexations no response came from our side, and the German Government, who disliked the resolution, found it so much the easier to set aside. A great opportunity of dividing the people and the Government of our principal enemy was allowed to slip because our representatives could not bring themselves to say a word of moderation. Not only has our diplomacy thus united the German people with its Government, but it has similarly compelled Austria—manifestly thirsting for rest from war—to remain locked in Germany's embrace. The repudiation by the new Russia of any desire for Constantinople, and indeed of all annexationist aims, opened up one of those opportunities for detaching an enemy from his alliance which statesmen pray for but do not expect. The opportunity was ignored, and Austria, forced to remain in the war, persuaded Germany to the conjoint attack on Italy. But even this was not the worst. Far more serious was the effect on Russia. The mere coldness and hostility of the greater part of the Press to democracy in general and to the Russian Revolution in particular would probably not count for very much among the great forces which have swayed the Russian people. What has without doubt counted is simply this: That the Russians ardently desired peace, primarily because of the exhaustion of the country, next because of the necessity of concentration on internal questions. But they were neither blind to the seriousness of anything like desertion of their allies nor to the ignominy of concluding a peace with an enemy well advanced upon Russian territory and likely to insist on retaining large slices of it. On the other hand, many of their popular leaders told them that this was a capitalists'

war, and that the Western Allies and the Germans were all
tarred with the same brush. The easy task for the Western
Allies was to prove this to be a lie, and the way to prove it
was from the beginning to enter into sympathetic discussion
of the Russian principle of peace without annexations, to
show the qualifications which the principle would need in
the case of the territories previously annexed by Germany,
but to give proof that the Allies wished to come as near to
the Russian standpoint as might be. In fact, the problem
for diplomacy here was simply that of maintaining contact
and understanding with the new influences among the
Russian people. But once again the deadly fear of moderation barred the way. To propose discussion was a stab
in the back; Stockholm was anathema. The Paris Conference might meet to discuss the methods but never the aims
of the war. We wonder what they have, in fact, been discussing to-day. These rebuffs convinced large sections of
Russian opinion that the extremists were right in denouncing
the Allies, and the upshot is that an armistice is now under
negotiation. Handled as it might have been handled, the
Russian Revolution would have given us a more faithful
ally, and might have reduced the number of our enemies.
Handled as it has been, it leaves us with Austria still on our
hands and the Russian situation that which we see to-day.

It is to the Russian situation, we take it, that Lord
Lansdowne's letter is primarily directed. Is that situation
hopeless? In the fog of the Russian news no one can say
that this is certain or that recovery is impossible. Apparently
the Cadets and Moderate Socialists are polling in considerable strength even in Petrograd. The peasants are, as we
may well suppose, for peace. But is anyone sure that the
peasants, or even the Maximalists themselves, will be for
peace upon German terms? Even the armistice is not yet
general; but suppose the armistice concluded, then the real
negotiations will begin. In these negotiations there are three
factors; all are unknown, and two are beyond our control,

but one, and it may be the decisive one, is in our power. The first factor is the German demand, the second the attitude of the Russian people to that demand, the third the attitude of the Allies. There will presumably come a moment when whatever Government is in power in Petrograd will ask the Allies what they have to say to the German proposals. Not even the Bolsheviks have yet proposed a separate peace. Their professed principle is a general democratic peace without annexation. What will be their attitude and that of Russians generally if they find they cannot get such a peace from Germany no one can yet predict. But the probability is that much will depend on the alternative proposed by the Allies. When it comes to fighting on or yielding, the Russians will ask what they are fighting for, and it is then that they will scrutinise carefully the Allied pronouncements. That is why Lord Lansdowne's letter, far from being inopportune, comes perhaps at the necessary moment. But to make use of it rests with others—men whose business lies not with the bandying of cheap words but with the serious problem of saving the Alliance from the most formidable loss which has yet threatened it.

THE DAWN

"THEY attacked with the dawn," said the Prime Minister of the Canadians on the Vimy Ridge, and he found therein a symbol and an omen. There is a lifting of the long night of Russia, where the people that sat in darkness have seen a great light. There is hope for the oppressed of Turkey and for the deliverance of Europe from the curse of a political system that has weighed upon it ever since the first Turkish Sultan crossed the Hellespont. There is hope for a new life of democracy in the fellowship of America with the Allies, and, finally there is the dawn, a dim red dawn, of hope for peace in the renewed vigour of the military attack. In all these elements of hope there are also elements of danger. Hope is not certainty, and it is our business to put our new and larger opportunities to wise and also to worthy issues if the dawn is to bring the brighter day. In part these opportunities depend upon us non-combatants at home. We do more to set the tone of the conflict than the men who are actually fighting and suffering in it. It falls largely upon us to maintain the spirit of the Alliance, to find a meaning for the new-born international democracy, and to conceive of a peace in harmony with the democratic idea. It is a mistake to think that these are matters of theoretical interest alone, or at any rate matters that must wait upon the military event. On the contrary, one of the most critical of immediate issues, the attitude of the Russian nation, will be largely influenced by the general temper of the Allies, by the kind of aims set forth in this and other Allied countries as the goal of the fight, and by the example which the older democracies may set to the democracy which is struggling for existence.

It is known that there are divergent tendencies struggling for the mastery in Russia. On the one hand there is the "Forward" Liberalism, somewhat Imperialistic in our phrase, which helped to make the revolution because it was

U

profoundly dissatisfied with the want of energy and
patriotism evinced by the old Government. On the other
side is the extreme Socialism which, idolising German Social
Democracy from of old, cannot bring itself to believe but
that all might go well if the Socialists of both nations could
somehow join hands across the trenches. So, indeed, it might
be, but the operation of joining hands across barbed wire
with the machine guns at play on both parties is one of some
difficulty. The more moderate Socialists, who have apparently been the backbone of the revolution, see this, and are
aware that there can be no future for Russian self-government as long as German autocracy holds the whole western
frontier in its grip. The result of this triangle of forces up
to the present has been so far as policy goes unexpectedly
favourable. The moderate view is in the ascendant, and if
this ascendancy is maintained it will mean that Russia
abjures any aggressive purposes, and the task of restoring
peace is so much the easier. The spirit of the new democracy
in Russia is what the spirit of democracy should be, but
what the spirit of actual democracies has not always been—
resolute on the defensive, but equally resolute against the
temptation of aggression. It is right that this temper should
be recognised and welcomed among the Western Allies
as the war spirit in which to approach the problems of peace.
It is common ground to us all that Germany made the
war with certain aggressive purposes, and if that is true
it follows that with the frustration of these purposes Germany is defeated, her militarism discredited, and her rulers
left to answer as best they can when their subjects ask
them, Why did you lead us out into the wilderness to
perish? What gains have you to show for a million and a
half dead? If we would work with the newly awakened
Russian people we must respond to the spirit in which they
are facing the problems of the war, and not, in relation to
the eastern front, be more Russian than the Russians. We
should also do well to show a more disinterested sympathy

in the Russian revolution itself. An old Liberal leader, Dr. Spence Watson, did much to educate British opinion in the iniquities of the old system, and with some understanding of the devotedness and endurance of the pioneers of this present dawn, of men like Stepniak, Volkhovsky, or Kropotkin. Apart from all its bearing on the war, the sense that the work of these men has at last borne fruit is an inspiring thing, and it is a pity that it has not been more fully expressed in our Press. There needs to be a real understanding between the democracies not merely for the remoter future but even for the vigorous and concerted conduct of the war, and the foundation of such understanding is that we are working together not merely in a mechanical alliance, each looking for help from the other, but in a real devotion to the same great human ends of peace founded on freedom.

To feel this deep and genuine sympathy with Russian freedom we must recover the sense of freedom among ourselves. If association with us has helped to liberate Russia, it may be feared that our politics have not gone wholly untarnished by association with the Tsardom. We shall not act as befits the democratic dawn if we, the most experienced of the great peoples in self-government, are content to use democracy as a theme of speeches and articles while practising autocratic arts, allowing the use of spies and informers in our courts, curtailing the freedom of the Press, persecuting men for conscience' sake, and abandoning the effort to treat Ireland as we applaud the new Russia for treating Finland. Of course in all these cases authority has a case. It has its reasons, which might be respected if there were not stronger reasons on the other side. Informers are useful in the particular instance, no doubt. But the legal system that is spy-ridden soon gets rotten, as the Russians know to their cost. A free Press has its inconveniences, but they do not compare with the loss to the nation involved in closing the springs of free discussion. We are sensitively aware of the difficulties in Ireland, but we forget that precisely

parallel difficulties are alleged in excuse of nine out of ten
failures to respect the freedom of the smaller nationalities.
Let us frankly recognise the "dawn" as in the first place
a summons to ourselves to wake once more the memories of
our own old freedom, lest, while we fight to save others, we
ourselves become castaways.

THE FUTURE LEAGUE OF PEACE

THE war will have been fought in vain if it does not lay the foundations of an assured peace. To all the civilised world there has come a calamity comparable only to one of the great historic pestilences, or to such a cataclysm as the Tartar invasions, which swept away whole peoples. War such as this the world believed to have become impossible. Such war must never recur if civilisation is to be maintained. How, then, can it be prevented? Short of a change of heart there can be no absolute security, but the condition of any success is the formation of some form of international organisation. How is any such organisation to be made effective without destroying the jealously guarded independence of the nations? In what shape can it be recommended to practical men, not as a Utopia but as something to be worked for here and now? The suggestion which has taken shape in America, advocated by ex-President Taft and approved by President Wilson, is the institution of a league of nations to enforce peace. Lord Bryce to-day lays before us a similar scheme drawn up two years ago by a group of Englishmen. We take it that we should not be far wrong in regarding the two schemes as sisters and Lord Bryce as the father of them both. The English scheme is, in fact, the elder sister, though its existence has been made known to the world later in time, opinion here in the midst of war having been less favourable for the calm consideration of the future than it has been in America, which till yesterday was but a spectator of the turmoil. Though earlier, the English scheme is the bolder and more advanced of the two, for it constitutes the league an alliance for common defence against any outside aggressor who refuses arbitration and conciliation, and it contemplates, though it does not positively enjoin, the use of the common force to give effect to its decision. The nature and extent of the divergence will appear if we briefly review the ground common to both proposals. This common ground is that as many of the Powers as will shall form a league agreeing to establish first a judicial tribunal and secondly a council of conciliation. To the tribunal all "justiciable" disputes are to be submitted, and the English scheme is distinguished by advancing a definition of justiciable questions, into which we have not space to enter, but of which we may say that it is at least a good experimental classification. It is, however, common ground that many of the questions arising between nations—questions of conflicting commercial interests, possibly questions of the treatment of incorporated or subject nationalities—do not admit of handling in a legal spirit, and, if a resort to force is to be averted, can only be decided by Parliamentary methods. Such questions both schemes would submit to a council of conciliation. It is common ground to both schemes to rely much on the moral weight of the decisions of the tribunal or the council and on the delay which discussion would interpose before there could be a resort to arms, and both schemes agree that the league as a whole should take part against any member who should refuse to resort to the tribunal or the council, whether by economic pressure or by the use of military force. But the American scheme does not go on to propose the same resort to the common force in the event of one Power rejecting the decisions of the common authority, nor does the English scheme provide directly that the decisions of this authority are to be enforced. But it prescribes that in such an event the Powers belonging to the league shall summon a conference to consider what collective action, if any, it is practicable to take.

Thus the English proposals go a step farther than the American in the direction of a common enforcement of decisions, as they do also in providing for collective action against a non-member of the league who refuses arbitration or conciliation as the case may be. But both schemes clearly hesitate to give direct collective enforcement to the decisions of the council. This is because they think that the council, in order to work freely and preserve itself from too much bias in favour of national interests or sectional alliances, must be a consultative body alone and have no executive authority. No doubt also they are cautious as to entrusting such power to a body which does not yet exist and of which no one can predict the composition, the capability, or the temper. At the same time the critic will point out that this lack of power may impair the council's authority, and even its sense of responsibility. The reluctance to trust it further engenders a machinery of cumbersome complexity. If we had stayed to deliberate in August 1914 the Germans would have been at Calais before our Expeditionary Force was across the water. Nothing in the war has been more alarming than the evidence of the rapidity of movement possible to a well-organised nation, and of the immense military advantage secured by the initial start. We incline to think that boldness as well as caution must be used in the formation of the league, and that the council, if it is to be a reality, must have a somewhat higher authority. We do not see why its action should be confined to the settlement of disputes which have already arisen. We incline rather to agree with the view, argued with skill by Mr. Brailsford in his *League of Nations*, that an international council to be effective must be an organ of change as well as of conservatism. It must be more like the standing Parliament to which all nations may resort for the redress of grievances or the ventilation of projects than an occasional court of conciliation called into activity from time to time only when disputes have already reached an acute stage.

It seems possible that if Lord Bryce's group were to meet again to-day they would find that the march of events had done something to ease their burden and make a bolder course seem less Utopian than it naturally appeared in 1915. For what has been happening during these years but the gradual formation in very serious earnest of something like

the general league for the suppression of the invader of
the common peace—the troubler of Israel? This country
went into the war not merely because Germany invaded
Belgium, nor because it attacked France, nor because it was
a danger to ourselves, but for all reasons combined. What
has sustained our efforts in the war has been the judgment,
repeatedly confirmed by the course of events, that Germany
was in substance committing just such offences against the
common peace as those which the proposed league contemplates as fit occasions for collective interposition. What has
sustained the spirit of the Italian people is no less the sense
of a common danger. What has finally brought America
into action is not the submarine itself but the evidence,
which the submarine clinches, that Germany as at present
directed is at war with the civilised world. Thus the league
of nations is gradually coming into being. It is a league
while the war lasts against Germany, just as in 1814 the
Allies were leagued against Napoleon. But after Waterloo
France was in substance admitted into the alliance, and so,
after this war, may Germany find admission into the league
if she seeks it and is prepared to conform to its spirit.
Moreover, unlike the Holy Alliance, which foundered on
its opposition to democracy and nationality, the league now
in formation is becoming a league of democracies in which
the recognition of nationality will be more and more felt
to be an essential principle, the Russian revolution and the
entry of America into the war having together laid the
foundation of a possible league of all self-governing peoples
to maintain peace among themselves, to provide for the
adjustment of questions arising out of their expansion, and
to resist the possibility of attack from an autocracy or a
militant empire, whether within or without their circle.

PRECEPT BEFORE EXAMPLE

SISTER AGATHA is a missionary born. She detects vice with microscopic eye, and reproves it with prophetic fire. In a manner all vice is fish for her net, which is cast as wide as its meshes are small. But if there is one vice more than another which moves her wrath and stirs her eloquence it is self-indulgence. Herself brought up in an atmosphere of wealth, she has from childhood recognised the vanity of riches and feels herself qualified by personal experience to explain to the poor how little they would add to their real happiness by doubling their income. It is pretty to see her on a wintry day passing down the village street in her rich furs, and glowing alike with the frosty air and the moral indignation within as she lectures some labourer's wife for spending half a crown on a new hat. Her own cost twenty guineas; but, as she says, she must go to her committees in order to do her bit, and she must have a hat to go in. The twenty guineas, I heard her very lucidly explaining to some unintelligent inquirer, was not, for her, luxurious expenditure, but virtually a contribution to public work. It was part of the personal cost incurred by her services to the seventeen committees which she adorns, and in particular to the National Committee for Restricting the Extravagance of the Working Classes, of which she is a mainstay. "Look at this car," she will say, as she is whirled from meeting to meeting. "It cost 600 guineas, and in one way or another costs some £300 a year to run. Now quite half of that is spent on committee work, which if I were poor I should do by tram and motor-bus, say, at 4d. a meeting. You see, I am doing my bit."

But in a day or two I found Sister Agatha much put out. She had been canvassing a street in one of her happy hunting grounds—Sister Agatha's paradise would hardly be complete unless largely laid out in slums conveniently accessible to visitors—to ask for spare pennies for her ornamental wooden leg fund. The actual supply of artistic footgear to wounded soldiers is, in reality, a secondary object of this fund, the main purpose being to keep down expenditure and sweep up any superfluous pennies lurking in corners of poor men's purses. Be that as it may, in the course of her visitations Sister Agatha seems to have happened on a household of an unexpected character. She was, for the first time for many years, taken unprepared, and did not like it. "The house," she said, "was very bare, but what furniture there was, though rather Victorian in character, was obviously much too good for the means of the owner, and I was beginning to make it the text of my discourse when the woman remarked, 'Yes, it is all we have been able to keep.' Evidently she had come down in the world, and the note to strike was quite different from what I had supposed. I spoke gently and sympathetically of her altered fortunes, touching lightly on drink and gambling as occasions of downfall, but pointed out that the opportunity for sacrifice on behalf of our common country was still not denied her. If she could do nothing else she could sell the oak dresser which stood up opposite the fire, and replace it with deal. And what do you think the woman answered? She made no excuses for herself at all. She declined to answer. She turned on me, and asked, 'And what have you got to sell?' Me! Asking me a question! I should think it the first time I've been asked a question—well, I mean, of course, in a house of that size—for years. I was so taken aback that I positively answered, which, of course, was an undignified thing to do. 'My good woman,' I said, 'I don't sell, I buy.' 'Yes,' she said with an unaccountable bitterness in her tone, 'I've got eyes in my head. What you have on would buy this house and all that is in it three times over.' This rather gave me the advantage. So I said, 'Well, you know, it is not very polite of you to make personal remarks to your guests, but at any rate you can see what it costs me to come here.' And what do you think she said then? With extraordinary glibness she just parodied me. She did not think it very polite to make personal remarks to one's hostess; as if she was my hostess—that woman—and as if I had made any remarks about her at all, except as to the unsuitability of her furniture. But I assure you that after this I could not get on a step. She had got the cue, and every single question I asked her she had the amazing impertinence to ask me back in a sort of parody. Naturally I wanted to know what her husband spent on beer, and she, if you please, must be informed how much I spend on wine. As if I had the smallest idea, or as if it mattered to her! I could not mention clothes without being asked impertinently about my own milliner's bill, or picture theatres without being asked the price of the dress circle—such ignorance, too. I suppose she never heard of boxes. Finally, when I asked her what time she had dinner, she openly flouted me by saying 'Eight o'clock'.

"Now, I always flatter myself that I know my limitations —it is the one poor little merit on which I do pique myself— and I could see that this was a stubborn case in which I could do no good. I got up to go, when the woman actually followed me and began to preach at me—me! Why, I have never been preached to—except of course in church—these ten years. But she took up her parables and she held the door latch, and would not be gainsaid. 'Listen,' she said. 'You come here in your car and your furs and your hat (as if I should come without a hat!) and grub up pennies from wretched women who pay to get rid of you. You talk about self-indulgence and thrift and patriotic sacrifice. Kindly listen to my story. My husband was in a business house. We had been engaged five years, and married when he had worked himself to a salary of £400 a year. Our second boy was born just after the war began. My husband had been a Volunteer in the old days, and when things began to go wrong he began to feel that he must go. I can't tell you the agony of doubt that he went through, torn between the children and me on one side and the country on the other, and every day being told he was a slacker and a shirker. We lived in a house—comfortable to our minds. You couldn't afford it—it would not have room for your philanthropy—but we were happy enough with our servant and a nursemaid, and the furniture that it had taken us five years of saving to buy. With the army allowances and the interest of the little money he had saved for, I have 30s. a week. We gave up the house, took this cottage, sold three-quarters of the furniture, kept what you see. I have the housework and the children to look to, and I have never been used to doing without a servant, but I manage to do a little for the hospital over the way. He is in Flanders, over the knees in mud when I last heard from him. Good-bye.' And before I could answer she had somehow got me out of the door.

"Did you ever hear of anything so uncomfortable? Somehow I can't get it out of my mind, Who was that man in the Bible—Nathan, Abram, or somebody—who had one ewe lamb? I must get my secretary to look it up. But of course, about spending, the woman's argument is utterly illogical. What I could not get her to understand is that my things are necessary expenses, and hers are superfluities."

"So that, in fact," I said, "the more you spend on dress or on motors the less you have to give away, while the woman who is too poor to have a motor and cannot afford a new gown has the money in her pocket, and ought to sacrifice it cheerfully to the State. The division of labour is that the poor do the saving and the giving, and you do the spending."

"I thought you were a serious person," she replied, "but now I begin to think you are a Socialist."

COMPULSION

WHAT right, after all, has the State to compel military service? The question has been raised in many minds as an issue that may at any moment become practical, and would be for many high-minded men serious. Different views have been urged by various correspondents. Some urge regular legal compulsion to military service as preferable to the indirect and unequal methods that no doubt have been used. Others believe universal service to be necessary if we are to win this war. Others admit conscription to be permissible in cases of necessity, but deny that the necessity has arisen. Yet others, probably a small but very important minority, deny altogether the right of the State to force the conscience of the individual. Some of them, taking their stand on the Gospel, maintain that Christ preached the doctrine of non-resistance, and condemned all meeting of force by force. They refuse all qualifications and metaphorical interpretations of the passages in question, declaring that the spirit is to them as plain and simple as the letter, and that, in fine, on their conscience as Christians they cannot and will not participate in bloodshed. Of this party I will not ask whether it is right or wrong. I merely take it from them—as all must who know the men and the history of the Society of Friends—that to participate in war, however just according to human standards, is against their conscience, and I go on to ask whether in that case the State has a right to enforce it upon them.

I must confess at the outset that I can find no simple and easy answer. The question is the final crux of political theory and practice, and I am not at all sure that it is to be solved by theory at all. I observe with amazement the acceptance by distinguished English writers on political philosophy of the State theory of the Greeks as containing the last word of human wisdom. Far from solving the relation of conscience to law, neither Plato nor Aristotle ever clearly raises it. They are a good deal concerned with the "good" of the individual and the "good" of society, and are at pains to show that properly understood the two coincide. The position of the good men in a bad State is also handled by Plato, and—cursorily and very inadequately —by Aristotle. But the sanctity of conscience, as the modern world has understood it, is as little in their minds as the possibility that the whole Greek form of the State will some day grow obsolete. Now, the authority of conscience and the moral autonomy of the individual form the kernel of the modern principle of liberty, and the theme of every English, American, or French writer on politics. The problems to which they give rise, far from being solved by the ancients, are not even stated by them. They may be insoluble, but to ignore them is to wipe out two thousand years of history, Christianity in general, Protestantism in particular, and as a mere appendix the entire struggle of the modern world in thought and in action, from the rebellion of the Dutch Calvinists to the protest of Herr Liebknecht in the Reichstag.

German thinkers eagerly adopted the theory of the onnipotence of the State, and the so-called idealists who have followed them in England have been ready to take up any stick with which they could beat Liberalism and political Rationalism. German thought as a whole does not differ from Greek thought in omitting morality from the aims of the State. On the contrary, Hegel, though always disparaging in his treatment of anything that savoured of rational reflection on morality, regards the State as the living embodiment and guardian of what is good tradition, good custom (Sittlichkeit). Treitschke certainly in some passages identifies the State with power, but in others he is, however inconsistently, quite clear that it has a moral end. This is not the essential mistake. The essential mistake is to regard the State—after all, in much of its constitution the product of historical accidents, and of all the passions, prejudices, and irrationalities of successive generations of men—as a kind of divine institution, the finest form of human association, justly indifferent to all interests but its own, and possessed of plenary authority over all its members. Why anyone should assign this mystic position to the State above any other form of human association passes my comprehension. I can understand men so thinking and speaking of their church. But to put the authority of the State on this pinnacle is wilfully to deify something manifestly human.

What, then, is the basis of State authority? Government can, of course, use force upon its members, but to plead power as a ground of moral authority is precisely to repeat Treitschke's fundamental mistake. What moral right, as contrasted with physical power, has the State to tell me to do what I do not like and do not think right? Well, the State is the organised expression of my country, of so much that has helped to make me whatever I happen to be, under whose protection lived my father and forefathers, developing the arts of industry and progress, evolving the very ideas which I have imbibed and the very language in which I now question the State's authority. It has protected and protects my person and property, my home and my children. It is the foundation of my ordered life. More than this, it is the keystone in the social arch. If I plead duty to mankind as a reason for disobedience, it may retort that to rebel successfully is to dissolve government into anarchy and to destroy those very social bonds on which I rely. Armed with a purely moral authority thus briefly and most inadequately analysed, the State may say, speaking through Government as its organ, "Our existence is at stake. We call on everyone to help us who is able, and all must serve alike." If the dissident replies, "Yes, but it is against my conscience. Call on all willing for this service. Call on me for any other, but not for this," Government may in turn rejoin: "Rules must be universal, not admitting of exceptions. If we begin with exceptions we must either act unjustly or let our scheme fall to the ground. We have thought the question out on all sides, and have come to the conclusion that this is necessary. We may be wrong, but someone must act for society as a whole, and it is our lot to do so. If you succeed in disobeying and so thwarting us you will, in our judgment, endanger the nation. Does that consist with your conscience?" These are arguments to which expounders of the rights of conscience have not always given the weight they deserve. Yet still there may be those who, setting the whole case before themselves far more fully and lucidly than it is presented here, may still say in the end: "No. I cannot bring myself to it. Do what you will with me." Admit that this case is possible, would, in fact, occur if conscription were introduced. What are the moral rights and wrongs? Who has right on his side, the individual who in the deliberate judgment of the Government endangers society, or the Government which in the deliberate judgment of the individual breaks the moral law and punishes him for refusing to do the same? Is it a paradox to suggest that both are right if both have in fact used all their resources to form their judgment aright? It is hard saying, for it admits that a man may rightly suffer for doing what he believes right. If it is true, one practical consequence follows: that Government must never let anything but insuperable necessity bring matters to such an issue. It must go a long way about to adapt State exigencies as it sees them to right and wrong as the conscience of some upright man judges them.

OPTIMISM

Of living men Martius is he whose temperament I am most often inclined to envy. To say that he never foresees evil would be a quite inadequate expression of the facts. When the evil which he always denied to be possible has arrived he sees it as a good. He was formerly an avowed Pacifist of the type which denied war to be possible in the modern world, particularly under a Government so wise, far-sighted, and consistently Liberal as ours. War was, in fact, for him an unthinkable calamity, until it broke out. When war became a fact I expected to find Martius a little dashed in spirits and shaken in confidence in his judgments. I was never more mistaken. War had become for him a great and glorious uprising of the nations in the cause of peace. It was a tragedy of the moment, no doubt, but the event could not long be deferred. Martius knew men at the front who said openly that they would be home by Christmas. Any hint of doubts or difficulties moved his patriotic ire. We had our leaders. There was the man on the spot, the man at the centre of affairs, the divinely inspired Cabinet holding all the threads together. To whisper of anything lacking anywhere in a scheme directed by omniscience was to play the German game. "No criticism" was the Martian motto. Time passed. Christmas came, the trench warfare developed, but found Martius serene as ever. Easter was now his date instead of Christmas. With the first dry days of spring the great conjoint advance would begin. While the Russian steam roller was moving with irresistible pressure from the east, the Allies would roll up the German lines on the west. By the end of May at latest it would all be over but the shouting. In point of fact we were recording small victories every day, and the sum-total must already be decisive. When private criticisms began to be echoed publicly, and, above all, when a leading Minister took the platform and told us definitely that unless we bestirred ourselves things would not go as we wished them, Martius, after being poised for a moment over an abyss of indignation and incredulity, flew off once more into the scene of exultation. Now we knew what had been lacking all along, as Martius himself had always suspected. In fact, he had told us so. None of us were keen enough. If we had listened to Martius we should have known that munitions of all sorts, particularly shells, were the one thing needed to complete our triumph. But we had been doubting Thomases, or mere slackers with whom the Government would now proceed to deal faithfully. A long pull and a strong pull and a pull altogether and we should put an end to the last desperate rallies of the enemy—every German effort is, according to Martius, desperate, and every success is a last frantic spasm —and all would be happily over. In fact, Martius knew a man at the front who had arranged to begin his holiday with his family at the end of July. There was something in preparation—Martius would not say what, but eked out the description with a nod as eloquent as Lord Burghley's.

Well, Martius has had nearly eleven happy months since the war began. Each victory has been to him an unqualified joy, and each retreat a masterly step destined to make the next victory more complete. When I compare him to Pluvius I almost think him the wiser man. Pluvius had seen Armageddon approaching for years, but found no satisfaction even in the prophet's triumph. He had not even the heart to say "I told you so" to his wife, and in the presence of Martius he habitually goes under. He made up his mind to a three years' war from the outset, but has not found eleven months of it any the easier to bear. He foresaw the fall of Lemberg from the beginning of the Galician thrust—not through strategic knowledge, but by emotional divination—yet he only listens meekly while Martius enlarges on the masterly tactics of retreat. He foresees now—what I decline to put on paper, and will only grudgingly admit when probed to the depth of his soul,

an underlying conviction that somehow we shall muddle
through. In sum, Pluvius has been as wretched for nearly
a year as Martius has been happy, and as far as can be
seen, the same contrast will continue indefinitely. Who
would deny that Martius is the enviable man?

Yet there is something on the other side of the account.
Martius and Pluvius, it is true, are both private individuals
with very little influence on affairs. But the great clans of
the Martii and Pluvii make up a considerable section of
public opinion, and of the two I wonder which have the
saner influence on events. Of Martius one thing is clear:
that he will neither initiate nor tolerate criticism. Everything being so much for the best in his world, there being
no defects, no remedies can be needed. We have only to
go on as we are, suppress croakers, and all will be well.
Also Martius is quite unteachable by experience, for
with him to be convinced that one of his ideas is wrong is
to be convinced that he has always rejected and denounced
it. Martius remains through life unaware of having made
mistakes. So the Gens Martia does not contribute much
to constructive statesmanship. Pluvius, on the other hand,
being perpetually aware of mistakes, failures, and dangers,
is also highly receptive to proposed remedies. He is too
easily alarmed, and his depression makes him troublesome
to live with in bad times. But he cultivates the spirit of
sceptical inquiry in the public. The Gens Pluvia numbers
only tens as against the thousands of the Martii. But it is
sufficient to secure a hearing for complaints and a support
for reforms. Between the two we want someone to mediate
—someone like, shall I say? Georgius Gallicus—who is
perfectly clear-eyed in his vision of existing difficulties and
dangers, but believes in ultimate success on the ground
that he is resolved to find the way to it, that he knows the
resources and temper of his fellow-countrymen, and is
determined to discover the means by which they can be
brought to bear. He is in a sense as confident as Martius,

but confidence with him is not a passive attitude, accepting all things as good. It is a practical attitude of resolve to make them good. He is as critical as Pluvius, but not as melancholy. Everything that he sees to be wrong stimulates him to effort, and suggests a means of hopeful exit. Yet he gets some help from Pluvius, who is always inclined to give him a chance on the ground that things can hardly be worse than they are already; while the Gens Martia presents a solid front of resistance, sometimes merely inert, sometimes clamorous, which he has to break or outflank before he can get forward. So when we consider Martius and Pluvius from the public point of view I am not sure that we must not reverse our judgment. Martius is the wiser in the inner man. He has so framed his own internal constitution as to yield him in all circumstances the greatest inward satisfaction. When I think of this I envy him. I would fain be built on the same lines. But as a member of the public I am afraid that Martius is of very little use. He does not contribute, on the contrary his crassness obfuscates. Pluvius, on the contrary, though he suffers needlessly, does help to dissipate the fog which the Martians create. He is not satisfied and he keeps things on the move. He could not run the country unaided, for he would despair too soon. But he helps to make a platform for the man who can run it. Pessimism is a bitter astringent, but taken in moderation, not more than once daily, it has its uses. Optimism is a soporific which should only be prescribed for those whose useful life is past.

THE PAST AND THE FUTURE

THE INFLUENCE OF NATIONALISM

NATIONALITY, Mr. Lowes Dickinson has lately said, is a Janus. It looks both ways—towards freedom and towards aggression. The struggles of subject nationalities with oppressors and conquerors have filled a great chapter in the history of freedom. Yet nationalities that have become free have often gone on to enslave others. A nationality feels itself to be one. It also feels itself or fancies itself to be unique, and as it can tolerate no superior, so when it has sufficient strength it is not very ready to tolerate an equal. It requires a very perfect drilling in principles of liberty to impose voluntary restraint on a nationality conscious of power. Hence the rise of nationality, essential in its first stages to political liberty—for, think what we may of it, national sentiment is a hard fact, and will not be kept under except by coercion—is also a permanent menace to peace and order. It is in particular the rise of nationality in Europe that has caused the succession of wars since 1815. Indeed, we ought to go back to 1793 and say that it was the assertion of French nationality, finding itself for the first time in the French Revolution and seeking to impose its type on Europe, that gradually called forth by reaction the national sentiment of one European people after another. The nineteenth century witnessed the successful emergence of two great nationalities, the German and the Italian, into consolidated political States, the successful claim of Magyar nationality to equality and internal independence, the liberation of Greece, the failure of Poland, and the partial success of Ireland. The later years of the nineteenth and the beginning of the twentieth century have seen the rise of the Slav nationalities into political prominence, and the problems arising out of this last movement have provided the occasion and in part the cause of the present war.

Few, if any, European States correspond accurately to national boundaries. But partly through grants of autonomy or through Federal or quasi-Federal arrangements, partly by transfers of territory, partly through a greater liberality in internal government, which tends to conciliate and so to overcome differences, there has been on the whole a tendency for the State and the nationality to coincide. Thus the typical State of the modern world is coming to be more and more a nation State. Great Britain, though comprising many racial strains, though including three peoples that nourish a strong and distinctive sentiment of patriotism, has yet been for many generations a true nationality. Scots, Welsh, English, are all truly one in sentiment as against the rest of the world. It is the general belief and hope that liberal measures have similarly incorporated Irish sentiment in a true national unity common to the United Kingdom. France has long been such a unity, though lacerated at one point by the forcible tearing away of two provinces. Germany includes Poles, some Danes, and Alsace-Lorraine, but for the rest is preponderantly German and permeated with an intense feeling for national unity. Italy is all Italian, though she does not include all Italians. All such States have elements of strength which Austria-Hungary, for example, wholly lacks. It is this fusion of living sentiment permeating the whole of the great majority of the population which gives to the State a new power, and a new unity. Patriotism has become a more general, a more spontaneous and a deeper feeling. The State has penetrated further and more sympathetically into private life than of old. Government no longer means in the concrete a king, a nobility, and a mercenary army that takes taxes, administers justice, and levies dynastic wars. It is much more truly an organisation of the common life, and this is no less true in semi-autocratic Germany than in semi-democratic England. Thus the national consciousness and the State consciousness have come to be one and the same thing. Each people has felt itself more at one, and at the same time has drawn the line more definitely between itself and others.

It is this heightening of national unity which has wrecked the peace programme of the old Manchester School. Cobden and Bright, whom it is the fashion to disparage as materialists, were in reality men of an intense spiritual vision. They saw a world becoming more intimately connected in all its parts by the growth of communication. They saw a peaceful commerce not only as an end in itself, but as a means to the development of a real sense of human unity. They taught—and Mr. Norman Angell, whose work has always been unjustly decried in the same terms, sought to revive their teaching—that separate national self-interest was not only wrong but illusory. They showed that in exchange advantage was mutual, that in the end Germany was not to lose by England's wealth, nor England to become poorer through Germany's expansion. They showed that Protectionism, avowedly an expression of national selfishness, was also a policy of class and even of individual selfishness. Their appeal was always to the truest interest of the widest community. In every tariff controversy the Protectionist has always the best of it as long as the argument is conducted on the lines of appeal to particular interests. The Free Trader has always to bring the argument back to the interest of trade as a whole, and even of the world as whole. Now Cobden and Bright were sanguine men who trusted much to human rationality. They believed that as Lancashire had followed them, and as England had followed Lancashire, so by degrees the world would follow England, and they looked forward accordingly to a reign of Free Trade and peace. In this they were mistaken, but in the principle underlying their argument they were right. The interconnection of Free Trade and Peace, of Protection and armaments, stands first. He who would think out a political map of Europe to-day which should give satisfaction to national claims is constantly pulled up by the contention that this or that outlet through foreign soil is necessary to the economic independence of a State. On principles of Free Trade there would be no such necessity. It could be a matter of no moment to Austria-Hungary to have a port in the Adriatic or to Bulgaria to have access to the Ægean or to Poland to have Dantzig as a harbour, but for the constant fear of the interposition of hostile tariff walls. But more than this, the Colonial ambitions of the European States, as distinct from our own, have been motived plainly by Protectionist principles, and questions of commercial rights or privileges have been among those which have made controversies as to aggression most acute. Protectionism and national sentiment have played into one another's hands, and between them have defeated reason and humanity.

Thus we have had a group of States, each consolidating itself more and more within, marking itself off from others by sentiments of national pride, and seeking economical aggrandisement at the expense of its neighbours by means of a tariff boundary. Meanwhile to these States there has fallen the prize of a derelict world as an apple of contention. Africa has been opened out. The Far East has been half opened. The Near East has been tempting with large unrealised possibilities. On all hands there has been the belief, three parts illusory, that the extension of territory in these defenceless or semi-defenceless regions redounds to national glory and economic advantage. Of this belief Protectionism has been the most solid support. But Protectionism, as we have seen, is itself at bottom an expression of national egoism, and so in the general impulse to plunder a new world we have an illustration on the grand scale of the side of nationalism that faces towards aggression and conquest. Perhaps the historian who reviews the last fifty years will marvel not that the crash came, but that it was averted so long. He will give their meed of credit to two statesmen who retained some of the traditions of older days—to Bismarck, who combined with all his unscrupulousness a certain moderation which disinclined him to adventure for its own sake, and to Lord Salisbury, who learned his lesson late in life from his chief opponent, Gladstone, and applied it so well as to carry through a peaceful partition of the greater part of Africa and to avert the imminent danger of China at the end of the century by insisting on the policy of the open door. But the equilibrium became more and more unstable. The new arrivals in the company of Great Powers were dissatisfied with their share, Germany most of all. They quickened the pace in the race of armaments. They drank in eagerly the new doctrines of lawlessness. They believed that the world was for the strong, and that they were the strong. They had just arrived, and were swollen with the consciousness of new maturity. Nor were they the first to overestimate themselves or undervalue their neighbours. It is not twenty years since it was fashionable in England to dismiss all the Latin peoples as dying nations, and to bepraise the Teuton as racially one with ourselves. If political memories are short, how much shorter is political foresight. The friends of France in those days would hardly themselves have ventured to attribute to her such rallying power as she showed in the dark days of last August and September, nor would they have found listeners if they had predicted a time not far off when we in England should be thankful for so staunch and virile an ally. Every nation in the days of its vigour and prosperity allows itself expressions of self-esteem and depreciation of others, which would not be tolerated in an individual, and comes through repetition to believe thoroughly in what it says.

So it was that in Europe at any time in the last dozen years there came together all the elements of disaster—a group of States inflamed with national self-consciousness, grasping at great prizes, discontented with each distribution, emancipated by their spiritual guides from all sense of law, indoctrinated with all the ethics of violence, ready to accept discipline and hardship only for the sake of over-whelming others, and sustained in their course, if every aggressive confidence flagged, by fear of the very rivals whom they despised and yet perpetually provoked. Such was the prolonged condition of moral warfare which we now see embodied in physical fact.

WAR AND LITERATURE

It is natural to suppose that great events, in particular any great and dramatic output of national energy, will be mirrored in national literature and art. The great artist wants a theme worthy of him, and a great theme might even stimulate into activity genius that would otherwise be dormant. If that is so, the colossal scale of the present war, the vastness of its tragedies, the pathos of the hundreds of thousands of young lives innocent of all military ambition given from sheer sense of duty, affords to the poets, the novelists, and the historians of the future an opportunity not easy to parallel. Yet if we look back on the great historical parallels we may doubt. In Greece, indeed, where every freeman was an active citizen and a soldier, we have one or two illustrious instances of great literary work directly inspired by great events. Æschylus was present at the battle of Salamis, and described it in a play. Yet his *Persæ* never won quite the same fame as his *Agamemnon* or the *Prometheus Bound*. After all, it would seem that the far-away heroic myths made at least as good subject-matter for the great dramatist as the actual world historic fight in which he played his part. No surviving play of Sophocles or Euripides deals with the great series of events which occupied the whole of the latter portion of their lives, and although Aristophanes deals with the Peloponnesian War, it isby way of satire and political pamphleteering. The Roman poets of the Augustan age have very little to say about the great civil wars or the personality of Cæsar, partly, perhaps, because it was not very safe to speak freely. "You are walking over fires hidden under treacherous cinders," says Horace to a friend who was meditating a history of his time, though Horace himself ventures a joke on his own performances when he was on the wrong side, and threw away his shield, too, in the flight. Virgil was undoubtedly inspired by the Augustan peace. It is the true theme of his

Æneid, but the wars of that epic are purely conventional Homeric or quasi-Homeric combats, in which the most Virgilian touches are the bits of local colour in the enumeration of the walled and turreted villages that send their quota of men. Historians, no doubt, stood in closer relation to contemporaneous events. The unfortunate participation of Thucydides in the Peloponnesian War hardly helped him much, and has even been supposed by some critics to have biased his account of Cleon. It is of literary interest mainly for the masterly impersonality of his reference to himself:

> Thucydides, who also wrote this history.

But besides failing in Thrace, Thucydides had the plague at Athens, and his description of that terrible episode could not have been written by anyone but an eye-witness and a sufferer.

In English literature the critics connect the outburst of the Elizabethan drama with the triumphant emergence of the nation from its struggles with Spain. The glory of Shakespeare is held to reflect the daring of Drake and Frobisher. If so, the connection is indirect. It may be that the atmosphere of sudden relief, of success, of triumph, disposes a people to welcome great creative art, and so makes that field which some men of genius never find. Yet Shakespeare's theme was not Elizabeth nor Drake. The series of his histories ends with *Henry VIII*, and his subjects, like those of the Attic dramatists, if not historic, are drawn from a world of tales and romances that are common property. Nor did Milton write about the Ironsides, but of Titans, angels, Gabriel, Abdiel, who merely as combatants were a good deal less interesting than the men of Marston Moor and Naseby. The last great war of Europe continued for twenty-two years, and was full of the most extraordinary achievements carried out by men of most striking personality. It coincided or was immediately followed by a period of great literary fertility, but it supplied very little of the subject-matter to the poets, novelists, and romancers of the day. Wordsworth, indeed, has given us some pages from the revolutionary days in his *Prelude*, but this is in strictness autobiography. Scott dealt with Napoleon historically, but went for themes of romance to the Jacobites and Covenanters, just as in France itself Dumas found the inspiration of his really great romance not in Danton, Ney, or Napoleon, but in Richelieu, Mazarin, and Louis XIV. We just touch the edge of the wave of great contemporary events in the *Antiquary*, where the ripples lap up into the quiet society of a Scottish seaport. We have no scene laid in the Peninsula, no story turning on the Hundred Days as its hinge. Jane Austen's case is even more remarkable. Her mild heroes seem lapped in sempiternal peace. Sir Thomas, it is true, congratulates himself on having escaped the attentions of French privateers on his way home to Mansfield Park, and in *Persuasion* the Peace is so far of importance in the narrative that it leads to the letting of Kellynch Hall to a successful admiral. Of Captain Wentworth, Anne Elliot mentions casually that he was "in the Trafalgar action". Will the heroines of the novels of to-morrow allude as tranquilly to the presence of their lovers in "the Ypres show"? On the whole, it may be taken as certain that the German scholars of two centuries hence, digging up Jane Austen from forgotten libraries, will prove to their entire satisfaction that the traditional dates of her life must be hopelessly wrong, for it will be clear to them from internal evidence that she wrote in a period of prolonged peace and profound national torpor.

Hitherto the Great War has certainly not produced much in the way of literary effort. The exclusion of the special correspondent has handicapped one class of writing which at its best may be genuine literature. But some of the Americans who have seen the war from the German side have given us vigorous descriptive scenes. Of poetry,

the "Song of Hate" will probably live. Of the original I
have only seen the first four lines, and thought them inferior
to the swing of the American translation:

> French and Russian, we hate them not.
> A blow for a blow, and a shot for a shot.
> We love them not, we hate them not,
> We hold the Weichsel and Vosges gate,
> We have but one and only hate—
>   England!

This translation will be remembered when the emotions
which provoked the original have come to seem incredible.
So also will be the equally stirring and spirited answer of
another American woman, which all Englishmen ought to
know:

> Pry the stone from the chancel floor,
> Dream ye that Shakspere shall live no more?
> Where is the giant shot that kills
> Wordsworth walking the old green hills?
> Trample the red roses on the ground!
> Keats is beauty while earth springs round.

But the question is not so much what the war will produce
while it is in progress—for the literature of controversy,
whether in prose or poetry, seldom, if ever, ranks among the
immortals—but how it will reflect itself in literature and
art when it is over. It is the rarest thing for the direct real
personal emotions of the artist to express themselves satis-
factorily in art. The artist expresses his own emotions
rather than by depicting the emotions of someone else, and
so we may imagine an age surcharged with the intense
excitement of its great events will rather seek at once expression and relief in handling something other than those events.
We may have a cult of the domestic and peaceful in literature and of beauty in art as opposed to the violence, disorder, and ugliness in which the imagination of the last
few years has so strangely revelled. There is only one quite

external and mechanical limitation which the war would seem necessarily to impose on our novelists. Their stories will have to date. They will either have to be before the war or after the war or during the war, for if the hero does not go or has not been to the front his literary censors will want to know the reason why!

DECADENCE

When Ajax hurled a stone upon the Trojan ranks, it was of such a weight as "not ten strong men of these degenerate days" could lift, but he just played with it single-handed. Thus in Homer's time degeneracy had set in. In the golden age of Roman literature, and in the beginning of that work of reconstruction which swept away a corrupt and brutal oligarchy, and founded the Empire which gave the principles of law and government to Europe, Horace declares that "the age of our fathers, itself inferior to our grandfathers, produced us more worthless than they, and about to yield a still more faulty progeny". According to the literary men, the world at any given epoch is degenerating. It is always losing its lofty ideals, its valour, its vigour. Its romance for ever dies. Mr. Kipling is beyond doubt right in throwing back the complaint to the Palæolithic Age:

> "Farewell, Romance!" the Caveman said;
> With bone well carved he went away;
> Flint arms the ignoble arrow-head,
> And jasper tips the spear to-day.
> Changed are the Gods of Hunt and Dance.
> And he with these, Farewell, Romance!

Men had taken to building huts for themselves, and the dim obscurities of the cave were no longer a delight and a terror to children. Cowards who would not face the enemy with bone-tipped spear were shooting at a distance with bow and arrow. Victory fell to the weakling. The race was degenerating, and must soon fall a prey to the mammoth or the grizzly bear.

But, after all, it was the mammoth that perished, and Neolithic man, no longer trusting purely to the keen eye and the swift foot in the hunt, but clearing the ground for seed, and afterwards tilling it and reaping the fruits of industry, laid the foundations of a life which was not only a little more secure but also a little larger and more free. He and his successors have never yet exhausted the wells of romance nor touched the barriers of the expansion of mind. But at every stage in the extension of peaceful arts, with every year in which men have lived for a while more happily and harmoniously, there has risen a wail from out of the sullenly retreating waters of barbarism: "You stay our flood with pitiful dams, behind which you lurk in fancied security. But the doom of rottenness is upon you. You shall wax fat and die. Peace shall be your ruin, for in its softness you shall rot." A more profound observer spoke of the most warlike State of his race in just the contrary sense. Sparta fell, said Aristotle, because the Spartans did not know how to live in peace. It was the one-sided cultivation of the arts of war that brought to its decline that city whose name has become the recognised epithet for endurance, fortitude, self-command, and discipline.

In our day the creed of decadence, like everything else, has swathed itself in the garb of science. The physical decadence of England was the subject of statistical demonstration. It was not merely assumed by Treitschke, who offered the abolition of the duel as one of its evidences, but it was accepted as demonstrated fact by our conscriptionists, our eugenists, our reactionaries. Revelling in their own forebodings, these prophets of evil wallowed in descriptions of the national decay that was to come from our objections to universal drill, our weakness in giving freedom and equality to dependencies, our humanitarian madness that kept the unfit alive, our insanely democratic jealousies that taxed the millionaire whose fitness was written large in the gigantic fortune which he had extracted by his financial skill from our less capable selves. We could not recruit our little army. We could not fill the complement of the Territorial Forces. England's day was over. Romance, farewell! Well, the Germans are said for many years to have drunk to "The Day"—the day that was to open the short, sharp, and decisive conflict between their youthful vigour and that Empire of ours which was, in Treitschke's words, "wholly a sham". The day dawned, and every German success was answered by an upward bound of the British recruitment roll. In spite of every War Office blunder, the young men came pouring in. The generation that even their fathers thought too much set upon amusement showed that the moment they were convinced of necessity they could give it up and go to drill. The "soft" young man from behind the counter took his place beside the miner, the spinner, and the schoolmaster, under canvas in the drenching autumn rains. The Oxford undergraduate left his football and his clubs to drill and be drilled. The City man abandoned golf and motor-car and money-making to make him ready for the front. We elders see them day by day in the streets, men strengthened by drill, fresh-faced and ruddy with the open air, clear-eyed, vigorous, and happy as though no tragedy of parting lay straight before them. Nor is theirs the courage of ignorance. Every man of them has read newspaper accounts by the score that tell that in the warfare of the trenches there is little glory and much of frostbite, rheumatism, filth, and fatigue—all that is most repugnant to the habits of civilisation. They know well what they are about, and they make no tall talk about it. When they get there they put off tragedy with a joke, and salt the grimness of war with the native wit of the London street. This is not the temper of a few picked men, but of the youth of England—the best product of a hundred years of general peace, the fourth generation born in the lap of security, the sons and grandsons of men nine out of ten of whom never saw a man killed in anger. War may destroy the virtues of peace, but peace cultivates the virtues that are required in war. As to the feats of individuals, can any soldier deed of earlier days match the flight over hostile territory to Friedrichshafen, or was ever a demand on constancy and

endurance and nerve to match the unceasing watchfulness
against torpedo or mine that may at any moment send a
whole ship's company to the bottom without the chance of a
blow in self-defence? These tests of courage are higher and
more exacting than those of the older warfare—not but
that the feats of those days are emulated. Did not a handful
of Frenchmen the other day hold a dug-out close upon
the enemy's lines, for all the world like D'Artagnan and
the immortal three at their breakfast in the Bastion of St.
Gervais?

Whatever else this war has done, let us hope that for a
time it has stopped the talk of decadence. There are good
things in civilisation which are often threatened with
decay, but physical vigour, courage, and enterprise are the
last qualities to be seriously endangered. Before the war any
cool-headed observer could see that, whatever else might
be threatened in our time, it was not manhood, vigour,
originality, enterprise. Consider the art of flying alone—
beyond reasonable question the most daring experiment
ever made by man—leaping from a dream to a reality in
five years, and yet requiring the most consummate union of
nerve, skill, and mechanical ingenuity. It is the gentler
and humaner elements of civilisation that are more often
in danger, and the cant of physical decadence is at bottom
a part of the campaign against all progress in the peaceful
arts by the active and plausible advocates of rebarbarisa-
tion. The triumph of this party is its logical undoing. The
test of war has justified peace. Yet the victory is but for a
day. In the next generation it is likely that men will be
wondering if their sons can fight as they did, if their boy
who is so keen on cricket (or whatever be the substitute
for cricket in 1950), and who smokes rather too many
cigarettes, could stand as they did in the trenches and joke
about Jack Johnsons as the huge shells dig their craters
near at hand. In 1950, as in 1914, there will be those who
lament that the old breed has died out, that the hardy

virtues of the fathers have perished, that the poor are coddled and the sick cured, and the feeble kept alive while the strong have to bear the burden. Lamenting over these signs of perishing manhood, they will look forward with apprehension to the day when the rising military Power of the time will challenge England's greatness and reveal it for an image with feet of clay, and with a sorrowful shake of the head the old men will turn from the outward sight of a decadent generation to the inward vision of those glorious days of national youth and vigour when George V was King.

NON-RESISTANCE

A DISCIPLE once asked Confucius whether one should recompense evil with kindness. "With what, then," the Master said, "should you recompense kindness?" "Recompense kindness with kindness, and evil with justice." The disciple was moved to the question by the teachings of Lao-Tsze, the originator, so far as history knows, of the complete doctrine of mystic Quietism. It was Confucius who became "the Master" to the Chinese mind, not Lao-Tsze, and his reply puts the point which appeals to the plain man not in his angry and resentful but in his more reflective mood. Lao-Tsze's doctrine is that of poetry and mysticism, the Confucian teaching that of practicality and prose. A poet perhaps is not bound to mere consistency, but it is noteworthy that in Lao-Tsze, as in all who have taught non-resistance, we seem to find two strains. At one moment it seems to be a simple acquiescence in the world as we find it that he is preaching. At another it is the superior efficacy of gentleness to force as a remedial measure. "The woman conquers the man by continual quietness", says the denizen of a strongly patriarchal society, and somewhere— unfortunately I have not the treatise at hand, and am quoting from memory—he speaks, I think, of water as the strongest of things because it is the most yielding. In a practical age and country it is fair to ask apostles of non-resistance on which leg they stand. Do they mean that it is not a man's business to try to set right the wrong? If so, they will be held to teach a retreat into the inner life which looks very much like a refined selfishness, and in any case they will find that the ethics of an active and vitally endowed race will make no terms with them. Not to prevent evil which is preventable is to share responsibility for it, and a people that has any confidence in itself and in the idea of justice will not readily believe that evils are unpreventable.

But do they mean that evil is to be resisted more effectually by forbearance than by force? This is quite a different thought. It is, to begin with, not a command at all, but rather a statement of fact—though one on which a rule of conduct may be based—and it is as a question of fact that it ought to be discussed. This has not as a rule been its fate. Non-resistance, love of enemies, turning the other cheek, have suffered the fate of other great spiritual ideas. They have become pulpit phrases which it is not quite polite to criticise seriously, but which it is universally allowed— universally, that is, outside small bodies of resolute enthusiasts—have no meaning for a world like this. The nearest we get to any genuine examination of them is an occasional discussion of the limits of literal interpretation of authoritative texts. It is probable that the mode in which they have been put upon the world has done positive harm, because it has suggested that the only alternative to force in many cases is a meekness so extreme as to be utterly unpractical, if not even somewhat repugnant. Thus, while a very few have accepted these principles in their entirety, the great majority have ignored them in their entirety. Rarely has anyone sought to investigate dispassionately the measure of truth which they contain. Yet if, as we say, at bottom they rather state a fact than utter a command, it should be within the resources of intelligence to examine that statement coolly and measure its truth.

So considered, is it so very paradoxical? Lao-Tsze's reference to women, though put with a certain Oriental quaintness, might almost pass for a platitude. When a Buddhist verse says:

> For never in this world did hatred cease by hatred,
> Hatred ceases by love: that is always its nature,

it is surely stating what we all know. Had Confucius been asked not how he should recompense evil but how he should conquer it, he might not have been so decided in rejecting the method of kindness. When John Bright said that "force is no remedy", his words became a motto for a very practical party as expressing the truth on a certain class of questions. In a word, there can be no doubt that where it can be put into effect the method of gentleness is infinitely more effective than the method of force. Who does not know the disconcerting effect of an unexpectedly mild reply to a furious onslaught, or the commanding authority of a low voice? Generally speaking, mildness is the method of the morally strong; force is the weapon of the weak, and to be driven to use force is to have failed in dealing with your case. The father who uses punishment has failed with his son. The schoolmaster who cannot keep discipline takes to the cane. Society, when it fails to maintain a certain standard by opinion, imposes legal punishment, and when moderate punishments fail resorts to severity. The kind of man who blusters about strong measures and spirited policies stamps himself an intellectual failure. War as such—not merely unjust war, or successful war, but war—is the failure of statesmanship, and the degree of force that has to be used for any purpose is the measure of the failure of mind in application to that purpose. "Can't schamy must lauster" is a Cornish proverb which, being interpreted, means that if you cannot carry a thing through by the use of your brains you must do it by hard bodily strength.

Every sane man therefore does his utmost to restrict the use of force, just as every silly man parades his forcefulness, but it is only the rarest type that can rely on success. There goes a touch of that "personality"—which none can acquire, but which is the offspring, like genius, of divine chance—to the compelling power of gentleness. Those may use it whose bare presence inspires the conviction that they are perfectly simple and perfectly unafraid, like a confiding child, who, in fact, possesses the compelling power in the highest degree. A State might have such a power if its record were unblemished, if it had never abused its strength, never grown rich at the expense of its neighbours, never sold gin and called it civilisation, never taken territory in the name of principle—in short, never done as all States habitually do. Unfortunately, in the matter of mere morality, States, much as their citizens love and admire them, perhaps because they are loved and admired so much—are on the level of rather inferior individuals. "If we had done for ourselves", said Cavour, "what we have done for Italy, we should be very bad men." This being so, States can exercise very little moral influence, and so their relations rest in the end on force. But this is only to say that the State is a weak form of human organisation, using crude methods to attain its ends even when the ends are good. There are political ends which cannot be attained by force—for instance, genuine loyalty; and in the more liberal States it has been possible to convince public opinion of this truth and to get Governments to rely on justice and freedom instead. But there are also ends which no one has yet shown us how to obtain without force; for instance, self-preservation. Advocates of non-resistance will never prevent the shedding of one drop of blood by telling us not to fight in our own defence. If they would really minimise warfare, they would do better to find a working ethics, a code of justice in international relations which men would accept. Of all statesmen Gladstone came nearest to this in his doctrine that the obligations of States were in principle identical with those of private persons. A code based on this principle, and a habit of detailed application to international politics in the interests of such a code, might build up the international institutions which alone, in the end, can supersede war. It might at least avert some wars, while the mere reiteration of an abstract principle averts none.

JANE AUSTEN

JANE AUSTEN, whose death a hundred years ago is being commemorated to-day in the modest and orderly manner which would have appealed to her, was a great worker on a small canvas. She knew a very limited society, and knew it down to the ground. Her world is the little trim garden plot of the upper middle class in the days when that class was untouched by any sense of problems or by any stir from the new industrial and political forces. The world was intensely alive, but of the "storms which raged outside their happy ground" the well-mannered gentlemen and elegant ladies (elegant is an epithet of praise in Miss Austen) moved about sublimely unconscious. Jane Austen's novels coincided pretty nearly with the epoch of the Revolutionary wars, yet there is scarcely an allusion to the great world-events that were in progress, and only a very occasional indication that they had any concern with the tranquil households who lived their placid and untroubled lives. "Persuasion", it is true, is indirectly concerned with the peace, because it is the peace which liberates the Admiral and enables him to take Kellynch Hall. Anne Elliott mentions that her lover took part in "the Trafalgar action" as a detail that might be of interest, but Sir Walter Elliott's contempt for admirals on account of their weather-beaten appearance is expressed with a *naïveté* which the novelist is, of course, ridiculing, but which would be quite impossible in the mouth of the most foolish man of the present day. In *Mansfield Park*, also, William Price is in the Navy, and there is a very amusing scene in which the question whether his boat has or has not gone out of port is the theme of a whole series of family announcements. In the same book the stately progress of Sir Thomas homeward from the West Indies is not unattended with anxiety as to capture by French privateers. In *Pride and Prejudice* there are soldiers, but they appear only as causing a flutter of excitement in

the feminine dovecot, providing agitation for Lydia and
Kitty. Throughout, one would say, if the contrary were not
proved by dates, that the novels were written and could
only have been written in a period of profound peace and
domestic tranquillity.

It is this atmosphere of peace which makes some of us
go back to Miss Austen again and again. There are no
problems here. The whole order of things is accepted and
settled; even individuals are scarcely to be seen pushing
their way up. The Coles were a family "that had been rising
for some generations into gentility", but when Mr. Cole
asked Mr. Woodhouse to dinner it was done with an
apologetic deference which completely disarmed Emma's
opposition. Lucy, in *Sense and Sensibility*, is perhaps the
only example of a successful social climber, and she is certainly drawn with a masterly touch. Lucy's vulgarity is
always kept well in hand. In the delightful scene where the
height of the little boys is compared, each mother is equally
convinced that her own boy is the taller, but out of politeness
gives the palm to the other. Each grandmother unblushingly
maintains the superiority of her grandson. Lucy's impossible sister gives the verdict as fast as she can in
favour of each alternately, but Lucy herself cannot conceive that there is the least shade of difference between
the two.

There are vulgarians in Jane Austen, but they are never
noisy, like the Brangtons in *Evelina*. The most insufferable
but also the truest type is Mrs. Elton, who speaks of Mr.
Knightley without the prefix, tries to patronise Emma, and
makes Jane Fairfax's life a burden by heaping on her
benefactions which she does not want. But even Mrs.
Elton has to keep within the bounds of decorum. One would
not imagine any characters in Jane Austen who would, as
Mr. Kipling says, "talk obstetrics when the little stranger
came", but we may be quite sure Mrs. Elton talked obstetrics in voluable detail to companies of matrons. All that,

however, was off the stage. Before the footlights Mrs. Elton is impossible but proper.

Lovers of Jane Austen dispute, as others do, as to the precedence of her books, but the dispute, I think, is limited to three of six novels. *Northanger Abbey* is amusing but slight, and I have never heard anyone claim the first place for *Sense and Sensibility*. There are those who love *Persuasion*, but Anne Elliott is a very sentimental heroine, and there are no great comic figures to be matched with Miss Bates, Mrs. Norris, or Mrs. Bennett. Of the three novels that remain, *Mansfield Park* fails both in its hero and heroine. Edmund and Fanny, to say the truth, are impossible sticks, and their loves do not interest. One has to abstract the main thread of narrative from the book to get what is almost perfection in comedy. Mrs. Norris, with her complicated meanness, her habit of prying into every little thing, her lectures to the gardener on his rheumatism, her pleasure in cutting off Fanny's fire for the mere pleasure of cutting down expenses, even if they were not her own, is as great a delight to the reader as she must have been a terror in real life. Lady Bertram with her pug dog, her sofa and her fancy work, is the complete picture for all time of vacuous indolence. Emma, on the other hand, is herself an interesting character study—the only one of Jane Austen's heroines who suggests the autobiographical type. One may imagine Jane Austen as a very young girl making the same sort of over-confident mistakes in the attempt to manage other people's lives into which Emma falls. In criticism of the plot of *Emma*, it may be said that it is much more amusing when you read it a second time, knowing the secret engagement of Frank Churchill, than when you come to it fresh, and expect, with Emma, that Frank Churchill is about to fall in love with her. There are a hundred of allusions so subtle that they escape on the first reading, but full of humour when you know the story. The novelist would have done better to have anticipated

Thackeray's method, and have taken the reader from the first into her confidence. What valetudinarian ever surpassed Mr. Woodhouse with his gruel, "thin but not too thin", his conflicts between the sense of hospitality and the dread of impairing the digestion of his guests, his dialogues with his married daughter, in which every speech of hers is a quotation from her doctor, and every reply of his is a reference to his own dear Perry? To some, however, Miss Bates bears off the palm, and William James took her as the supreme example of a certain psychological type —the type of mind which utterly fails to get to the essence of things because it reproduces every incident, however irrelevant, in the details surrounding the case.

"But where could you hear it?" cried Miss Bates. "Where could you possibly hear it, Mr. Knightley? For it is not five minutes since I received Mrs. Cole's note—no, it cannot be more than five minutes—or at least ten—for I had got my bonnet and spencer on, just ready to come out —I was only gone down to speak to Patty again about the pork—Jane was standing in the passage—were you not, Jane? for my mother was so afraid that we had not any salting-pan large enough. So I said I would go down and see, and Jane said, 'Shall I go down instead? for I think you have a little cold, and Patty has been washing the kitchen.' 'Oh, my dear,' said I—well, and just then came the note. A Miss Hawkins—that's all I know—a Miss Hawkins, of Bath. But, Mr. Knightley, how could you possibly have heard it? for the very moment Mr. Cole told Mrs. Cole of it, she sat down and wrote to me. A Miss Hawkins——"

I think that is the passage which Professor James quotes, and it certainly illustrates his point.

There remains *Pride and Prejudice*, not quite so rich in comic characters, but with the most charming heroine in Jane Austen. Elizabeth was a great deal too good for Darcy, but she took the conceit out of him before their marriage, and we may trust her to have kept it well out afterwards. Some say that her parents are a little over-drawn. It is difficult to conceive such a girl as Elizabeth growing up with such a mother as Mrs. Bennett, and with a father who had no weapon of defence except sarcasm, but in Jane Austen we do not raise questions either of heredity or of environment, and we are content that Elizabeth should be Elizabeth, and that Mr. Collins should meet her refusal with the dictum that it was the "established practice of elegant females" to meet every offer, even though secretly determined to entertain it, with an apparent refusal. Some find Mr. Collins a caricature, but I do not think that he carries comedy into burlesque. It is a master stroke that he takes quite seriously Elizabeth's remark that his patroness, the great Lady Catherine, would not approve of her. "Were I indeed to think, Lady Catherine," he begins, "but, no——". The attitude of a certain type of clergyman, whom Jane Austen knew well, to the dispenser of bounty is but too faithfully reproduced.

In sum, Jane Austen's novels are an oasis to which the world-weary may repair for a season. Someone thanked God that he had given tired men Dumas It seems strange to bring the fevered activity, the melodrama of D'Artagnan and Porthos, into a comparison with the peaceful retirement of Mr. Woodhouse and Mrs. Dashwood, but in Dumas one seeks relief from questionings and sorrow in the vivid movement of a spontaneous life that takes no thought of the future or of its own purpose and meaning; in Jane Austen we have the garden plot where the lawns are trimmed to perfection and even Mr. Woodhouse may take his one daily walk sheltered from the wind. Let us walk with him for an hour and envy the man who has no fears but that his gruel may be thicker than Perry would approve, to be rewarded, let us hope, before the hour is out by a glimpse of Emma herself, the model of a culture perfect just because of its limitations.

THE ARTISTIC FALLACY

THE divorce between the plain man and the artist in matters of taste has received less attention from critical writers than it deserves. For the most part it serves merely as a commonplace text for some thrust at popular Philistinism. The wrongness, banality, futility of the popular view is taken as axiomatic, and the justice of the taste of the particular school to which the critic adheres is equally assumed. Yet omniscience is often to be found divided against itself. How many of the dogmas which Ruskin lavished from the stores of his certitude would raise anything but a smile from the critic of to-day, and how long will to-day's canons of criticism endure? If anyone flinches from his own judgment under the lash of the critic, let him take courage from the contemplation of these diversities among the pundits. Let him enjoy the picture, the poem, the music of his choice, and not let himself be shamed into an abjuration. It is better to read the *Idylls of the King* with genuine enjoyment than Meredith's sonnets with artificial critic-engendered appreciation.

But how does the divorce come about? A recent article in this column by Mr. Horace Taylor has for me at least thrown a new light on the question. An artist describes a sunset sky—for most of us plain men the consummation of earthly beauty—as a "raspberry jam effect". What is beautiful to us is contemptible to him, contemptible to the professed student of beauty. The reason suggested is that the artist has been studying subtler effects of colour, to which we plain men are insensible all day long. His eye is attuned to the subtler and nicer shades which we miss. But as a result it would seem that he is in danger of losing certain broad effects which we enjoy. The balance of gain and loss is doubtful. On the whole it seems to me to be against the artist. I would not myself barter my power of enjoying a sunset over the Cornish coast for any increased sensibility to the play of colours on a whitewashed wall. Like others who are not artists, I imagine, I have at times noticed the effects of such a play, but as it is not my business to attend to them or reproduce them, they have not disturbed my enjoyment of the sunset glory. And I am glad that they have not, as in a world of many sorrows and cares one would rather have two sources of enjoyment than one. I feel a little sorry for the artist whose main interest in life is in the realm of beauty and who yet seems destined to lose at one end as much appreciation as he gains at the other.

None the less I believe Mr. Taylor's analysis to be just as applied to a great many artists, and to explain why painters are enthusiastic over pictures which the plain man would never look at if he were not taken by the shoulders by the critic, planted down before them, and held there till he says "Beautiful!"; why the musically erudite derides the melody which entrances us vulgar; why we find the stylists for whom the critics reserve their highest praise obscure, verbose, tedious, and in a word—if we dared to utter it— unreadable. The answer is, in essentials, the same in all cases. The artist is hour by hour straining his vision, or rather the sensori-motor apparatus that connects hand and eye, to follow up and reproduce the subtleties of form and colour; the musician's mind is working on intricacies of harmony which render him impatient of the simple and straightforward; the stylist exerts himself unceasingly to choose just the right word, and perhaps does not find it in the accustomed vocabulary of such as you and me.

If this is so, it means that the energy which the artist puts into the mechanism of his art is withdrawn from his appreciation of its broader and simpler issues. Either there is a fatigue engendered by continuous application, or there is a certain narrowing of interest such as we find in all specialism or professionalism. But it would seem to be only of second-rate artists that this is true. The greatest

men always seem able to appeal very directly to the plain
man as well as to the initiated. Shakespeare, for example,
wrote I know not how many lines which have become for
us parts of ordinary speech. As such they have no doubt
lost for us their special beauty and charm, but it must have
been for that special charm that men first caught them up
and began to quote them. They said just the right thing in
a way that everyone could understand. Matthew Arnold, I
remember, quotes somewhere a number of lines from various
poets as illustrations of the supreme art. All are exceedingly
simple, and in a sense, obvious. You feel like Mr. Partridge
when he saw Garrick, that there was nothing in the performance, because any man—Mr. Partridge himself, for
example—placed in the position of Hamlet would have
behaved just as Garrick did. It was so simple. Partridge's
admiration was reserved for the Player King. Mr. Arnold
chooses from Homer two lines which follow Helen's
prayer for her two brothers, who, unknown to her, are
already under the ground far away "in Lacedæmon, her
dear fatherland". The pathos is so apparent. It must have
moved the contempt of the Greek critic. But a good deal
of life consists of the obvious, and when the common is
lighted up by genius, the common man perhaps feels his
ego exalted.

On the whole, then, we may doubt whether the divorce
between the artist and the ordinary man is altogether the
fault of one party. Might it not be contended that the
artist, among other things, should help us to interpret
ourselves and our own sensations rather than compel us
to reject them as vulgar, illiterate, or Philistine? Fra Lippo
Lippi in Browning's monologue boasts to the captain of the
guard that with a bit of chalk he would soon make him see
his follower's face as the painter sees it. This is to make the
artist go before the plain man, find out new meanings, and
make them plain. It is the opposite ideal to that of the
artist as living in a world of his own too precious for the

vulgar eye, or ear, or brain (as the case may be) to enter.
I cannot help thinking that it is a part of the natural impulse
of the artist to be understanded of the people, and that it is
principally because in modern times he is cockered up
by the critics who have discovered the advertising value of
abnormality that he is content to move in a world apart.
At any rate, when he has lost his enjoyment of the beauty
that is apparent to all normal men, he will do well to question
himself, just as he would upon the discovery of any abnormality of his organs. He should certainly be faithful to his
artistic conscience, but he need not pique himself on the
extent to which that conscience leads him apart from the
ordinary ways of men—"housed in a dream at distance from
the kind".

THE PRINCIPAL WORKS OF L. T. HOBHOUSE

(1) BOOKS

The Labour Movement, with a preface by R. B. Haldane. pp. xii + 98. Fisher Unwin, London. 1893.

The Labour Movement, with a preface by R. B. Haldane, M.P. Second edition. T. F. Unwin. 1898.

The Theory of Knowledge. A contribution to some problems of logic and metaphysics. pp. xx + 627. Methuen & Co., London. 1896.

The Theory of Knowledge. Third Edition. pp. xxvi + 627. Methuen & Co., London. 1921.

Mind in Evolution. pp. xiv + 415. Macmillan & Co., London. 1901.

Mind in Evolution. Third Edition. pp. xix + 483. 1926.

Democracy and Reaction. pp. vii + 244. T. Fisher Unwin, London. 1904.

Lord Hobhouse; a Memoir, with J. L. Hammond. pp. 280. Edward Arnold, London. 1905.

Morals in Evolution: a study in comparative ethics. 2 vols. Chapman & Hall, London. 1906.

Morals in Evolution. Third Edition. pp. xvi + 648. 1915.

Social Evolution and Political Theory. pp. ix + 218. New York. 1911.

Liberalism. pp. 254. 1911 (Home University Library of Modern Knowledge).

Liberalism. Reprinted 1919 and 1923.

Development and Purpose. An essay towards a philosophy of evolution. pp. xxix + 383. Macmillan & Co. 1913.

Development and Purpose. Second Edition revised. pp. xxix + 494. Macmillan & Co., London. 1929.

The Material Culture and Social Institutions of the Simpler Peoples: An essay in Correlation (with G. C. Wheeler and M. Ginsberg). pp. 299. 1915 (London Monographs on Sociology. No. 3).

The Material Culture and Social Institutions of the Simpler Peoples: An essay in Correlation (with G. C. Wheeler and M. Ginsberg). Reprinted 1930.

The World in Conflict. pp. 104. T. Fisher Unwin, London. 1915.

Questions of War and Peace. pp. 223. T. Fisher Unwin, London. 1916.

The Metaphysical Theory of the State: a criticism. pp. 156. G. Allen & Unwin, London. Macmillan & Co., New York. 1918.

The Elements of Social Justice. pp. 208. Allen and Unwin, London. 1921.

The Elements of Social Justice. pp. vii + 247. H. Holt & Co., New York. 1922.

The Rational Good: a study in the logic of practice. pp. 165. Allen and Unwin, London. 1921.

The Rational Good. pp. xxix + 237. H. Holt & Co., New York. 1921.

Social Development: its nature and conditions. Allen and Unwin, London. 1924.

(2) ARTICLES

Experimental Certainty. *Mind*. O.S. Vol. XV. 1891. pp. 251–260.

The Principle of Induction. *Mind*. O.S. Vol. XVI. 1891. pp. 80–91.

Induction and Deduction. *Mind*. O.S. Vol. XVI. 1891. pp. 507–520.

Some Problems of Conception. *Mind*. N.S. Vol. VI. pp. 20–22.

Faith and the Will to Believe. *Proc. of the Aristotelian Soc.* N.S. Vol. VI. 1904. pp. 87–111.

The Law of the Three Stages. *The Sociologival Review*. July 1908.

The Value and Limitations of Eugenics. *Soc. Review*. October 1911.

Democracy and Civilisation. *Soc. Review*. Vol. XIII. No. 3. 1921.

The Historical Evolution of Property in Fact and in Idea. In *Property: its Duties and Rights*. 1913. Macmillan.

Law and Justice. In *Representative Essays*. Ed. H. R. Steers and F. H. Ristine. 1913.

Sociology. Article in *Hastings's Dictionary of Religion and Ethics*.

Comparative Ethics. *Encyclopædia Britannica*. 14th Edition. Vol. VI.

Comparative Psychology. *Encyclopædia Britannica*. 14th Edition. Vol. VI.

Aristocracy. Article in *Encyclopædia of the Social Sciences*.

Christianity in its Sociological Bearings. Article in *Encyclopædia of the Social Sciences*.

The Roots of Modern Sociology. Inaugural Lecture. 1908.

Sociology. In *The Mind*. A Series of Lectures delivered in King's College, London. 1927. Edited by R. J. S. McDowall. pp. 282–316.

The Ethical Basis of Collectivism. *International Journal of Ethics*. Jan. 1898.

Competitive and Social Value. *Economica*. Nov. 1924.

Über einige der primitivsten Völker: Eine vergleichende Studie. *Zeitschrift für Völker-psychologie und Soziologie*. Edited by Richard Thurnwald. 1929.

Are Physical, Biological and Psychological Categories Irreducible? *Proceedings of Aristotelian Society*. 1917–1918.

The Place of Mind in Nature. *Aristotelian Society*. *Supplementary Vol. VI.* 1926.

The Philosophy of Development. *Contemporary British Philosophy*. 1st Series. Edited by J. H. Muirhead. pp. 149–188.

INDEX

For Product Safety Concerns and Information please contact our EU
representative GPSR@taylorandfrancis.com
Taylor & Francis Verlag GmbH, Kaufingerstraße 24, 80331 München, Germany

www.ingramcontent.com/pod-product-compliance
Lightning Source LLC
Chambersburg PA
CBHW060138280326
41932CB00012B/1560